IT'S FUN TO BE

SMART

IT'S FUN TO BE

SMART

A Parents' Guide to Stress-Free Early Learning
From Birth Through Age Five

Dr. Florence Baccus

Library of Congress Cataloging-in-Publication Data

Baccus, Florence, 1928-
  It's fun to be smart: a parents' guide to stress-free early learning from birth through age 5 / Florence Baccus.
    p.   cm.
  Includes bibliographical references and index.
  ISBN 0-945847-04-1
  1. Education, Preschool—Parent participation.   2. Education, Preschool—Curricula.   3. Child rearing.   I. Title.
LB1140.35.P37B33   1991
649'.68—dc20   91-2174
                                                                                    CIP

Edited by: *Dianne J. Borneman*
Interior design and typography by: *Dianne J. Borneman,*
    Shadow Canyon Graphics, Evergreen, CO
Cover design by: *Ruth Koning*
    Shadow Canyon Graphics, Evergreen, CO

Printed in the United States of America

First Edition
1   2   3   4   5   6   7   8   9

QUANTITY DISCOUNTS are available on bulk purchases of this book for educational, business, or promotional use. For more information, please contact our special sales department:

Vade Mecum Press
5200 DTC Parkway, Suite 260
Englewood, Colorado 80111
(303) 935-6703

Contents

Developing a lifelong love of learning; strengthening the parent-child bond; avoiding the first-grade teacher risk

An "insurance policy" for early learning; accentuating PEEEHK (pleasure, excitement, enjoyment, enthusiasm, hugs & kisses) and eliminating SPPPAN (stress, pressure, pushing, punishment, anxiety, negativism)

The benefits of sensory stimulation together with more than 150 activities for pleasure, excitement, and learning

Chapter 4: SELF-EXPRESSION THROUGH SPEECH 113

Developing and projecting personality through speech; providing
opportunities for vocal self-expression; the importance of sound-play;
turning the Terrible Twos into the Terrific Twos

Chapter 5: TEACHING YOUR CHILD TO READ 129

Myths about reading readiness; word-play, phonetics, and other early-
reading techniques; beginning a love affair with books

Chapter 6: TEACHING MATH TO YOUR CHILD 155

Eliminating math anxiety; math in the everyday world; games that
encourage math development

This book is dedicated to my loving son, Stephen A. Baccus, whose achievements have, I believe, resulted from a mastery of the precepts and techniques set forth in this book. His rapid ability to learn together with his insatiable desire to learn; his enthusiasm, industry, leadership, application, and courage, have inspired me to write this book for the benefit of any parent who may wish to learn how to educate a child to his or her fullest potential.

This book is also dedicated to my dear friend Deborah Lampert, whose loyalty and assistance made this book possible.

The Author

F lorence Baccus served as a teacher, counselor, and drug specialist in the public schools for nearly three decades. She has also directed numerous seminars and courses for parents on early learning techniques and has recently begun a series of early learning readers for young children. Following extensive research on the history of giftedness in children, Dr. Baccus earned the Doctor of Public Administration degree, which credentials her to serve as a superintendent of schools.

Preface

"Mrs. Baccus, I'm sorry to tell you this . . ."

My heart raced as I waited for the doctor. Was it really possible? After ten years of a blissful but childless second marriage, could I at last be pregnant? In between daydreams of cribs and diapers, I kept wondering what was delaying the doctor. Certainly nothing could be wrong. I was an old hand at childbirth. After all, I had already given birth to three sons. Now I was beginning to get annoyed. What was keeping that man?

After what seemed like an eternity, but was more likely only minutes, in he strode, looking at once both at me and through me. My nerves were beginning to fray when at last I heard those three words that I was longing to hear: "You are pregnant."

It was then that I noticed the doctor fidgeting his fingers. His voice became strangely patronizing as he unloaded his message all at once, almost like gunfire. "Mrs. Baccus, I'm sorry to tell you this," he began to speak as my heart began to sink, "but your baby has three strikes against it." Funny, I thought, he calls a baby "it." Not "him" or "her," but "it." In only a second, as the doctor raced on to complete his verdict, I learned why he was speaking about my long-awaited child in such dispassionate tones.

"There is every likelihood that your child will be born retarded. You are forty years old, and we now know that one in fifty mothers your age gives birth to a Down's syndrome child."

Strike one. While my mind reeled, my palms began to sweat.

On he went, without stopping for a second to consider either my shock or my pain. "You already have retardation on your side of the family."

Strike two. I didn't know it then, but the panic that began to overtake me at that moment was to continue unabated for many months.

"You know that your husband also has retardation in his immediate family. Now to me, that's strike three. Where do you want to go for your abortion — New York or California? Those are the only two places in the United States where abortion is legal."

The year was 1968, and the doctor was certainly right about two things. First, he had his medical facts straight. As an educator myself, I knew that his pessimism was well founded. And second, had I agreed to an abortion, I would indeed have been forced to travel either to California or New York.

What the doctor failed to consider, however, was a third fact: This was my second marriage, and, having waited ten years for this child, my husband and I intended to birth him, to know him, and to love him — even if the odds suggested that he might never know or love us.

Once I made this fateful decision, despite my physician shaking his head and muttering under his breath, I made another decision as well. And it was this second resolution that has made all the difference in my life — and in my baby's life as well.

I realized that if my baby was born profoundly retarded, he might have to be institutionalized. After all, my husband, a lawyer, and I, a former teacher and then school guidance counselor, worked full-time to support our four other children. But I also knew that I had a mandatory six-week maternity leave. And I was determined to use those six weeks to teach this new baby everything I possibly could. And when I returned to work and would have to leave the baby with an elderly neighbor, I was likewise determined to use nights and weekends to further expand my baby's seemingly limited horizons. Then, if at six months it seemed as though an institution were the only answer, I would know that I had done my best and offered this tiny infant whatever learning his brain might feebly absorb.

My son, Stephen Baccus, was born on February 25, 1969. As I held him in my arms that winter's day, I silently prayed for the strength to do my best for him.

On January 19, 1986, less than seventeen years later, Stephen graduated from the Law School of the University of Miami.

What happened between the somber day in the doctor's office and that glorious day on which my son became the youngest lawyer in the

United States is the subject of this book. Happily, this is one extraordinary "success story" in which all our children, yours and mine, can
share.

— Dr. Florence Baccus

Introduction

You should be congratulated. Whether you're a parent or expectant parent, a grandparent, an educator, a care giver, or simply an individual who recognizes that children are our greatest natural resource, you merit a good deal of credit for deciding to expand your understanding of the nearly limitless intellectual potential of children. Stop and think a moment. How old were you when you when you learned to read? Five years old? Six? Older? In the United States, most children are taught to read between the ages of five and one-half and six and one-half. If that sounds about right to you, then ask yourself a second question: How old were you when you were taught to speak?

Perhaps you think that you weren't taught to speak. Speaking, you may believe, "just comes naturally?" But if that's so, then why doesn't reading "just come naturally"? Along this same line of reasoning, when you were in school, perhaps math was troublesome to you. Is math still troublesome to you? If so, why hasn't math "just come naturally?"

What is it about speech that makes speaking child's play, while reading and math remain behind locked doors? What's different about reading, math, science, foreign languages, and all the other subjects that children and young adults are eventually taught in school?

Nothing. That's right. There's no difference between the subjects currently taught to six-year-olds — or sixteen-year-olds — and a utility like speech that we believe is naturally acquired by infants and toddlers.

Think about it. Did you ever take a foreign language in high school or college? Most of us find these courses fairly difficult. Yet we all know very young children who are bilingual or even multilingual. Why is a three-year-old able to perform an intellectual feat that stymies most thirty-year-olds?

This presents an interesting dilemma. Are we wrong to say that speech is learned naturally? Would we be more accurate to say that speech is taught to a baby? Or, are we wrong when we say that other subjects cannot be learned naturally? Is it somehow possible for a young child — two or three or four years old — to learn to read . . . naturally?

The truth is that while all of us possess a certain amount of innate knowledge — and doctors and scientists still argue about what that innate knowledge consists of — most of what we know is, in fact, learned. And we know something because we have been taught it. The teaching need not be formal. In fact, very often the best teaching is informal, the kind of teaching that accompanies our very acts of living. In that way, the lessons that we need to learn are absorbed easily, happily, and, yes, naturally.

If children are our greatest natural resource, then what do we owe them to ensure that they will not merely survive, but flourish? We owe them a secure physical environment, nutritious food, the best available medical care, and the love and support of family and friends. These are a child's birthright. But every child is entitled to more.

Every child — your child, my child — is born with approximately 12 billion nerve cells in his or her brain. And every one of those 12 billion cells has up to 5,000 synapses, or contact points, across which nerve impulses are transmitted. How many interconnections are available in a child's brain? More than the grains of sand on all the beaches in the entire United States!

Knowing that this literally astronomical number of transmitters exists in a child's brain on the day of birth gives rise to a growing realization that brain structures develop and mature earlier than we had ever imagined. That's why very young children can become fluent speakers of several foreign languages while those of us many decades older may fail French 101. *More importantly, if the young child is not exposed to appropriate learning experiences at the time when the structure matures, then the structure begins to deteriorate.*

The optimal period of time when specific brain structures mature and are capable of learning is known as a "sensitive period." Near the end of each sensitive period is a time known as a "critical period." Neurologists and other professionals who study brain development suggest that when a sensitive period is ignored, a critical period develops. At that time, unless the brain structure is stimulated into use, particular brain networks may be lost forever. In the case of language acquisition, for example, these brain networks combine to form a structure called a Language Acquisition Device (or LAD). The time between the ages of about eighteen months and four years is a sensitive period for language acquisition. That's why young children can learn one, two, or even more languages fairly easily. About the age of three and one-half to four, a critical period develops for language acquisition. When the LAD facility is not used by that time, a child's ability to learn a language may be impaired permanently.

If children's lifelong ability to know themselves and their world depends on early intellectual stimulation then isn't this stimulation a child's birthright — as vital to human functioning as food, clothing, shelter, and love? Of course it is.

While the physiological and psychological evidence for terms like "synapse" and "sensitive period" may be recent, the belief that infants and young children benefit from early intellectual stimulation is anything but new.

Throughout recorded history, many renowned statesmen, artists, philosophers, and scientists were the products of early childhood education. We may admire, praise, or stand in awe of individuals such as Alexander the Great, Cicero, Raphael, Bach, Mozart, or even Franklin Delano Roosevelt, but it would be more fitting if we praised the parents of these remarkable individuals, all of whom actively educated their children from infancy. In fact, this early childhood education is the common link shared by the most respected and remarkable individuals of historical record.

Very little of this now-vast research was known to me in 1969 when my son, Stephen, was born. At that time I had completed my first decade as a teacher and guidance counselor, and when I thought of education, I thought of the school system.

My doctor's insistence that Stephen would most likely be born retarded forced me to reevaluate my old beliefs. I wanted the best for Stephen, whatever his handicaps might be, just as all of us want the best for our children.

Even though I was an experienced mother as well as a professional educator, I don't want you to think that those first few months were easy. There were so many highs and lows that conflicting emotions nearly tore me apart. One moment my whole being was filled with love for this infant and I knew in my soul that I could never relinquish him to an institution. Then the dark thoughts rushed in and I wondered how I could possibly keep a profoundly retarded child at home. The child would grow older, the problems would mount, the other children would pay the price, my husband might . . . , my husband might . . . ; I didn't have the courage to finish the sentence.

During the first months of Stephen's life he did have several physical problems. As I took him from specialist to specialist, and heard his heart-wrenching screams as they examined him, I concluded for perhaps the hundredth time: "No, I just can't do this! I cannot bring him up!"

Thankfully, those moments passed, and despite full-time employment, I was resolved that my role as mother necessarily included the role of teacher or stimulator. I began, from the first moment that Stephen was placed in my arms, to develop his human potential. That's right — human potential, not merely intellectual potential. yes, I wanted Stephen to be as bright as he could be, even though I thought that his capabilities might be limited. But I also wanted him to be as happy as he could be, and as healthy, and as fulfilled.

What I did was to develop a plan where Stephen and I (and the rest of the family) participated in events — games, travel, even housework — through which he learned comfortably and naturally. I couldn't wait to get home from my work at school and begin my *real* job of educating Stephen. However, educating Stephen was no job; it was a joy, because I didn't really "teach" in the conventional sense. I challenged, I demonstrated, I guided, I offered, I suggested, I gave a million hugs and kisses, and I provided praise and encouragement. I didn't know it then, but I've since learned that my educational plan stimulated Stephen during virtually every sensitive period of his childhood.

Days turned into weeks and months and years, and at every turn, Stephen's reactions rewarded my efforts. First, I began to hope and later to know that Stephen was not retarded. Soon I began to recognize that, owing to my techniques, Stephen's intellect and temperament were developing in ways remarkably different from those of his siblings. Even in Stephen's infancy I was amazed to behold an uncommonly happy, contented, and self-reliant child. Every day became a new time of wonder.

Stephen is now twenty-one yers old and is a talented dancer, a singer, an accomplished stage and film actor, the recipient of a master's degree in computer science from New York University, and a practicing attorney who was admitted to the Florida State Bar at age seventeen and the Federal Bar at age nineteen.

You may wonder what this book can do for you. I've spent nearly three decades expanding my understanding of early childhood learning and perfecting these techniques in seminars and workshops with hundreds of parents. From these parents, I've learned that ALL CHILDREN can learn an extraordinary amount in the months and years after birth. When exposed properly to the excitement of knowing, all children are avid learners. Best of all, the earlier a child is educated, using appropriate techniques such as stimulation and focusing combined with lots of hugs and kisses, the happier that child will be. This happiness is *every* child's birthright. This book will give you the knowledge and specific tools to make this right a reality for the children whom you know and love.

In this book, you'll learn how early education strengthens the parent-child bond and reinforces your child's lifelong feelings of respect and trust toward you. On the other hand, if you've thought that early childhood education is the sole domain of kindergarten and first-grade teachers, you'll come to understand why your faith in conventional educators may pose a significant risk to your child.

Even if you're convinced, as I am, that early learning is a child's birthright, remember that there's a right way and a wrong way to pursue your goals. *Attitude* is the key. But how can you develop that smiling, even-tempered, nonjudgmental attitude that is crucial to your child's well-being? In Chapter 2, you'll learn that accentuating PEEEHK (pleasure, enthusiasm, enjoyment, excitement, hugs, and kisses) and eliminating SPPPAN (stress, pressure, pushing, punishment, anxiety, and negativism) will keep you on the right track. Best of all, developing the right attitude toward early learning will help you to optimize the time that you spend with your child, whether the time is hours each day or only minutes.

If your child is a newborn, an infant, or a toddler, then stimulation and focusing techniques will form the core of your early activities.

You'll learn dozens of ways to enhance children's awareness of their own identities and of the world around them.

As children grow, speech isn't merely a parent-pleasing development; it's the primary means by which humans (both children and adults) express their self-awareness and their awareness of the world. Activities that bolster speech refinement serve children well throughout their lives, by enhancing their self-confidence and self-esteem.

Later chapters, which address the needs of toddlers and older children, focus on tested methods that make reading, math, and other subjects as accessible to children as speech. If this sounds incredible to you — or, worse yet, unnatural to you — stop for a moment and reflect on the fact that the world surrounding your child is filled with the stuff of knowledge: the numbers of fingers and toes; the sizes and shapes of toys; the letters in a bedtime storybook; all the shades of green in the park. It's obvious that your child will encounter these reflections of his or her universe every day. Making these encounters *happy and meaningful,* for your child and for you, is the aim of this book.

All childhood learning is a family affair. That's why you'll be introduced to both everyday and out-of-the-way places to visit with children. They'll provide easy, yet stimulating answers to the perennial question, "What will we do today?"

Finally, we'll look to the future. In preparation for that day when your child enters school, we'll survey the educational alternatives available to you and will suggest methods for analyzing their benefits and drawbacks.

Perhaps you think that these methods worked with Stephen because he's an exceptional child. You're right; he is. But so, I assure you, is your child. On many occasions, when I've led seminars and workshops, parents have questioned whether their own children would benefit significantly from early learning techniques. My answer is always the same: while all children learn at a different pace, I promise that your child will derive extraordinary pleasure and intellectual growth from early learning and that your satisfaction with your child's progress will amaze you.

Over the years, the stories that I've heard from these parents are consistently heartwarming and encouraging. A bright but "problem" child has developed an eager and even temperament. A child once thought "slow" has shown exciting enthusiasm for his surroundings.

The children are different, but their stories are the same. Theirs are stories of joy. And, because every child is another grand beginning, your story will be one of joy as well.

The Rationale of Early Learning

C an you imagine waking up one morning after a sound sleep only to find yourself in a foreign country, one nestled high in the Himalayas, for example? Despite the awesomeness of your surroundings — or even because of them — your first reaction would probably be one of trepidation. As you continued to look about, your reasons for concern would multiply: you can't read the signs; you can't even speak the language; the people and their customs are amazingly alien to you. Wouldn't it be the answer to a prayer if along came a translator, a tender and caring guide, who spoke your language and who would serve as both instructor and buffer, at once introducing you to the loveliness of this new world while sheltering you from its dangers?

While you may not remember the details, each of us has indeed found ourselves in just this circumstance. We call it birth. And if we were fortunate, we had a tender guide or two — a parent, a grandparent, or other care giver — who paved our way in what would otherwise be an alien and threatening environment.

Venture back to the Himalayas again and try to visualize your mountain guides. If they gave you food, clothing, and shelter, you might feel relieved and satisfied, at least for a time. Your fears would be assuaged. But what about your curiosity? As apprehension gave way to awe, as concern ebbed and curiosity flowed in its place, wouldn't you want to explore your mountain home and meet its people, learn their language, and experience and understand their culture and environment? Of course you would. And, if it eventually occurred to you that you were never going to return to your former home, your desire to comprehend the world about you would grow to an imperative. You would want to become an integral member of your surroundings in order to survive and to flourish. Your very happiness would be intertwined into the fabric of that world. And, if your guides helped you to achieve this nearly magical entrance into a realm of wonder, then your lifelong love and admiration for these individuals would be assured.

So it is with a child.

If all of us recognized this allegory of Shangri-la and understood its relevance for children, we parents would have become early learning guides long ago. But, somewhere between the fairy tale and the reality, a vital concept has been lost, and it is this concept that can make all the difference in a child's life.

"Survive" Versus "Flourish"

There's little doubt that our society spends billions of dollars and nearly endless effort to ensure the survival of infants and children. Thanks to advances in medical technology, for example, infants, some born so prematurely that they weigh less than a pound at birth, now regularly survive. Better understanding of prenatal care likewise ensures that increasing numbers of babies and children will be healthy enough to survive childhood.

So children survive — but do they flourish?

How can you even recognize children who are flourishing? They're the children who are happier and better adjusted than many of their peers. They're eager to learn, are well-behaved and considerate, and are quick to make friends. These are children who, as they mature into young adulthood, are praised, respected, and sought after. Because they associate learning with pleasure and not with deprivation, they manifest an innate, insatiable desire to learn. They are more apt to become tomorrow's leaders, to find the cure for a disease, to create a work of art, to write a book, or to patent an invention. Their intelligence and self-reliance go far to ensure both their material and spiritual success. These flourishing children are a joy to their families, to their friends, and, most important of all, to themselves.

I remember reading, in a book about galaxies, the opinion that science progresses best when our observations force us to alter our preconceptions. I admit that early learning was not a priority with my first four children. I also admit that my determination now to make early learning the number-one priority for all parents is the result not only of my experiences with my son, Stephen. As an educator — a teacher, guidance counselor, and drug specialist for twenty-nine years — I must have read about 13,000 records of children. And from this mountain of information, I observed that children who were the products of early learning — and especially children who could read by the time they entered school — were still the brightest and best-adjusted students in high school. At first, the number of such early learners was fairly low, but in the last ten years, their numbers have increased dramatically. And these children aren't merely taking honors courses and qualifying for college scholarships. They're also more likely to be well-adjusted and they're the most likely to be drug free.

Yet, if these children are such a delight, then why aren't all children flourishing? It certainly isn't from lack of effort or interest. Today, mountains of information are available to parents and care givers. Many moms and dads-to-be (and even grandmoms and granddads-to-be!) read more about infant and child care than do many child psychologists. Their babies will be fed the right food, at the right time, and will be burped right on schedule. And, as the months go by, the child will see more and know more. And the parents will beam. And the grandparents will brag. And everyone will say that milk and cookies alone really are the keys to parenting.

And one day the beloved child will start school. And, the statistics show, there's a one in three chance that this lovable, wonderful child will never learn to read properly and that school will become an uncomfortable chore. And the temptations to find pleasure outside of school and outside the family will grow. If your child lives in a state such as Florida, there's an even chance that he or she will never graduate from high school. And all the shining dreams will begin to tarnish around the edges.

*My gardener worked on my yard every other Saturday morn-
ing, and he brought his young son with him. That little boy's
knowledge was wonderful to observe. He knew the generic and
scientific names for all the Florida grasses. He could talk at
length about fertilizing. He knew all the scientific names for the
trees and flowers. I remember that he could look up into a clear,
blue sky and know that it was going to rain. He explained why
it's hottest at midday, why water is the best drink, why people,
like plants, shouldn't drink too fast. In addition, he was an
uncommonly polite little boy, always thanking me for a snack,
a drink, or a little extra gratuity for helping his dad.*

*I recognized, of course, that the boy's father had been his
teacher and that this man had taught his son naturally and
lovingly. The boy loved to learn and looked forward with anticipation to first grade.*

*But the father had not taught his son to read — "the school
will do that," he told me — and he was bitterly disappointed
when he was called to school. The first-grade teacher of this
wonderful and eager little boy told the astonished father that the
child was "dumb" and that he would "never learn to read." Not
only was the boy kept back in first grade, but after another year
the teacher began to mumble that the boy should be placed in
a school for retarded children.*

*What a dreadful sentence to pass on to so seemingly bright a
child!*

For heaven's sake, what went wrong? In many cases, the gremlin is
a single word: readiness.

The Tyranny of "Readiness"

Let's face it, raising a child can be a terrifying experience. Always,
there are the "what if" fears. What if the child doesn't walk when he
should? What if she doesn't talk when she should?

To alleviate these fears, most "baby books" suggest time frames during
which events ought to occur. If your baby stands in the crib by month
x, then everything's okay. She's right on schedule. If the little princess

stands in her crib earlier than month x, then that's really terrific. You can brag about the miracle to everyone in the office. But, what if month x passes and the little tyke doesn't stand up? What happens if months x plus 1 and even x plus 2 pass by and the child still won't get her bottom off those sheets? Then, you keep quiet. Or you lie. Because all of us have been told that children are supposed to do things on schedule.

These are physical acts. What about mental abilities? Well, the "experts" say that your child should be talking by about twelve months. So you keep cooing "mommy" and "daddy" over the crib rail and, if your wonderful baby, who is only nine months old, coos back anything that vaguely resembles an "m" sound or a "d" sound, well, you break out the champagne.

What comes next? What about reading? Or math? Or world geography? Oh yes, the book says that children will learn these things in school. Why can't *you* teach these things to your child? After all, *you* taught the child to speak, didn't you? It seems that you're a pretty good teacher so far.

The reason why you can't teach these subjects to your child, so we've been told, is because the child isn't "ready." If you ask a first-grade teacher when a child is "ready" to read or write or do arithmetic, that teacher will most likely respond, "The child is ready when he or she enters my classroom." Such a familiar remark indicates that many teachers, consciously or subconsciously, resemble other authority figures — certain doctors, lawyers, or politicians — who want to keep their power to themselves. After all, if virtually any parent can teach virtually any child to read, then the mystique of the first-grade teacher certainly lessens. Largely to defend their domain, teachers and school administrators have invented the theory of readiness. In the past year or two, this jargon has been expanded to include the phrase "developmentally appropriate practice," indicating once again that educators believe it their exclusive right to decide when children should pursue certain academic endeavors. Don't let a well-meaning term scare you into believing that only older children should learn to read, do math, or enjoy other intellectual challenges.

In my own case, I was faced with a monumental dilemma. As an educator, I was only too well aware of the theory of readiness. Yet, as my pregnancy progressed, I was confronted with the doctor's verdict that I was likely carrying a retarded child. I was a working mother with four other children, my three sons and stepdaughter, whom I could not sacrifice to a potentially retarded sibling. I was resolved to devote my six-week mandatory maternity leave to this infant. I also decided to devote an additional four and one-half months of effort to my baby's "education," which began each day in the early morning and continued after I returned from work. I was saddened by the fact that if, after six months, my baby was in fact severely retarded, I might have to place him in an institution.

I did not have the luxury of "readiness," of waiting for the school system to teach my child. In all likelihood, I thought, my son would never confront a school system. If he was to learn anything at all, I would have to teach him, and I had given us a six-month reprieve to show what I could do.

Ties That Bind

My first delight in early learning has proven to be the most meaningful. I have enjoyed an extraordinary bond with Stephen, a bond at once stronger and more flexible than I've shared with my other children. In retrospect, it's easy to understand why. My activities with Stephen developed an innate awareness between us. We could then — and can to this day — "read" each other's thoughts and emotions and communicate with one another using an almost uncanny shorthand. There are no buffers or barriers between us; that's what I mean by a bond.

You may wonder why I speak of early learning, but I don't usually mention the phrase "early teaching." After all, if the child is the early learner, isn't the adult the "early teacher"? Not always. One of the great pleasures in being an early teacher is that you always remain an active *learner*. As your child grows, *you* become increasingly excited by knowing things. *You* want to investigate more and more interesting facts and ideas to share with your child. The benefit for both of you is intense and abiding. Not only do you satisfy your child's immediate desire to know more about the world, but you serve as an exceptional role model for your child — demonstrating firsthand that learning and the love of learning are joyous, lifelong projects.

Thus, the parent-child bond is doubly strong. First, you expand and satisfy your child's insatiable curiosity about the environment. It's an interesting phenomenon that the more a child learns, the more a child wants to learn. When your child begins to spend less time with you — when you return to work or your child begins school — you still remain your child's closest confidante and mentor. That's because from the very first day of your baby's life, you have been his or her guide and teacher.

Remember our trip to the mountains? When someone is helpless, like a baby, the person who satisfies basic survival needs becomes tremendously important. Later, however, when these basic needs have been met, the individual begins to search farther afield for someone to satisfy increasingly more sophisticated yearnings. The individual or individuals who satisfy these new desires gain precedence over the original care giver. That's why so many children, as they mature, look first to their teachers and then to their friends as role models or inspirations. However, if *you* are the individual with whom the child associates the satisfaction of his or her innermost desires — the primary desire being the yearning to understand the world and to express that understanding — then your bond with your child can only grow stronger and more meaningful as your child matures.

If your child is now an infant, totally dependent upon you, then it may seem impossible for the parent-child bond to weaken. But look around you. Everywhere you see children who view their parents and families as enemies. Many of these children bow to the peer pressure which suggests that drugs or alcohol or adolescent sex are good substitutes for the parent-child bond.

In my quarter-century as a school guidance counselor, and specifically as a high school drug specialist for five years, I seldom encountered an "early learner" child who had succumbed to these pressures. Why not? Well, I've come to realize that when a parent participates in early learning with his or her child, the parent-child bond remains uncommonly strong. Because you are an intimate witness to the flowering of your child's emotional and intellectual development, you are cognizant of the smallest changes that may, if left uncorrected, signal later danger. From this intimacy, you come to trust your child — and your child comes to trust you — in a way not typical in today's society. As an example, if your child has difficulty in school, such as with the work, with the teacher, or with another child, he or she is better prepared to share this difficulty with you because he or she knows: 1) that you respect the importance of the problem and 2) that you inherently and rightly believe that your child is telling the truth because you feel as your own the emotions of your child.

> *I was not so lucky with my older children. One day when my son Michael was about ten years old, I was called to school by his teacher. She told me that Michael was not able to keep up with the class; specifically, she said, he was having a great deal of difficulty with reading and arithmetic, especially with subtraction. I was puzzled, because, while I did little educational work at home with Michael, he had never displayed any reading or math problems in my presence. Still, the teacher persisted, so I went home, confused and annoyed, to confront my son.*
>
> *Michael loudly protested his innocence, but I kept repeating to him the teacher's conclusions. Finally, he demonstrated to me that reading and subtraction posed no problems. I later learned that this was all a case of mistaken identity; the teacher had the wrong folder on the desk when I arrived for the meeting.*
>
> *Michael resented my lack of trust, and rightly so. All I can say is that this sorry encounter would never have happened with Stephen.*
>
> *As a high school drug specialist, I know that many parents are not so fortunate. I once encountered a sixteen-year-old girl, a lovely girl, I thought, who had serious problems with school. Heading the list was a major drug problem. After some time I gained her trust, and she confided to me that drugs were an escape from a home life fraught with terror. She said that her father had sexually molested her and I sensed that she was telling the truth.*
>
> *The girl's mother, however, felt differently. "She's a liar," the mother shot back. "Always has been, always will be." I really believed that girl, however, and looked for a way to begin to resolve this terrible situation. I had an idea. With the defiant mother sitting before me, I issued a challenge: "Will your husband submit to a lie-detector test? Your daughter is willing to take one today."   As the mother dissolved into tears and guilt and recriminations, I could only sit and sadly reflect that had this mother and child developed an early bond of mutual trust, this*

*hideous situation might have been prevented or alleviated. My
sadness only increased when the child psychologist appointed to
the case reported to me that what was more devastating to the
girl than the physical attacks of her father was her mother's
refusal to believe that she was telling the truth.*

The Dilemma of the First-Grade Teacher

Whatever your reservations about the school system, one day you
must relinquish your child to its grasp. So I ask you, do you know the
name of your child's first-grade teacher? In fact, do you know anything
at all about this person? When your child's first-grade teacher attended
college, was he or she an excellent student or a mediocre one? Does
your child's first-grade teacher truly enjoy teaching, or is the job simply
a financial necessity? What's going on in the teacher's life? Is his or
her home life tranquil and productive, or is this person facing some
personal crisis that cannot be left at home?

Beyond these more intimate characteristics, what's going on in the
classroom? Are most of the children brighter than your child, which
means that your child may feel pressured? Are some children so slow
that the teacher is forced to adopt an endless repetitive drill technique
that quickly bores the rest of the class and extinguishes their desire to
learn? Are there several children in the class who are consistently
disruptive, stealing the teacher's time and energy for themselves?

What is the teacher's own philosophy of education, and what
philosophy has he or she adopted from his or her own college classes
and brought into the classroom? Does the teacher follow the "executive"
approach, which asserts that children learn only through step-by-step
instruction, by accepting authority and repeating endless drills? Or
does the teacher adopt the Gestalt method, which suggests that children
achieve insights by perceiving patterns of experience? Some teachers
believe in operant conditioning, that children learn only through endless
cycles of reward and punishment. Others are Lockeans, hoping that
simple, repetitive drills hold the key to more complex associations. Is
the teacher a follower of Kohler, or Dewey, or Piaget; is he or she an
advocate of Sartre or Maslow? Does the teacher agree with the cognitive
education theorists who believe that children learn in exactly the same

way as a computer intakes data? These teachers believe that a child's mind intakes information, stores it, retrieves it, and outputs it, just like your personal computer. If such a view is not to your liking, then take heart — your child's teacher may be a liberationist, a believer that the child's mind should be left alone to find its own solutions.

Which philosophy does your child's teacher accept? Every philosophy works some of the time; none of them work all of the time. Even the most rational philosophy simply may not work for your child. But your child will spend all of his or her educational time with this person. Who is this teacher?

Think about it. Your child's ability to read, to write, to add and subtract, or to engage in a dozen other major intellectual undertakings may depend on this person. Whether your child views school as a lifelong adventure or an ongoing punishment may depend on this person. Your child's ability to make friends, to assert his self-esteem, and to articulate her hopes and aspirations may depend on this single individual.

Yet, you don't even know who this person is! Let me ask you candidly: Are you willing to place your child's future in the hands of an individual whom you don't even know? Knowing that learning to read and write is more difficult by age six, is this a risk that you are really prepared to take?

Why not ask the parents of 180 schoolchildren in the Washington, D.C. metropolitan suburban area? The national media reported that these eight- to twelve-year-old children, when surveyed, could name more brands of alcoholic beverages than presidents of the United States. It seems as though these parents have risked their children's educations to the school system, with disastrous results.

Was this a random incident? I think not. That same week, a survey of incoming freshmen at a local university found that only 15 percent could locate the Persian Gulf on a map. One coed smartly pointed to the waters off the coast of Argentina! Yet these same students, when asked to name their most important life goal, chose success. They chose success over family, over service to others, and even over wealth [*Miami Herald*, August 29, 1988]. What success, however, awaits a young person who believes that the Persian Gulf, the hottest area in the political world, lies adjacent to Argentina? We can point accusing fingers, but the conclusion is always the same: the school system, so relied upon by parents, has failed these children.

I was a teacher and counselor in the public schools for three decades, so I'm not here as a teacher-basher. But let's face facts. Let's imagine that your child's first-grade teacher is today still in college. Is she an A student or a C-student? Is he a vital or involved student, or does he cut class when the opportunity presents itself? Let's hope for the best, which does happen perhaps 20 percent of the time. Your child's teacher was indeed a good student and has formed both a coherent theory of education as well as an expertise in what to teach *and* how to teach it.

Then, D-Day occurs — the first day of school. As the teacher stands smiling at the classroom door, twenty-five to thirty-five teary-eyed children march in. They are remarkably bright, just about average, or learning disabled. They come from stable, caring homes or traumatic, crisis-filled environments. They are shy, aggressive, sullen, well-adjusted, or sadly maladjusted, looking for attention or shunning any notice at all. And somewhere in this possible maelstrom of personalities stands your child. Every basic skill that your child will need to know in order to make learning meaningful, now and in the years to come, must somehow be communicated to your child in this environment.

It's a well-known fact that students who find first grade easy and satisfying tend to find the remainder of school easy and satisfying as well. Children's senses of achievement and success, their good attention spans, their problem-solving skills, and even their creativity must be engendered by first grade if they are to emerge at all. If your son or daughter learns what he or she should, then you breathe a sigh of relief. If not, you should get used to sighing, because the next twelve years may be trying ones.

How can you turn the odds in your favor? How can you ensure that the first-grade experience will be a joyous, adventure-filled cap to early learning rather than a sorry introduction to the world of education? The answer is radiantly simple. Even though you have no control over your child's first-grade teacher, *you have total control over your child's first teacher, because that person is you.*

> *You remember my gardener's child? We left him about to enter a school for the retarded. When I heard this, I was shocked! I asked the father if I might attempt to teach the boy to read. He gratefully agreed to let me try and left his son with me all day Saturday and Sunday. In two days, that boy was reading! What did I do? I began by walking around my yard, asking the*

boy for the names of the plants and grasses. As he began to feel comfortable, I took a piece of paper and wrote down the words, one at a time: "grass," "water," "palm," "rose," even "fertilizer." Within a single session, the boy could recognize all these words and could read the schoolbook he had brought with him. What had gone wrong within his first-grade classroom? To this day I don't know. Perhaps the teacher began with phonics and this confused the boy. Many children cannot learn to read by beginning with phonics. By the second day I did introduce phonics with fun games, pictures, and stories, and the boy assimilated this new information without difficulty. What went wrong before I never knew. But I do know that the boy never failed reading again.

"But I'm No Teacher"

I have heard this refrain so often. It has many variations: "Shouldn't I leave teaching to the experts?" "How can I be my child's teacher if I work full-time?" "What if I do something wrong?"

Memorize these points!

1. You *are* your child's teacher, whether or not you accept the position.
2. No one — absolutely no one — is more of an expert on the subject of your child than you are, or can be.
3. Even if you work full-time, even if you spend only minutes a day with your child, you can make those minutes infinitely rewarding for both you and your child.
4. If you use common sense, and if you bring to your teaching role the proper attitude suggested throughout this book, it is *impossible* for you to fail; it is *impossible* for you to do anything wrong; it is *impossible* for your child to suffer.

What are your teaching credentials? In fact, you have three impressive credentials: you have observed this child more intimately than anyone else has; you can individualize your approach to meet the needs of only this child; and you and your child, not the school system, share the greatest stake in your child's success and happiness. You have the most to gain — or the most to lose.

Thanks to these credentials, you don't need any "theory" at all. Instead of the right theory, what you need is the right attitude — an attitude which suggests that learning is exciting and pleasurable for both the learner and the teacher. Then, you simply engage in any of the extraordinarily wide variety of activities suggested in this book. There will be no tedium or boredom; if your child isn't interested in one type of activity, try something else. As you do, you'll see that these activities build on one another to form the patterns of learning that inherently or naturally appeal to the developing structure of your child's brain. As these activity patterns develop, you'll see that they perfectly match your child's "sensitive" periods, those times when the brain and nervous system are expanding in ways that make learning quick, easy, and intensely pleasurable.

How can you tell if your child is learning? That's easy — perhaps too easy for some rigid individuals. There are no tests, no standards, no guidelines. Nothing hurts a child more than comparison, whether it's comparison to another child or to some prescribed criteria for achievement. You'll find none of that here. You only need to remember this: If both you and your child are smiling, then I promise you that your child is learning.

As you share this fantastic journey with your child, you'll witness a miracle: the coming together of a perfect teacher, one with much to give, and a perfect child, one avidly ready to learn.

When Stephen was four years old, and after fourteen years of marriage, my husband and I took our first extended vacation, a drive through the Southern states. Most of our stays were at inexpensive motels, but we planned one night at a deluxe hotel that had advertised fireworks. Our beautiful room had a large balcony, and we looked forward to the fireworks as much as Stephen did, so we were both surprised and disappointed when Stephen became petrified at the noise of the fireworks. Had we explained beforehand what was going to happen, we probably would have alleviated his fright, but as it was, nothing we said could placate him.

The next night there was a tremendous rainstorm, replete

with thunder and lightning. Probably because it reminded him of the fireworks, Stephen was again terrified.

I had become a bit agitated myself, but my husband had an idea. He put Stephen on his lap and said, "I'm going to explain to you exactly what's going on up there." I thought that this might be a bad time for a science lesson, but my husband continued: "You remember when we read the stories about Atlas and Hercules, about how strong they were?" Stephen nodded in agreement. When my husband suggested to Stephen that Atlas and Hercules were merely having a bowling match in the heavens, and that the huge pins falling down were the cause of the thunder, Stephen was delighted. Atlas and Hercules were his old storybook friends, and bowling was certainly an innocent diversion. We had fun with this make-believe explanation, but some time later Stephen's dad explained how lightning and thunder really occurred. At the library I checked out a book on weather, and Stephen and I took long walks discussing the science of the wind and clouds around him. For many years after that, however, whenever there was a thunderstorm, my husband or I, and finally Stephen himself, would always remark: "It's just Atlas and Hercules bowling in the sky."

"How Can I Be a Teacher? I'm Not Even Sure Who Atlas and Hercules Are!"

At one of my seminars on early learning, one or two people will invariably tell me that although the idea of early learning seems like a good one, they are concerned that they may not be capable of carrying it out. A mother may be concerned that she has had little formal education herself. A father may mention that his own grades were never the best. Two career parents, especially those with their first child, are worried that they cannot have a meaningful conversation with a very young child.

These concerns are invariably heartfelt, but they are also unwarranted.

What will you discuss with your child? If you're a computer programmer, some days you'll discuss binary codes and hard disk drives. If you're a construction worker, you'll talk about steel and concrete. Are you a waitress? Children love to hear about food preparation, about the customers you've served, and about the money you've handled. Wherever you work — an office, a factory, a hospital, on an airplane, or in the great outdoors — it sounds like Disneyland to your child. Your coworkers, whomever they are and whatever they do, can be as fascinating to your child as Mickey or Minnie.

Even if you don't work away from home, you'll share wonderful things with your children, from the garden outside the kitchen window or a walk around the block to the inexhaustible children's library which we adults call a supermarket.

The true key to early learning is *communication*. And communication happens in one of two ways — either you enter your child's world, or your child enters your world. When your child is an infant, the scales are tilted more toward your entering the child's world. But very shortly, before your baby is even a toddler, you'll find increasing opportunities for your child to enter your world. And because your world is an extraordinarily wonderful place for a child, you'll derive an impressive array of benefits when this happens.

You'll notice that your child is less cranky or fretful. That's because he or she is more stimulated and less bored. In an early learning environment, no two days are ever exactly alike, even when certain activities are repeated. There will always be the opportunity to derive increased pleasure through more complex understanding. Your child's relationship with the world will be marked by an ever-expanding sense of place, just as his or her relationship with you will be marked by ever-increasing respect, self-esteem, and love.

Every belief has some exception, so I must admit that not all adults are ready for a child to enter their world. When Stephen was twelve years old and was attending New York University, he and I spent Saturdays strolling about the city. One day we were walking along Broadway when Stephen spotted a bookstore. The sign said "Adult Books." Stephen told me that since he was a college student, he thought he could read adult books. Of course, he had no idea of the true connotation of "adult" bookstore. Before I could set him straight or even stop him, in he marched. A rather unsavory-looking man yelled, "Kid, get outta here!" Since Stephen was wearing his NYU shirt and ID pin, he never imagined that the man was talking to him. The man yelled again: "Kid, scram!" Again, Stephen ignored him, walked up to a clerk, and — since Stephen loved games and brainteasers — asked the clerk: "Do you have a magazine called Games?" The two men picked Stephen up and escorted him to the door. I laughed so hard that tears ran down my cheeks.

As I said, not all adults are prepared for such bright children!

The Importance of Attitude

Are There Any Risks in Early Learning?

From time to time, you may hear of an early childhood "expert" who expresses apprehension about the wisdom of early learning. Their concerns take on three main forms:

1. If you practice early learning continuously, you will rob your child of his or her childhood.
2. If you practice early techniques incorrectly, you will impede, rather than foster, your child's desire to learn.
3. If you practice early learning techniques unremittingly, your child may become egocentric or socially maladjusted.

Honestly, can any of these dreadful things happen? Honestly, yes they can. But they happen for a reason, and if you understand the reason why it's possible to get poor results from good intentions, you'll know how to prevent any of these misfortunes from happening.

The key to success is an eight-letter word: ATTITUDE.

Today we are conditioned to think of relationships in terms of "benefits." We are told to enter into relationships that will benefit our employment, our social life, and our bank account. Unfortunately, this idea of reciprocity may become distorted in a parent-child relationship.

It is crucial to remember that we do things for children so that they may do for *themselves*, not so that they may do for *us*. No dreams for your child are too far-fetched as long as they are your child's dreams, too. A child is a singular human being, unique in creation, here to do his or her own bidding. You must never consider children or their accomplishments as status symbols or as monuments to your investment of time, effort, or even money.

For what may be the first time in your life, you enter a relationship giving all and expecting nothing. Your child is here primarily to *be*, not to do. And when your child does, he or she does for himself or for herself, not for you. Thus, you are the role model and the benefactor; your child is the recipient. What makes parenting unique in all the universe is that it may be the only true example of a win-win relationship: when your child benefits, so do you. In fact, the only way that you as a parent can benefit is if your child benefits also.

Some educators today express the belief that early learning is harmful to a child's emotional development. Rarely have these individuals actually participated in early learning activities. Instead, they comment about the "case studies" that have been brought to their attention. When several different academics voiced this concern, I was puzzled. My own results had been substantiated over the years by scores of parents. Why, suddenly, was early learning being called on the carpet?

Yet, as I analyzed the writings and lectures of these academics, the facts became clear. Early learning was not to blame. A mistaken, short-sighted, and, I'm sorry to say, selfish attitude on the part of parents was always the culprit. These so-called early learning "failures" were children who were pushed too hard and too fast, for all the wrong reasons. In fact, the problem was that they were pushed at all.

If your picture of early learning includes a weary child sitting at a desk, throw that picture away! Early learning has *nothing* to do with either pushing or tedium. Quite the contrary. You should approach early learning as a joyous, happy, exciting, fun-filled experience. It was for me, and it has been for the parents whom I've directed. Teaching Stephen was the greatest adventure of my life! It was pure pleasure. At any moment I would rather have been with him than with anyone else I knew. Best of all, these enjoyable experiences have been shared by other parents who practice early learning techniques.

If this sounds too good to be true, let me assure you that bringing up my other children — three sons and a daughter — was the most difficult time of my life, a time of constant battles, shouting, and tears.

"Hurry up!" "Get dressed!" "Stop fighting!" "Stop crying!" "Stop whin-ing!" "Eat!" With these four earlier children, I constantly hoped that the next stage — infancy, babyhood (oh, those terrible twos!), child-hood, preteen, and so on — would be better than the stage we were living through at the time. I always hoped that this next stage would be happier, better, easier, and calmer when the child was finally a little older. My hopes were rarely rewarded. None of that was present with Stephen.

One day when Stephen was about four, I took him to the park. He was playing in the sandbox with several other children when I called him over for juice and cookies. I poured a little of the juice into a cup and told Stephen to take one-fourth of the cookies. There were eight cookies in the package, and Stephen selected two of them. Immediately, the other mothers sitting on the park bench questioned me about Stephen. Finally, one mother remarked, "I never see him here so I guess he never plays. You must keep him working all the time."

I was hurt. The truth was that this park was not near my home. My husband and older sons had gone there to play baseball, so I had taken Stephen to the adjacent children's playground. In fact, Stephen and I went to the park near our home almost every day. Another mother added, "You're robbing him of his childhood, you know," and her friend concurred, "He looks like a nice boy, but you never know."

Later that evening, still feeling stung by those remarks, I asked my husband to show the home movies we had taken of Stephen. When I saw reel after reel of a happy and smiling boy playing on the beach or in the park, with his friends or siblings, I knew that I hadn't robbed Stephen of anything. Quite the contrary, I had fulfilled his birthright, his right to comprehend the world around him.

About six months later we returned to that park and I once again met one of those mothers. She confessed to me that she had started teaching math to her three-year-old daughter and was delighted by the child's response.

This attitude, that early learning somehow "robs" children of their childhood, is an aggravating, pernicious, and downright dangerous misconception. This misconception is never uttered by parents who have actually participated in proper early learning activities. Rather, this is always the belief of an individual who has never come into contact with *healthy* early learning, but who may have encountered those unfortunate children who were made the unwilling pawns in their parents' game of self-aggrandizement.

What these critics are observing is not the failure of early learning, but the failure brought about by an unhealthy *attitude* toward learning. When parents seek to inflate their own egos through the acts of their children, the results are rarely beneficial either to the parent or the child.

Thus, a child may be pushed beyond his or her own interests or abilities in a parent's zeal to create a super-child. One mother pushed her young daughter into so many activities — swimming, gymnastics, tennis, ballet, French lessons — never considering either the child's desires or her stamina, that the girl verged on physical collapse. Another mother used flash cards to excess, assaulting the child during virtually every waking moment. While these reported cases of overzealous instruction are different, they do have a common thread. There was no sense of moderation. In fact, there was no common sense at all on the part of the parent. The goal was never to produce a happy child or a child in whom intellectual, physical, social, and emotional attainments were balanced, but rather to produce a child who could "show off" for relatives, friends, and co-workers.

Again, the fault is not early learning. The fault is improper attitude. If I were forced to imagine examples of these unhealthy attitudes, I would never conjure up fantasies as bizarre as the truth. For example, the state of Florida has recently announced that it is sponsoring deer hunts for children. Why would a child who not so long ago cried over *Bambi* now want to kill deer? The answer, suggested an animal rights activist, is that "Rambo" parents are pressuring their children to hunt animals. Incidentally, why would the state of Florida concoct such a strange activity? Because, they say, a deer hunt will "train youth in the proper respect for wildlife . . . preservation"!

One day Stephen and I went to the traveling library that stopped a few blocks from our house. They had many fine books, and Stephen picked out several to read. I thought that there might be a limit on the number of books he could check out, and I told him to ask the librarian. When we reached the librarian's desk, Stephen asked, "May I take all these books?" The librarian smilingly replied, "Do you sit still when your mother reads to you? I know that my son runs everywhere when I try to read to him." "No," I answered, "I don't plan to read to my son; my son plans to read these books himself." The librarian stared at Stephen, who was four years old at the time, and with saddened eyes she pouted, "My, what a smart little boy you are, but don't you have any fun?" Puzzled at her remark, Stephen looked at me and said, "Mommy, it's fun to be smart!"

Why would anyone think that learning and playing are contradictory or mutually exclusive? This prejudice may be the result of some of our own sorry school experiences where learning certain subjects was difficult because they were started too late. Your child doesn't know the difference between learning and playing. That's part of the miracle of childhood, and it's also a bonus that early learners can take with them into maturity.

For example, do you think that your child would rather play with that new red truck you've just bought, or would he rather learn about spatial concepts? He'd much sooner play with the truck, you think? After about three minutes of wheeling the truck back and forth, isn't he going to become bored? Isn't he going to start banging the truck on the floor moments before he finally abandons it? When you think about it, rolling a truck back and forth isn't really much fun after all.

Let's turn playing with that same truck into a learning experience; specifically, a lesson about spatial concepts. You can talk about under and over, for example. Can the child put the truck under something else? Suggest rolling the truck under a chair or sofa. Can the child place something over the truck? You can suggest a pillow or towel. What's bigger than the truck? How about another truck? Well, if you have a red truck and a blue truck, how many trucks do you have? What you have is a math lesson.

Where else has your child seen trucks? On the highway? What do these trucks carry? Food? Gasoline? Where does gasoline come from? Why do we need it? Can you find the place on the map or globe where gasoline comes from? Next time you go to the service station, the child can understand why you gas up the car. Isn't this kind of play a lot more fun than simply rolling that truck back and forth?

In the same way, other toys can form the basis for lessons. Stephen loved balls and must have had at least fifty of them. I think that we bought every ball he ever saw. He learned spatial concepts from small balls and large ones; he learned colors and patterns; he learned to count; he learned texture, material, hardness, and softness; he practiced concepts such as over, under, and beside; he learned to add and subtract, and even to multiply and divide. Beyond providing opportunities for mental dexterity, those balls also provided occasions for physical activity and creativity. Balls can be thrown, caught, bounced, and rolled; they're fun in water, sand, or grass.

While playing with toys is a traditional childhood pastime that can provide valuable learning experiences, the best "toys" that children possess are their minds and their imaginations. Their own mental resources can fashion inexhaustible toy chests filled with ever-new, ever-exciting experiences. Recognizing this, you see that I never "robbed" Stephen of his childhood. Instead, I enhanced every possible opportunity for fun and learning. By every "possible" opportunity, I mean that I respected Stephen's moods and my own. I never began learning activities if he was tired, and I tried to avoid them if I was tired. Certainly, I laid low if Stephen was ill. But even during illness, children can learn valuable lessons. They can learn about sickness and, more important, about recovery; they can learn exactly how strong the parent-child bond really is and that their parents will not desert them when they are ill.

> When Stephen was only a year old, he contracted pneumonia and had to be hospitalized. I could make this a "learning" story by explaining that I did not bring any new toys to the hospital. Rather, I let Stephen choose his favorite picture cards, toys, puzzles, and books to bring himself. In this story, however, I'd rather you learn a more important lesson. You see, in this hospital, parents were allowed to visit but were not allowed to stay with seriously ill children. The nurses insisted that I leave. I stayed. They sent a janitor who removed all the chairs from the room. I sat on the floor. At night they demanded that I leave. I slept on the floor under the crib. I tenaciously resolved that Stephen must never — not ever — think that he couldn't depend on me.

I wanted him to know that I could always be depended on.

Of course, I hope that you're never confronted with an incident like this, but I want you to understand that all early learning is built on a foundation, and that foundation is the parent-child bond. If you weaken that bond, then recovery, if it comes, may be slow.

Coincidentally, Stephen's friend contracted pneumonia at the same time. The difference is that his mother obeyed the hospital authorities and left the child alone. I observed that it took that little boy more than a year to recover from those few days of trauma. He cried whenever his mother left the room; his moods and temperament changed; he lost ground socially, emotionally, and mentally. What had happened? It wasn't only the illness; the greater trauma was the recognition that he couldn't always rely on his mother, that she wasn't there when he needed her the most. That's why your attitude toward every event that faces your child is so critical.

There are several prerequisites to a healthy attitude about children in general and about your own child's early learning in particular, but the most important is to recognize that your child is an individual human being with a unique personality. Your son may be gregarious, always smiling at everyone, or he may grouse or whine at the least provocation. Perhaps your daughter is active, never in the same place for more than a moment, or she may be passive, quiet, or moody. Your own attitude may be uncommonly pessimistic or critical and that is bound to have an effect on your child.

Just as personalities and physical types differ, so do children's mental abilities and interests. From this observation derives our first rule of healthy parenting:

1. Avoid comparing your child's progress to that of other children. If you can't avoid observations, at least avoid judgments.

From this precept derives another, just as important:

2. Never set definite goals based on time. Never expect any accomplishment to take place by or before a specific time, because this leads to unnecessary pressure.

Of course, always report suspicious symptoms to your pediatrician, but recognize that *childhood is not a race.* It doesn't matter what your neighbor's son or your sister-in-law's daughter has already accomplished, because your child is following his or her own clock, not theirs. Finally, here's a third rule to complement the other two:

3. Don't give tests.

You are a parent, or an individual filling the parent role, not a professor or a drill sergeant. Tests imply right and wrong answers, passing and failing. That's not what early learning is all about. An incorrect answer should elicit no negative reaction; instead, wrong answers are merely opportunities for both of you to consider what the correct answer may be.

If you simply take it for granted that a child is learning, you'll soon learn that you're absolutely correct!

The Keys to Success: PEEEHK and SPPPAN

When I recall my earliest years as a teacher, I always think of a tenth-grade basic math course. The students were about sixteen years old, nearly all of them ready to drop out of high school. I wish that critics of early learning could have seen these children. None had ever received even a C on a report card; Ds and Fs were all they knew.

And so it might have been with me. I had given five tests and, not surprisingly, every student had failed every test. I unloaded on my principal. "What these kids need is a psychologist or maybe a psychiatrist, not a teacher. I can't teach them anything. The class is absolute bedlam. The kids throw erasers. They scream at one another. They turn the lights off. I'm at a loss. All my other classes — the business education classes — are fine. But I absolutely cannot teach that class!"

The principal shrugged, muttered that no one else was available to teach the class, and insisted that I return. "Do what you can" was his only admonition.

For some reason, I decided to go to the counselor's office and read the cumulative record folders for those students. These assessment folders had traced the children from first grade. As I read true-life tales more incredible than fiction, tears came to my eyes. My God, I thought, it's a miracle that these children are alive. One child, as an infant, had hot water poured on him and was left to die. Another child was allowed to swallow nails before he was finally placed in a psychiatric hospital. A third had been beaten unconscious with a cane. On and on the stories went, and at last I made a crucial observation: these children had never once met with success. Not ever.

With the zeal of a missionary I returned to the principal. "Those children," I adamantly told him, "are not going to fail anymore. In my class they will only receive praise. If you check their folders, you may see that they're still doing F work, but they are not going to get another F!" The principal, grasping at any straw, agreed. "Do it," he assented, "do anything!"

It was like a miracle. In truth, it was a miracle. A child psychologist had told the mother of one of these students, "If your child ever learns any math, it will be a miracle." Well, I must be a miracle worker because this woman's child did, in fact, learn math.

They all learned. And they learned because I praised whatever they did. They never failed. Every test they took, they passed. Of course, these children were neither stupid nor naive. At first they knew that they hadn't earned the grades. Furthermore, they knew that it wasn't right to receive a grade that they hadn't earned. But, as time passed, they started working to earn the grades that they were already receiving.

I tacked their papers on the bulletin board. I called in their mothers to brag about their papers. For most of these parents, the visit was a shock. Here they were called to school for the umpteenth time, and they had already steeled themselves for the inevitable criticism. I could see by their body language that they were stiff with tension and battered with despair. I wish that you could have seen the expression on a mother's face when I opened my mouth and said, "Mrs. Jerome, I had to call you here to tell you how fantastic your son is. His progress is absolutely wonderful!" This poor woman was so shocked that she nearly fainted. And I repeated this meeting with every parent. I encour-

*aged them to praise their children — whatever small action they
might find to praise — because the children, wanting to continue
hearing that praise, would eventually take steps to earn it.*

*One day, years later, Mrs. Jerome gave me a call, and on
that day my tears were ones of joy. "Dr. Baccus, I wanted you
to know that my son and I graduated college on the same day
last week."*

The right attitude: with it, every good thing is possible; without it,
no good thing can survive to maturity. Because of the importance of
proper attitude in early learning — indeed, in all child care — I've
endeavored over the years to define what is meant by "the right attitude."
The most universal definition that I've offered to parents throughout
the years is:

Embrace PEEEHK and Avoid SPPPAN!

What is PEEEHK? That's simple — each letter stands for a word.
Praise. Excitement. Enthusiasm. Enjoyment. Hugs. Kisses.

Think about these words for a moment. They form a complete
emotional response to your child's learning. That's why you shouldn't
try to separate these concepts, because what you want to offer your
child is an intense, genuine, spontaneous reaction that embodies your
mutual pleasure in learning.

In the quiet of our home, I still scream out loud when Stephen does
something great, whether he passes the Bar exam with a high score,
receives a perfect score on a graduate record exam, or wins a difficult
legal case. I still hug and kiss him when he plays a beautiful song. And
you can do the same for your child. If you're the type of person who
generally can't show enthusiastic affection, then it's even *more* important
that you try to do so. Your child will be excited and impressed by your
efforts.

Not only that, but your child will want to see you get excited again and
will want to see you get excited again and will want to be praised again.
That's what makes early learning so much fun. It challenges, excites,
and satisfies a child's limitless imagination, plus it offers so many
pleasurable opportunities for parental enthusiasm. So success leads to
success, in matters both large and small.

It doesn't matter *how much* your child learns, because your son or daughter certainly knows more than he or she did yesterday. Every child wants a mother's or father's hugs, kisses, praise, and other signals of love. Children want this more than they want anything in the world. Always find ways for your child to succeed. Make your suggestions so simple that your child must succeed. Once you start, it is virtually impossible to extinguish this winning attitude. Once a child learns to win — to succeed in accomplishing something — and once your child learns how great it *feels* to succeed, your child will always *want* to succeed.

Many parents ask about giving children material rewards for certain accomplishments (learning new words, getting good grades, or the like). First, let's distinguish between a reward and a bribe. A reward comes after the fact; a bribe comes before the fact. Take the example of good grades. If your child gets an A in a difficult subject, and, spontaneously, you give the child a small gift for that A, that's a reward. Occasional small rewards for good performance are typically harmless as long as they supplement, but do not replace, parental enthusiasm and excitement. You should not give your child a gift *instead* of your affection simply because you're "too busy" to invest your time in an enthusiastic personal response. The best gift is always a part of yourself — your praise, your attention, your enthusiasm, your time. But an occasional material reward will not undermine this.

Bribes, on the other hand, can be destructive. A bribe is a promise made in advance — if you get a good grade, I'll give you a new bike. When you bribe a child, the pleasure of learning is never a goal. The goal is always the promised article. Children who must be bribed in order to accomplish something subconsciously internalize a negative concept. They conclude that they don't have the talent or initiative to accomplish anything unless they're bribed.

Bribes are especially negative when they're teamed with requests to perform. Some children, sooner or later, enjoy displaying their abilities. For many parents, however, this moment cannot come too soon. From the time a child learns to say "Mama" or "Dada," the entreaties and enticements to perform always seem to be present: "Tell Daddy what you told me;" "Tell Grandma;" "Tell Auntie." Tell. Tell. Tell. Do. Do. Do.

When an occasional request turns to unbridled petitions, children turn off. These childhood episodes are probably the original chapter of performance anxiety. Many children do not like to perform or show off even for relatives, and especially for strangers. Children have a unique way of refusing anyone who asks them to perform something that they consider irrelevant. Nor can most children comprehend how much pleasure their performances give you. More often, requests for performance are seen by children as tests to be passed, and children, wanting to avoid possible failure, refuse to say or do anything at all. Later you will read about one child who even refused to read for his mother.

You'll learn how to overcome these hurdles. In general, parents are best advised to avoid these requests or to at least couch them in the form of a question: "Would you like to count to ten for Aunt Anna? You're a terrific counter!" That way, the child has already received praise (not a bribe, just praise), and the child can simply say no; the parent might then respond, "Well, maybe next time. I know that you know your numbers very well."

Some parents, however, are embarrassed by their children's rebukes and seek to remedy the situation by bribing the child: "If you count to ten for Aunt Anna, then we'll go for ice cream." This sets up an endless cycle of bribes and performances that can destroy individual initiative and zest for learning. Invariably, most children will one day feel comfortable expressing what they know. Don't use bribes to hurry that day along.

If there is any way to encourage a child's speech or other abilities, it's by PEEEHK (pleasure, excitement, enjoyment, enthusiasm, hugs, and kisses). In that way, whenever the child accomplishes anything, you ensure that the *child* receives pleasure. When you ask a child to perform, however, *you* are the one seeking pleasure, a fact typically unimportant to your child. So you rely on a bribe to balance the scales. Don't belittle your child in that way.

Critics of early learning adopt their beliefs after exposure to *miseducated* children. Is there some way that you can avoid this miseducation and practice risk-free early learning? The best way is by adopting PEEEHK, because when your child sees the gleam in your eyes, hears the enthusiasm in your voice, and feels the love in your hugs and kisses, then early learning experiences must be the most pleasurable that you and your child will ever share.

But parents always ask, "Isn't there some other insurance policy so that we don't unknowingly do the wrong things?" Yes! In addition to

embracing PEEEHK, avoid SPPPAN: Stress. Pressure. Pushing. Punishment. Anxiety. Negativism.
Remember:

NO STRESS!
NO PRESSURE!
NO PUSHING!
NO PUNISHMENT!
NO ANXIETY!
NO NEGATIVISM!

Early learning critics tend to base their views only on observations of children whose parents *adopted* SPPPAN rather than *avoided* it. Let me repeat this point, because it is so vital. When a child suffers at the hands of an overzealous parent, early learning is never to blame, because early learning does not demand a competitive, stressful environment. True early learning can flourish *only* in a noncompetitive atmosphere marked at once by enthusiasm and moderation. Thus, in these textbook cases of parental fervor, the parents' attitude is the source of the problem. Many people in Miami, for example, are familiar with the hard-nosed news commentator who always pressured his young son in front of friends and relatives to "speak up;" "make sure that they hear you;" "let 'em know you're my kid." The child not only bore the brunt of his father's harassment but other people's annoyance and displeasure. This negativism should have been directed solely to the father, but it was directed unfairly toward the son as well.

Furthermore, while it is logically impossible to generalize from these extreme cases, some early learning critics do just that. They remind me of a noted group of nineteenth-century psychiatrists whose only patients were schizophrenics or psychotics. Instead of realizing that they were seeing only a minute subsection of the population, these psychiatrists erroneously assumed that all individuals have schizophrenic or psychotic tendencies. Today their assumptions may seem laughable, but the sorry fact is that their beliefs colored the practice of psychiatry for nearly a century.

It is much the same today with early learning critics. Instead of counseling parents in *correct* early learning techniques, as I have always done, they believe that the path of least resistance is to teach *nothing at all.* They consider this course the safest. And they might be right, except for one fact: Children learn many things, whether they're exposed to early learning or not. But children who are *not* exposed to early learning, who roll a truck endlessly back and forth on the floor for example, only learn that the world is a boring place, that time is something to be filled with endless repetition, that each day is pretty much like the day before.

Thus, the decision *not* to practice early learning invariably leads to parent-child stress. The parent invariably (and naturally, I might add) wants the child to give evidence of increasing mental agility, but the child, having had few opportunities to learn anything, is nearly powerless to respond. This sets up the first of many confrontations to come. Teachers also expect to see evidence of learning. However, the child who is forced to begin learning at the age of five or six, not when learning is easiest, but when it is most difficult, now associates all learning *not* with *pleasure*, but with stressful and unpleasant situations.

That's why it's so vital — and also so easy — to integrate early learning into the natural activities of childhood. If at an early age your child associates learning with pleasure and self-esteem, you'll give your child extraordinary powers: the power to reason, the power to make decisions, the power to express feelings and thoughts, the power to become increasingly self-reliant, the power to make sense of the universe. Aren't these powers a lot more wonderful than the power it takes to roll a truck back and forth?

So it is that psychiatrists today apologize for their mistaken colleagues of an earlier century. I'm convinced that as we approach a new century and a new millennium, early educators will one day apologize for early learning antagonists in just the same way. By that time, however, it may be too late for your child.

> One Easter I decided to have an Easter egg hunt for the neighborhood children. Stephen, along with his brothers and sister, had boiled and colored the eggs the day before. I was delighted to see Stephen's siblings join in the early learning. They would ask Stephen how many eggs there were, how many eggs there would be if they divided that number in half, how many colors Stephen could name, and so on. It was a lovely scene and I beamed as I observed it.
>
> The day of the hunt found the children anxiously waiting for

a little girl who lived down the block with her grandmother. When the little girl failed to appear, I went to her house and was astonished to find her crying. The girl's grandmother had insisted that the little girl make her bed before she went to the Easter egg hunt. The girl had obliged, but the grandmother could only repeat, "You call that making a bed?"

I offered to help the girl make the bed. No good. I asked if the girl might go to the hunt first and remake the bed later. No good. I pointed out that the bed was made pretty well considering that the girl was only about five years old. Still no good. I asked the grandmother to show the child how to make the bed and was met with an icy retort, "She ought to know how to make a bed!"

I ask you, which environment was more stressful — the early learning in my home, or the absence of learning in that grandmother's home?

Some attitudes that adversely affect children are far less obvious and far more subtle. So let's review the key components of SPPPAN so that you can recognize and eliminate these threatening attitudes before they adversely affect your child's development.

The first deals with stress. The absence of stress is a key ingredient in successful early learning. That's why early learning is not goal oriented; it's child oriented. If you're a hardworking and industrious parent, as most of us are, it may be difficult for you to undertake any action that fails to have an immediate goal. Certainly our careers are always goal oriented. We, or our employers, want to see results. Don't bring this attitude home to your child. Early learning always brings results, today, tomorrow, and next year. The key is *not to look for results* but to concentrate on the wonderful time you're having with your child.

When you become goal oriented, when you add stress to the early learning equation, the child senses this immediately. Then, the fear of failure colors every situation and learning is no longer fun. Instead, it becomes drudgery, a task to be accomplished in order to keep mommy and daddy happy. Remember, NO STRESS!

Pressure is a little different than stress. Pressure typically involves coercing a child to do something that the child does not want to do or coercing a child to do something longer or more often than the child wants to do it. Another principle of early learning is that you don't do more than your child wants to do; instead, *you do less*. The "do less" principal is the same theory adopted by a producer who wants to leave the audience hungry to come back for more. When you decide that an activity has gone on long enough — that is, the activity has excited your child but has not become boring — stop. That's it: stop. Go on to another activity, preferably in a new physical location, "Let's start to make dinner," or "Let's see if the mailman came," or "Let's see if the roses are blooming."

That way, if there's any pressure in the early learning environment, the pressure comes from the child. Your daughter will want to hear another story and still another one. Your son will ask you to teach him more words. That's good pressure. Pressure that originates with you is bad pressure. Remember, NO PRESSURE!

If there is any single word associated with faulty early learning, that word is "pushing." Pushing is a "too" word: too hard, too long, too many, too advanced.

> *Stephen, even as a very young child, expressed an interest in acting. I was certainly no stage parent; the idea of acting would never have occurred to me had Stephen not made the first suggestion. Over the years, he has appeared on television, in motion pictures, even on the stage, and the reviews of his work are wonderfully positive.*
>
> *One of the more interesting roles that he had as a young teenager was that of the Nazi youth in the play* Tomorrow the World. *At the time, I wondered if the role would be too emotionally draining for him, but he was intensely interested in portraying this menacing character. I went to a performance and, during intermission, overheard two women discussing the play. Specifically, they were discussing Stephen. "He's such a nasty boy," one of these ladies remarked; her friend nodded and then adamantly added, "You can tell he's a nasty boy in real life too!" I couldn't believe my ears! I turned around to the two of them and set them straight!*
>
> *At that time, I was satisfied that Stephen could handle the emotions inherent in the character he was portraying. But I was not satisfied on an earlier occasion. Stephen was about eight years old and, because he showed an interest in acting, was attending a local drama school. The director instructed each*

child to assume the part of a child of divorced parents.

I observed that Stephen immediately rejected this role. He told the director-teacher that such a role was too far-fetched for him. He could never imagine his parents divorcing. The director insisted that Stephen choose one parent with whom to stay. I saw that Stephen was becoming upset as she told him, "I can't let you get away with this. You have to do this part. Now, pick a parent and tell us which one you've chosen."

Stephen, tears streaming down his cheeks, answered, "I guess I'd pick my mother because she would be better able to take care of me."

I felt no pride at being the "chosen" parent. What I felt was rage because my child was pushed into doing something that he was emotionally unprepared to do. Stephen never returned to that drama school.

Pushing is nearly always the result of a parent who wants a child to show off. Children who undertake too many activities that they themselves do not care to do, or who undertake activities that are too physically strenuous for young children, are typically trying to win their parents' approval. Such children are pushed, consciously or unconsciously, by the signals received from their parents. The signals say, do more, do better, and then I'll love you.

Ask yourself this question and be truthful in answering it. Do you want your child to succeed, or do you want your child to be happy? Today, the answer to this question very often hinges on success. Parents ask me, "Are success and happiness mutually exclusive?" or "Doesn't success lead to happiness?" The answer, of course, is that they're not exclusive and that yes, happiness is often based on successes — big ones and little ones. But success does not invariably lead to happiness. The successes must be appropriate for your child, undertaken because, in fact, they make your child — not you — happy. Remember, NO PUSHING.

"Punishment" is a word that usually elicits a deep-gut, emotional response from parents. Many parents assume that the general absence of punishment means the withholding of discipline, and they invariably set up a "what if" situation. Of course, children need guidelines and they also need discipline when they exceed those guidelines. However, many parents unwittingly set up situations that later require discipline.

For example, if your daughter is a proficient crawler, you have two choices. You can remove hazards from her path, or you can spend all day yelling "don't" and slapping her wrist when she does. Children want to learn about their world. That's the natural tendency on which all early learning is based. And you can't expect a child to discern that multicolored puzzles are great fun while multicolored glass vases are forbidden.

If you remove offending objects from your child's environment, you'll accomplish two great things. You'll reduce the tension level in your home as you refrain from making the child's entire day one long string of "don'ts," and you'll increase the effectiveness of warnings and of discipline because you'll reserve them only for necessary occasions.

If you live near water, for example, then your child must understand that it is forbidden to go near the water. However, if your "don't go near the water" warning is couched in the middle of dozens of other "don'ts," then your child fails to grasp the special importance of this one warning. Protect your own nerves and your child's safety by eliminating as many attractive hazards as you can.

What about punishing a child who refuses to learn or who learns poorly? My answer is only one word: Never! I asked Stephen just the other day if he remembers ever being punished or hit. He thought a moment and said, "No, never." Stephen was never bad, not because he was a saint, but because he was so eager to learn that it didn't occur to him to misbehave.

> *Of course, when I say "never bad," I mean that Stephen was never violent or aggressive. He had a rambunctious nature like most children, and always enjoyed a harmless — if annoying — practical joke.*
>
> *Such jokes or teases were naturally directed toward his brothers. As a young boy, one of Stephen's favorites was propping a pail of water atop Clifford's bedroom door. Clifford would enter the room, the pail would fall, and Clifford's "I'm going to get you!" screams would reverberate throughout the house.*
>
> *One day I had had enough. "Stephen," I offered adamantly, "if one more pail of water spills on your brother's head, you are going to be punished." I knew that this would be the end of it because Stephen, after all, was not a disobedient child.*
>
> *I was, therefore, somewhat taken aback when, a few days*

later, I once again heard Clifford's angry yells. Resigned to the fact that Stephen had disobeyed me, I angrily summoned him to me.

"Didn't I tell you not to drop a pail of water on your brother's head?" "Mommy, he offered sheepishly, "I didn't." "Then why is Clifford screaming? Answer me that, Stephen!" "Because," Stephen told me, trying to conceal a grin, "this time I put sand in the pail, not water."

All children want to learn, but at any given moment a child may be bored or tired, just plain ornery due to illness or some other event, or even overly excited by the day's events. The activity may be too advanced or presented poorly. *You* may be bored or tired or just plain ornery because of physical or emotional problems. When this happens, simply put the activity away. Early learning relies on an atmosphere where there is NO PUNISHMENT!

When I suggest no punishment in the early learning environment, however, I do not mean that you should not punish hostile or defiant acts. A child who is learning is almost always a delight, but certainly you need to use common sense in dealing with negative or aggressive behavior. For instance, you cannot allow a child to destroy property or to hit, bite, or kick you whether it is a learning situation or not.

Eliminating anxiety comes next. Anxiety, realistically defined in terms of a child's perceptions, is the fear of failure. In early learning you can eliminate anxiety by eliminating opportunities to fail. Never test. Never ridicule an answer. Children say correct and incorrect things all the time, but by nature they speak what they believe to be the truth. Children are generally incapable of cunning or subterfuge. If your child consistently says incorrect things, then perhaps you aren't presenting him or her with the information from which the correct answer can be deduced.

Pay continuing attention to your child's body language. If your child squirms, seems distracted, evades your eyes, yawns, or turns away, then your child is very likely bored, tired, ill, or otherwise emotionally or intellectually unable to cope with the current activity. Don't correct or reprimand him or her. Simply call the activity to a halt and begin again at another time. Analyze these signals from your child. Is the material too difficult? Does the child prefer to learn in another way? Recent evidence suggests that a child who turns an ear to you — and who does not have a hearing problem — may actually learn better through hearing than through the other senses. Try not to allow opportunities for failure to exist. When they do occur, make sure that your child understands that everyone makes mistakes and that the child is not a failure as a person. Everyone breaks a toy, drops a ball, gives the wrong response, or forgets an answer. That's okay. You love your child all the time, not just when things are right.

> *Once, when my washing machine was broken, Stephen and I went to the laundromat. I took him out of his stroller so that he could participate in the chores with me. He was helping me transfer the clothes from the washer to the dryer, and I asked him to try not to drop anything because the floor was pretty grimy. Stephen did his best, but wouldn't you know it, he dropped a washcloth on the floor. As huge tears welled in his eyes, I immediately dropped a towel on the floor and said, "You see, Stephen adults have accidents and make mistakes too. It's no big deal. We'll put these things in the next wash, but first, let's see if we can shake the dirt out."*
>
> *Later at home, we counted the towels and washcloths. In both cases, there were eleven clean items instead of twelve. I reminded him that we had to rewash the washcloth and towel that we had dropped and that we both had to learn to be more careful. We started to shake out the laundry as though it were dirty again, and we both dissolved into laughter.*
>
> *Children feel bad enough when accidents happen. Don't make matters worse by chastising or punishing them. Instead, say and do the kinds of things that boost morale. You'll find fewer accidents happening in the future.*

Never convey by words, gestures, or attitude that you are disappointed in your child. Nothing is so dispiriting to a child as parental displeasure. When you give a child a new toy or puzzle, for example, don't walk away, leaving the child to his or her own devices, only to express disdain when the toy is broken or the puzzle completed incorrectly. Be there with your child, at least at first, offering encouragement and boosting your child's confidence and self-esteem. Praise the child's observations and early attempts. That's what fun is all about. And early learning is all about fun, the unending fun of a magical universe. Remember, NO ANXIETY!

Negativism can be conveyed by both verbal and nonverbal behavior. Most literate adults understand the awesome power of language. What some of us don't realize is that we adults have many defense systems to protect ourselves from negative language. If someone says something negative to us, we can refute the authority of that person. We can walk away; we can explain or argue our own case. Children have none of these defenses; as a result, negative words are destructive to children.

Negative words associated with learning ("You're wrong;" "Try harder;" "You still don't know the right answer") are viciously destructive. If you eliminate stress, pressure, pushing, punishment, and anxiety, you will have gone a long way toward eliminating many possible occasions for negativism.

Be aware, however, of more subtle negativism. One indirect but potent form of negativism is what some parents would call "justified" disinterest. Let's face it, we're all busy people, and children often ask for assistance at hectic moments. You know the responses: "I'm busy now;" "Mommy is on the phone;" "Daddy's getting ready to play tennis;" "I have to get ready to go out;" "I want to watch this TV program;" "I'm cooking dinner." Certainly these occasions happen to all of us, but if your child is *consistently* hearing these messages, then you're working as hard to undo the parent-child bond as you once worked to strengthen it.

Of course you're getting dressed to go to work, but can't you take sixty seconds to answer a question or offer a word of encouragement? Realize that you can get dressed and tell a story at the same time. Cooking dinner? Have your child help. Watching TV? Hoist your child onto your lap and explain why the show is so interesting. Virtually every negative situation can, with a small amount of effort and interest, be turned into a pleasurable experience for both parent and child. Remember that the heart of early learning is not drill or rote, but response — your response to your child's desire to know about the world. Remember, NO NEGATIVISM!

Whether you practice early learning or not, SPPPAN can impoverish your child's life. It can destroy self-respect, self-confidence, and self-reliance. It will destroy any later attempt to learn. And the sad truth is that when you don't give your child the gift of early learning activities, there are simply many more occasions for SPPPAN in your child's life. On the other hand, avoiding SPPPAN and embracing PEEEHK in an early-learning program will ensure that childhood is an enchanted experience whose shared joys, spontaneous pleasures, and steadfast bonds will last a lifetime.

Today, more and more parents want to give these gifts to their children. Now that you understand the rationale of early learning and the attitude that guarantees its success, you're probably asking, "How do I begin? What do I do next?"

Take a deep breath. Seriously, take a deep breath . . . let it out . . . now, relax. The following chapters will teach you everything that you need to know to become the very best teacher in your child's universe.

CHAPTER THREE

Stimulation and Focusing

What exactly are stimulation and focusing? Perhaps the best way to explain is with an analogy. Imagine, if you will, a sumptuous buffet at an elegant restaurant. A sparkling table perhaps sixty feet long is filled with delicacies from around the world: steaming, medium-rare prime rib of beef, its burgundy juices running onto a silver tray; golden-crusted quiche filled with leeks and asparagus and truffles; vegetables — red and green, purple and gold — fresh from the garden; buttered herb breads, hot and crusty. And the desserts! Milk chocolate, white chocolate, amaretto chocolate bursting from souffles and cakes and mousses, all topped with lacy cascades of fresh whipped cream.

That sensory ecstasy is *stimulation*.

However, while this vast array of sensory delights excites your eyes and whips your salivary glands into overdrive, you realize, perhaps sadly, that you can't eat everything. You have to make a choice. So you look up and down that table and finally make a selection: toothsome ripe strawberries nestled in a chocolate-cognac sauce. As you down the first bite, you concentrate on that exquisite blend of flavors: the sweet tang of strawberry mixed with the heady darkness of French chocolate and 100-year-old liqueur. Every bite is the same, yet every one is different, each possessing an infinitely different proportion of the enticing ingredients. Before the last bite is swallowed and the magic gone, you concentrate on the incredible taste, willing your palate to remember this moment forever. This concentration, of course, is *focusing*.

So I ask you, if life can be just this kind of banquet, filled with extensively pleasurable stimulation and intensively delicious focusing, then why should you, so to speak, feed your child a fast-food hamburger every day?

The point I want to make is crucial. In my exhaustive research on gifted children, I examined the backgrounds of virtually every historical figure who has been considered a genius, a savant, a prodigy, or any other synonym that we apply to an intellectually talented individual. I was gratified to learn that seldom were these people "born brilliant," despite our popular misconception that they were.

Historically, the intellectual and cultural leaders of any society have, in fact, owed a debt to their parents, but the debt is not a genetic one. In virtually every case, the parents of these world-renowned persons provided exceptional early learning opportunities for their children. Some parents hired tutors, but most took on the jobs themselves. And, tossing aside another misconception frequently asserted by critics of early education, few of these children were ever forced to submit to vigorous, narrow, or pedantic learning. Whether the teacher was Aristotle, perhaps the greatest intellect in western civilization and tutor to Alexander the Great, or simply any of the remarkable but unpretentious mothers who nurtured some of America's greatest statesmen, their methods, I learned, were very much alike.

Basically, these people said to the impressionable children in their care: "The world is a pretty remarkable place, and I'd like to share some of that wonder with you."

That's it? Yes, to a great degree, that is it.

These observations gave rise to an important realization in my own thinking. Most parents do not abandon their children. Typical parents spend many hours "playing" with or at least being with their children. Why, I wondered, don't all children exhibit the benefits of early learning? The answer has much to do with purpose. Activities are a kind of self-fulfilling prophecy. If the activity is designed to challenge, it challenges; if it is designed to fill up time, that's just what it does.

Yet, how can we distinguish the activities that provide the greatest opportunities for stimulation and focusing? This question has often led me to review the notes that I kept on Stephen's early progress. I jotted down the activities that I or the family shared with Stephen and made special note of the activities that elicited progressively more advanced physical or mental responses. My earliest goal centered on my doctor's fear that Stephen might be retarded. If, in fact, he would have to be institutionalized, I wanted to pass on the most accurate information about the activities that he found physically or intellectually challenging. Later, when I realized that Stephen was not only *not* retarded but was advancing at an incredible rate, the educator in me came out, and I continued to maintain my journal, hoping to share the information with other parents and educators.

Today, neurobiologists (scientists who study the physiology and development of the brain) confirm the importance of early stimulation and focusing. A baby is born with a complex but largely inactive brain. Through the first two years of life, the baby's brain increases its activities *in response to stimuli.* The greater the stimuli, the greater the response. In fact, by the time the child is two years old, he or she has more synapses (transmitters that carry nerve messages) in the brain than that child will ever have. Like me, you may find it wondrous to learn that a two-year-old child has *twice* the number of synapses as an adult.

Where do these relay stations of the brain go? Why do they disappear as children grow older? Scientists tell us that the brain, like many parts of the body, has a built-in conservation system. When the brain observes that certain networks are not used, it begins to shut them down. Between the ages of two and five, a child's brain seems to be at work every moment culling out these unused pathways. Thus, by the time a child is ready to enter kindergarten, virtually millions of unstimulated brain synapses have been destroyed . . . by the brain itself! And it is at this very moment that we say to the child, *now learn.* This really does seem unfair, doesn't it?

The destruction of these precious synapses continues throughout childhood until, by about the time of puberty, fully half of the synapses in the brain are lost. On the other hand, a child whose brain is stimulated early and often with appropriate activities is sending the brain a far different message: "Wait a minute! I need all those synapses. Don't destroy anything!"

Thus, early learning activities actually change the biology of the brain itself, ensuring that virtually all possible synapses or learning highways are available throughout childhood and into maturity. It is not so much that "gifted" individuals are born brilliant; we are all born brilliant. Those persons who we call gifted have merely *sustained* the brilliance that their minds, like everyone's mind, grasped at the moment of birth. So often we have argued over the relative importance of heredity and environment. Now we better understand that the most crucial element in education is the *learning environment* that we bring to the heredity handed to us.

Most of this scientific evidence was unknown to me when Stephen was an infant. Certainly it was unknown to the parents of historical figures who we now call "great" men and women. I believe, however, that many of us sensed that neurological development proceeded in just this way and, as we began an early learning program for our own children, these intuitions were amply justified and rewarded.

Why, then, doesn't every parent or educator think the same way? In one sense, the blame is attributable to a single individual, the Swiss observer Jean Piaget. To many educational theorists, Piaget is something of a divine being. Rather than assume anything about the nature of a child's intelligence, Piaget decided to observe children at various ages in order to determine at what age a child might "naturally understand" certain concepts or be able to perform certain intellectual operations. From these observations, Piaget concluded that teaching a child certain concepts before this "natural" time was largely a waste of effort. The child was not "ready" to learn. In fact, the concepts of "readiness" and "developmentally appropriate" can largely be traced to the influence of Piaget.

So Piaget himself, together with dozens of his followers, observed children in "natural" environments and concluded that early learning is a contradiction in terms and that the schools have been right all along: You can't teach a child anything until the school teaches it.

Are you beginning to recognize the subtle but critical distortion in thinking that Piaget's work has occasioned? Remember, Piaget did not act as an educator; he was an observer. He did not attempt to teach anything at all to the children who he observed. For example, if he observed a young child rolling a truck back and forth, he said nothing to the child. He never discussed color or speed or spatial relationships. He never suggested counting the tires on the truck or filling the truck with sand to see how much it would hold. So it's not surprising that Piaget observed that young children do not participate in early learning. They can hardly be expected to participate in something that they know nothing about!

Later, Piaget observed these same children in school as they were taught counting and volume and all the other activities. Lo and behold, Piaget surmised, if you teach a five-year-old child to count, he learns to count. So at what age does a child "naturally" learn to count? At age five, of course.

Poppycock, yes, but this is insidious poppycock, because it deprives a child of learning activities at the very time when the brain is best prepared to absorb them and translate them into meaningful experiences. You must realize by now that simply allowing a baby to lie endlessly in a crib or allowing a young child to "amuse" him or herself with an endless string of meaningless motions is actually a form of child abuse. Such inactivity does not ensure a happy childhood; rather, it is a formula for permanent deprivation because never again will the child be able to develop his or her brain with such ease and delight.

Fortunately, you hold the keys to your child's development in your own hands. And I'm not simply talking about intellectual development. Physical development, social development, even aesthetic and moral development can all be formed, challenged and guided, even in infants and very young children. You alone can decide whether your child merely survives and copes . . . or flourishes.

The activities in this chapter are designed primarily for children from birth to about one year of age. If your child is already older than this, you should still read this chapter, because many of these activities remain appropriate or can be modified for older children. If your child is older and you're ready to proceed with specific activities such as reading or math, then this chapter will introduce you to the patterns of stimulation and focusing that form the crucial foundation for later achievement. If you believe that your child may be deficient in any of these areas, consider sharing these activities whatever your child's age.

Above all, remember that the time frames suggested in this chapter and elsewhere in the book are simply that — suggestions. Each child is an individual universe, learning some things more slowly and other things with dazzling speed. In addition, many children learn advanced concepts more easily and at an earlier age than they learn simpler concepts. If you are bound by time frames or age frames, you are likely to shortchange both your child and yourself.

I recall one mother who took my seminar. She had a four-month-old daughter and a sixteen-month-old son. Despite my suggestion that she could easily present activities to both children at the same time, and that each child would learn from the other, she preferred to teach the children separately. She later told me that she had shown the four-month-old a card with five circles on it. Because she felt that the four-month-old was not really interested, she went to put the cards away. Her sixteen-month-old, who was observing the "lesson," snatched the card from her and shouted, as he pointed to each circle card: "Mommy! One. Two. Three. Four. Five." She had never before heard her son count numbers.

Focusing and Stimulation for Newborns

At 2 a.m., and with the experience of several pregnancies behind me, I had those familiar pains. My husband, Jimmy, drove me to the hospital, where I confronted a belligerent labor nurse — I swear that she came right out of a Gothic horror novel — who examined me and asked me, straightfaced: "Why are you here?"

Somewhat puzzled, but not wanting to make a scene, I responded, "I'm going to have a baby." Honestly, I didn't know what to say. All I knew was that I was in no mood for Twenty Questions.

"Oh no, you're not," Godzilla responded, "you're not even in labor," and out she walked. At that moment an intense contraction racked my body and I yelled for her to return. In she marched, asking, "What do you want now?" I told her that the pains were stronger. "Hrumph," she offered, feeling my stomach, "lie down if you want, but I think that you should go home. I just hate it when doctors give mothers-to-be their due dates. They're never right." She gave me a little bell to ring if I needed her and offered, as she left the room, "You're no more in labor than I am."

A short time later the pain became excruciating and I rang for The Lady in White. In she marched, and, as she began to examine me, she started yelling too. Now we were both yelling the same thing at the same time: "Oh my God!" At last she gave me that blessed shot.

The next thing I knew, I was in a room with another woman. I began to yell for the nurse, and she finally entered the room, yelling back that I had had the baby. "Is it a boy?" I asked. "Is he all right?" I must have repeated those questions fifty times, but all I ever heard was, "Didn't I already answer you?" If she had, I couldn't remember the answers, so I kept yelling. Perhaps it was the worry about the baby being retarded, or perhaps it was my experience with the labor nurse, but there seemed to be no adequate response to my distress. Finally, two nurses stood over me, both saying the same thing: "We told you about the baby."

I simply did not understand what they were telling me and I was rapidly becoming hysterical when one nurse suggested to the other, "Maybe if we bring her the baby, she'll understand and be quiet."

When they handed the baby to me, a complete calmness enveloped my soul. And then it hit me — that total, all-encompassing love that doesn't even seem possible. In fact, it had not always occurred with my other children. But at that instant, I knew that I would never part with this baby, that I would spend my entire life loving him.

As I looked into his beautiful eyes and saw him return my look, I told him, "Stephen, you have two beautiful eyes." I held up his tiny hands and gasped a little when he looked at them. "Stephen," I whispered, "here are your two beautiful hands." I hadn't done that kind of thing with my other babies. In fact, before Stephen was born, doctors had long assured mothers that newborns could not see. Only recently have they corrected their judgment.

As I stimulated Stephen by gently massaging his entire body and focused him by pointing to the parts of his body and reciting their names aloud, he seemed to evidence a pleasure that I had never seen in a baby before. My husband was the first to remark that the baby was uncommonly alert and content. I'm not sure that I believed him until I observed the other babies and overheard their parents remarking about Stephen: "He's so alert." "So wide awake." "So contented."

And I began to think, can this baby really be retarded?

1

Newborn stimulation can actually begin before your baby is born. Much research supports the belief that the growing fetus can respond to various forms of external stimuli, the most typical being music — especially classical music. In addition, the mother-to-be's body releases a number of chemicals into her bloodstream that are carried to the fetus. Scientists tell us that the proportion of these "good chemicals" may be affected by several conditions: the mother's diet, her mental attitude, her stress level and so on. Discuss these issues with your physician. Explain that you intend to provide an early learning environment for your baby, and ask your obstetrician's help in planning a healthful and stimulating prenatal environment.

2

So much early learning can take place in the hours and days after birth. That's why the new birthing centers available in many hospitals can be a boon for parents. In most birthing centers, the conventional labor, operating, and recovery rooms are eliminated. Instead, the mother stays in one private room throughout. Her spouse or coach (and, in many cases, even her other children) may stay with her as long as she desires. After the baby is born in the birthing room, the mother decides if she prefers the baby to stay with her or be placed in the nursery. Find out if your hospital has a birthing center, and ask your physician's advice on reserving one of these rooms for your delivery.

3

When your baby is brought to you in the hospital, or when the baby awakens if he or she is in the same room with you, always say the same thing, perhaps varying a word or two. Remember to include the baby's name in your greeting: "Adam, Mommy is so happy to see you," or "Mommy wants to feed you, Adam," or "Adam, you make Mommy very happy." This constant repetition of your name and the baby's name encourages stimulation and focusing and strengthens the parent-child bond. That's why it's important that Daddy do the same thing every time he sees the baby.

4

Tactile stimulation — touching — is of extraordinary importance. Babies immediately sense your reactions or feelings by the pattern or pressure of sensory stimulation on their skin. A lack of touch will result in sensory deprivation. On the other hand, rough handling will arouse fear and displeasure in an infant. Warn an overzealous father or grand-father that the baby isn't a linebacker yet.

5

If your newborn seems cranky, try to increase your touching. Exper-iment holding different body parts — his hand, his foot, even his tummy — until you find the spots which quiet your baby. The impor-tance of touching in strengthening the parent-child bond cannot be overemphasized. Think of the native mother who carries her child secured to her back. Their motions and touching become so interming-led, her knowledge of her baby's moods and signals so intimate, that she knows the precise moment to take the baby into the grass before the baby can soil the swaddling cloth. This intimacy cannot be achieved except by repeated and direct physical contact.

6

Another truth that we can learn from native mothers is that some babies seem to miss the protective cover of the amniotic sac or womb and enjoy being swaddled — gently wrapped in a soft cloth that is tucked around them with slight pressure.

7

If you have a private room, play soft music, especially classical music, for your baby. The beat of this music parallels the baby's first, nearly year-long musical experience — hearing your heartbeat.

8

If you continue to talk to your baby and hold him (or her — every time I speak about boys, I also mean girls, and vice versa), you'll soon notice that he begins to move his head about, looking around the room. For many years doctors insisted that newborns could not see and that these motions were merely random or were vague responses to light or sound. We now know that newborn infants can, in fact, see and that many of them, especially those in early learning environments, can see very well if objects are held close enough to their faces. Evidence now suggests that even very young infants can only distinguish white from black. Those lovely pastels in the baby store — pink and blue and peach and yellow and seafoam green — are, in fact, largely lost on an infant. So bring a black-and-white toy, like a zebra, to the hospital. Move it slowly back and forth across the baby's field of vision. Tell the baby that this toy will be in her crib when she gets home.

9

Begin to point out the features on your own face: your eyes, ears, nose, mouth, even your smile. Within about three weeks, your baby will look longer at your face than at any other object. You may be tired, sore, or even panicked, but try to let your baby see you smiling. Throughout his or her entire life, that smile will serve as a beacon of love and safety.

10

Holding your baby seven to ten inches from you, look right into her eyes and speak slowly but rhythmically. Rely on the softness and modulation of your natural speaking voice. Tell your daughter how beautiful she is — how wonderful, how special. Let your voice mirror your emotions.

11

Infants love laughter. Find reasons to laugh with your newborn. If nothing comes to mind, simply hold her hand, look into her beautiful eyes, and say "Ha! Ha! Ha!" You'll see a happy infant looking back at you!

12

Now is the time to begin minimizing stress in your baby's environment. The best way to do this is by soothing the baby whenever she cries. Never leave a baby to "cry it out." Your baby is crying for a reason, and even if you can't immediately determine what that reason is, there is, in fact, a reason. You can still offer your infant love, warmth, and consolation. All babies are different. Some will stop crying if you point to the black-and-white toy in the crib. Others like to hear a song or just want to hear your voice or be rocked.

13

That old-fashioned rocking chair, largely ignored by modern parents because it doesn't match the decor, can be a lifesaver when a baby is cranky or ill.

14

The decision to bring an infant into your own bed is a personal one. Many parents who need their sleep have reported that this is the best idea of all.

15

Some babies, of course, are "walkers." No, the baby doesn't do the walking — you do. Stephen was a walker, and I often relied on my husband and four other children to share the load. If you aren't this lucky, come to grips with the fact that a walker, at least for a time, will not be placated by any other activity. So don't wear yourself out trying things that you know will not work. If you do, you'll be so tired and cranky by the time you pick the baby up that the baby will sense your hostility. Then, of course, nothing will quiet him down. If you have a walker, pick him up when he starts to cry, begin walking, and continue talking in soothing tones. Every time this happens, make the walk a little shorter but the soothing talk just as emphatic. Eventually, you will reach the time when the walk can be eliminated and the soothing words will be all that is needed. Trust me, that day will come!

16

Even newborns are easily bored, so alternate between stimulation and focusing. For example, stimulation may mean placing a number of toys in the crib; focusing may involve removing every toy except one and then talking about that toy: "Jenny, this is a zebra. The zebra is black and white. Jenny, did you know that zebras live in Africa? A zebra looks a lot like a horse. One day, Jenny, we'll go to the zoo and see the zebras." What has your infant learned from this encounter? First, her own name has gone into her memory bank again and again. Second, the toy's name — zebra — has been repeated frequently so that the association between a sound and an object is reinforced. Third, Jenny has become more accustomed to the sound and animation of her mother's or father's voice. She can sense her parents' delight in talking to her, a delight that she should recognize every day of her life.

17

Introduce counting into the natural environment. Don't merely count your baby's fingers and toes — let him hear you counting slowly and rhythmically. For example, show your baby his feet and count, "One, two," and say, "You have two feet." Repeat this with hands, fingers, and toes. Ask Daddy to join in, because it's important for a baby to hear the same language, or an approximation of the same language, from more than one person.

18
If you can, include other people, especially siblings, in your baby's environment. Sisters and brothers, or aunts and uncles, can continue the counting games and other activities right in the hospital. Allowing older children to help you with the newborn can boost their own self-esteem at a time when they tend to feel ignored or abandoned.

19
While promoting your baby's senses of sight, sound, touch, and taste, don't forget smell. Babies are especially sensitive to smell and may not like the smell of strong perfumes, so wear a light scent or lightly perfumed powder. Clothes that you have worn have a scent that your infant can detect easily. Try placing a piece of your clothing that you have worn recently in the crib of a cranky infant. This can be the ultimate security blanket for newborns (and older babies and children, too!) who will cling to that piece of apparel as they drift blissfully to sleep.

20
Recognize that you are introducing the world to your baby. Babies are born with all of their sense organs functional, whether to a greater or lesser degree. Let your baby know from minute one that the world is a terrific place filled with loving people and interesting objects. Don't wait "until the baby understands." Your baby understands NOW! When I researched my doctoral dissertation, I found that pediatricians and educators throughout the world found a significant correlation between early learning (especially newborn learning), strong parent-child bonds, and later giftedness.

I encouraged each of my children to come upstairs, one at a time, to see their new brother, and each was prepared to do one activity with this latest sibling. Michael, who loved to act like a clown, put his face about ten inches from Stephen's and began to make those really exaggerated faces that are the natural property of thirteen-year-old boys. Michael would open his mouth, turn his head, and bob it up and down. I was delighted to see Stephen's eyes following Michael's movements. Once, when Stephen was only fourteen days old, Michael stuck out his tongue at Stephen, and I was shocked to see Stephen trying to stick out his tongue at Michael! Michael said, "My brother will be an actor," and I replied, "I hope so."

On another occasion, Nolan came upstairs and found Stephen awake and alert. Nolan has always been the strong, athletic type. He placed his finger on Stephen's hand and, as Stephen swiped at the muscular finger, Nolan gently moved it back and forth and said that Stephen would be a great ballplayer. At this early time Stephen still had the doctor's verdict of retardation hanging over his head, and I wasn't sure that Stephen would ever be a "great" anything, in the world's sense, except a great love to his family. When Nolan put his face right up to Stephen's crib, Stephen responded by trying to grab it. "Wow," said Nolan, "you almost knocked me out. Maybe you'll be a fighter." If Nolan placed a finger on Stephen's foot, Stephen's toes would grasp that finger so hard that Nolan was certain that here was a future long-distance runner. Or, when he moved his hands back and forth over Stephen's body, gently caressing his younger brother, Nolan would always say, "Mom, with those muscles I just know that Stephen will be a great athlete." I could only smile and offer, "I hope so."

The next time that Stephen was alert, we invited Clifford to share himself with his brother. What would Clifford think of, the boy who loved music, who loved to sing, who played the piano at home and the tuba in his high-school band? Clifford came up the stairs singing and carrying a music box. He sang a song to Stephen, accompanying himself on the music box. Stephen seemed mesmerized and Clifford concluded, "Mom, I just know that Stephen will be a musician." I gently responded, "Yes, I hope so."

My stepdaughter, Deborah, had offered me extraordinary help with Stephen. One day, when he was awake and crying for the fourth time, Deb came upstairs. I asked her to pick up Stephen and hold him while I warmed his bottle. When I returned, Deborah told me that Stephen had stopped crying the moment she had begun to touch him. She rationalized that Stephen understood that he was going to be picked up and anticipated his bottle; therefore, she said, he no longer had any reason to cry. "Stephen," she proclaimed, "is going to be very smart," to which I could only sigh and offer a silent prayer, "Yes, I do hope so."

I'm not sure when I first realized that all of their predictions had come true. Perhaps it was the time when Stephen could first catch and throw a ball with great accuracy. Or perhaps it was his first performance as a professional actor and singer. Or when he made his first TV commercials. Perhaps it was the time my wide-eyed twelve-year-old told me that he had been accepted at New York University. The realization had to have come by the time I saw my tall, handsome, seventeen-year-old son sworn in to practice law in the courts of the United States.

Whenever it came, the realization was always the same. My children were right, and my doctor was wrong. And thank God for that.

21

Stimulate and focus, but don't overstimulate or overfocus. How can you tell the difference? That's easy. What's boring to you is very likely boring to your child. Certainly you can't maintain the same encouraging tone of voice if you're counting your baby's fingers and toes ten or twenty times a day. Most infants focus longer on new things than on objects or activities that they've repeated many times before. Take it easy! It isn't necessary to go through your entire storehouse of activities every day. Always leave your child and yourself wanting more.

22

Musical toys, record players, tape players and TVs have their place but are no substitute for the human voice. Most newborns seem to respond most positively to the higher range of voices — voices of moms, grandmoms, or sisters. Any human voice, however, produces a happier reaction than a mechanical one. You can occasionally introduce soft music, especially the rhythmic sounds of classical music. In fact, many babies who fall asleep to the sounds of classical music continue the practice even into adulthood. The best forms of auditory or sound stimulation come from the human voice and soft music. While some children react positively to toys that make noises, like squeeze toys, many other children are frightened by them. Don't try to force your baby to like a toy simply because a favorite aunt has purchased it. If the toy frightens the baby (if the baby cries more than once upon hearing the noise) then by all means remove the toy, at least for a time.

23

Bath time can be a delicious experience for both parent and child. Avoid initial fears by talking your baby through the entire bath experience. "Water is wet, Brian. Here comes the nice warm water over your beautiful body. See the water cover your two feet? How many toes do you have, Brian? Ten. That's right! And you have ten fingers too. First the water covers five little fingers. Brian, how many fingers are left? Five fingers. That's right! Brian, you are so smart and wonderful!"

24

Notice that the above conversation is carried on as a one-person question-and-answer session. The modulation or tone of your voice introduces your baby to various intellectual situations: asking questions, giving information, receiving wonderful praise. Today you are furnishing everything — the question, the answer, the praise. Eventually, your child will join in the experience, delighted to do so because your favorable response has been assured as well as ingrained in his psyche.

25

There is no such thing as a "baby" expert. There is only a "your baby" expert, and that person is you. If you practice reading your baby's face and body language, you'll soon find that you can foretell your baby's moods. You'll know when he's beginning to become tired or fretful or hungry, and you'll adjust activities accordingly. As your baby grows, you'll be amazed to find that the cranky periods diminish rapidly because you're actually forestalling them, avoiding activity when he's tired and picking up the pace when he's alert and interested.

26

If your baby is having a rough day — if she seems to be fretful and you're unable to find the cause — try to put yourself in your baby's place. Use all of your senses to experience exactly what your baby is experiencing at that moment. Is the room a little chilly? Babies are uncommonly sensitive to cold. Is something spicy cooking in the kitchen? Most babies react negatively to strong or uncommon odors. Is a dog barking outside? We have accustomed our ears to block out the background noise of the world, but infants haven't yet developed this ability. Trying to duplicate the sensory impulses that bombard a baby is a good way to seek out and eliminate the offending problem.

27

Expand opportunities for black-and-white focusing. Newborns focus better on black and white because the retinal cones in their eyes are too underdeveloped to discern differences among pastels. Black-and-white bumper guards are a good idea; so are black-and-white mobiles. If you can't find these items ready-made, you can make you own. Black designs on white paper, especially paper plates, are easy to make. Consider also black-and-white sheets, pillow cases, toys, and similar objects. Stuffed zebras and panda bears make excellent toys. If you can't find these objects in the toy store, call the gift shop of your local zoo.

28

After the first weeks, your baby's attention span will increase from four to ten seconds to about sixty to ninety seconds. Lengthen activities accordingly. At two to three weeks, babies begin to imitate actions. Provide simple body movements for your baby to copy — smile, stick out your tongue, reach out your hand, point with your index finger, laugh.

29

Keep repeating your baby's name. One way to introduce your baby to new voices is to have people repeat the baby's name together with a remark that you usually make. Thus, grandpa should say, "Adam, what a beautiful boy you are!"

30

Ask your baby questions ("Are you wet?" "Are you hungry?"). If the baby makes any sound at all, give a big smile and exclaim something like, "What a beautiful sound!" Your enthusiasm will encourage future attempts at noises or sounds that help to strengthen the baby's throat muscles and vocal cords.

31

Increase your baby's sensitivity to sound by whispering happily. Note the baby's attempts to look toward the direction of the whisper and offer enthusiastic congratulations.

32

Don't separate early learning activities from care-giving activities. Instead, incorportae learning into care giving. So much of a new parent's time is spent feeding, changing, and bathing a baby that these activities are the most natural times for learning.

33

Begin reading books to your baby. The natural modulation of a reading voice is soothing to an infant. Read stories in which you are interested so that your voice will actually sound interested. Alternate children's books, which tend to have short sentences with a sing-song rhythm, with adult books that feature extended narrative and more sophisticated speech patterns. You can even read *The Wall Street Journal* to an infant with a twofold benefit: You will sound interested because you are, and your infant, slowly but surely, will become accustomed to the patterns of intelligent and sophisticated speech. When Stephen's dad brought work home from his law office, he would often read law books to Stephen who, from about the age of two, followed along with his finger as his dad read the book.

34

Once a month, change the location of the baby's crib. This will provide an entirely new field of visual stimulation.

35

Alternate crib toys every few days, and place no more than two or three toys in the crib. Always try to have at least one black-and-white toy in the crib. If you can't find the zebra or panda, use a waterproof, nontoxic marker to paint black lines on a white ball or black wavy lines on paper plates that you then attach to the sides of the crib. You can also tie black-and-white ribbons to the sides of the crib. The toys should feature different shapes and textures. Identify the toys by name whenever you place them in the crib.

36

If you have other children, encourage them to talk to their baby sister or brother. Depending on their ages, they may simply repeat the simple things that you say or may engage in extended conversation. If you have a six-year-old, for example, have him tell his baby sister about his day at school. Assure the older child that the baby really does listen to what he says, and if he protests that the baby cannot possibly understand him, point out that her listening to his voice makes his sister happy. Activities such as these encourage the development of a caring sibling bond. You may be astonished to see the older child deriving as much benefit as the baby.

37

When anyone talks to the baby, they should use the principle of "repeat and expand." This means that you shouldn't say words once but should repeat key words in different contexts: "I know you're hungry, Susan. Here's your bottle of milk, Susan. I know that you love your bottle. Susan, the milk will make you nice and strong. Susan, I love you." The next time you give Susan a bottle, you can repeat the key words — "Susan" and "bottle," perhaps — and then add new key words: "warm," "drink," etc. Repeat all the key words — "Susan," "bottle," "warm," "drink" — when you give Susan a bottle of water, expanding with a new word: "water." This building-block approach mimics the natural connections that the brain always endeavors to make.

38

You can increase stimulation by changing mobiles every week or two. If you can't find at least one black-and-white mobile, make one from scratch with cardboard or paper plates, a marker pen, string, and a hanger.

39

Begin taking the baby for walks, first around the room and then around the house. Point out objects as you go along. Especially point out similar objects in different rooms — pictures, pillows, chairs. Remember that pictures should be no more than seven to ten inches from the baby's face.

40

Put a large photograph of the baby on the wall, at least 8x10 or poster-size if you can. A black-and-white poster is best. Point to the picture and say, "That's baby! That baby is Kevin. Kevin, that baby is you!" Point to the parts of the baby's face and say, "That's the baby's mouth;" "Those are the baby's eyes;" "Kevin, you have beautiful eyes." Point to the mouth on the photograph and say, "mouth;" then point to the baby's mouth and say, "mouth."

41

When the baby is about two weeks old, show the baby a poster featuring one circle or one square (or any simple shape that you prefer). You can make a one-circle poster by taking a 9x12 sheet of white paper and pasting on or coloring a black circle about three inches in diameter. Hang the poster on the wall as you do other pictures. When you point to that poster, simply say, "one." Don't say, "one circle" or "one square," just "one." You'll learn more about these shapes, and about the value of counting, later in this chapter and in the math chapter.

42

Provide objects for your baby to touch and hold. He may hold a rattle for only a second and then drop it, but attempting to hold lightweight objects will help to strengthen finger and arm muscles and will encourage manual dexterity.

43

Whether you nurse or bottle feed your baby, in the first few weeks, don't interject other conversation or activities at feeding time. Allow your baby to focus entirely on sucking. After a few weeks, introduce soft conversation at feeding time.

44

If you can find a large mirror, hold it about eight to ten inches from your baby's face. Point to the baby's reflection and say "baby" and your baby's name. Point to your own reflection and say "Mommy" or your name. If your baby is disinterested, try this again at a later date. Also, be sure to introduce all the people in the house to the baby. Include not only a spouse, siblings and grandparents, but also a housekeeper or anyone else who will regularly come into contact with the baby. Be sure, of course, that no one who comes into contact with the baby has the sniffles!

Let's catch our breath for a moment. Must you do all of these activities? The best answer comes from the ancient religious masters: Do as much as is comfortable for you. You may have more time with your baby or less. At any given moment or age, your baby may have more or less interest in these activities. I only want you to know that these are the kinds of stimulation and focusing activities that are available. Generally speaking you should choose the ones that you enjoy, but from time to time, branch out into a new area. You may be pleasantly surprised by the results.

Another point is equally important: Trust yourself and your own instincts. Everyone will have an opinion about every facet of babyrearing. Smile and thank them for their interest, then add, "Of course, you'd want me to do what I think best."

Last, try your best to get enough rest yourself. Very little good occurs when *you* are the tired and cranky one. How can you avoid fatigue? You should assign priorities to all tasks and only do those that top the list. Also, try to share the burden with others — your spouse, your family, your friends. A friend who stops by for a cup of coffee may be an imposition, while a friend who does emergency grocery shopping for you is a godsend. Most people are willing to help; find ways for them to do just that.

Focusing and Stimulation
at About One to Two Months

The past month has been an incredible time for both you and your baby. If you could see your baby's brain at work, you would see that as each day goes by, the brain absorbs glucose from the baby's bloodstream in order to fire more and more electrical activity. As the synapses, or bridges across which electrical energy passes, grow in number and complexity, the baby's capacity for learning also grows.

Once stimulated, a baby's attention span will expand for longer and longer periods of time. We now know that an increased attention span is less the result of age than of stimulation. Babies who are understimulated may have only brief attention spans throughout their lives. On the other hand, babies who enjoy stimulation and focusing activities from birth or during early childhood tend to develop the mental reflexes which, in the past, were erroneously believed to be reserved only for gifted children.

Now is a good time to emphasize again that no two children are identical, nor do they develop in identical ways. That's why the time frames in this chapter and throughout the book are only broad references, not report cards on which to identify your child's "score."

As the months pass, you may begin to notice that your baby exhibits certain learning patterns indicative of "right-brain" or "left-brain" prominence. The human brain is divisible into two hemispheres, or parts, each of which contributes in a different way to the acquisition of knowledge. Simply put, the right half of the brain seems more visually oriented, while the left half is more word oriented. In many cases, predominantly right-brain children will become left-handed and left-brain children will become right-handed. That's because each half of the brain controls the motion on the opposite side of the body.

While it is important to recognize that no child is entirely right- or left-brained, many children do reflect a preference. Extensive research supports observations that right-brain children do best working with pictures and images, abstractions, intuition, improvisation and emotions. It has been suggested that many of these children become artists and musicians or possess similar creative talents. Left-brain children generally do best working with words instead of pictures; they prefer facts, logic, step-by-step thinking and practical tasks as opposed to intuitive or artistic tasks. Left-brain children often evidence greater dexterity with language than do their right-brain counterparts, and many left-brain children go on to become attorneys, scholars, or other language-dependent professionals.

It is important that you do not categorize your child as either right- or left-brained, because this nearly always implies a limitation rather than an expansion of activities. Why mention it at all? Because, if you become an intimate observer of your child, you may begin to see patterns emerge. While you should still offer stimulation for both parts of the brain, if you recognize that a child is having difficulty with a certain activity, you can rethink the activity in a more suitable way. A child (or even a baby) who is easily bored by shapes or colors isn't "slow;" she may actually show more interest in numbers or letters. Other babies react poorly to a loosely scheduled day; they prefer everything to be done at precisely the same time each day. Recognizing these idiosyncrasies of brain development may help you to devise a schedule uniquely suited to your infant.

1
If you haven't done so before, introduce a soft ball, preferably black and white, into the crib. Never use a golf ball, Ping-Pong ball, or other ball so small that it may wedge in the baby's mouth. Look for labels that say "nontoxic" and "washable." Begin to gently and slowly roll the ball in the crib, allowing the baby's eyes to focus on the trail of the ball.

2
Carry the baby around the home to experience the difference types of light that can be seen during the day or early evening. Open the refrigerator or oven to see these lights. Be careful to avoid bright light and sunlight. Infants focus better in light that is not too strong.

3
During the first month of life, you placed objects about eight to ten inches from the baby's face. Now you can generally move objects ten to twelve inches away to slowly encourage distance vision.

4

Whenever you can, continue to encourage others to talk to the baby. Allow the baby to become accustomed to the sounds of different voices and to begin to grasp the idea that speech is a universal human function.

5

Some babies actively like noisemakers; others don't. If yours does, then place rattles or noisemakers about ten inches from his face and shake gently, allowing him to focus on the object. If your baby is fearful of noisy objects, increase your black-and-white activities instead. Make a paper garland from rings of black-and-white construction paper. Gently shake it in front of the baby and allow him to focus on its movement. If the baby seems to avoid focusing, either move the object slightly or gently turn the baby's head to encourage eye contact with the object.

6

Whenever you plan to nurse or feed the baby, announce it, then feed or nurse immediately. Eventually, whenever you announce a feeding time, the baby will focus on your breast or on the bottle.

7

Babies' eyes focus more easily on objects that are moved in a horizontal or across motion rather than in a vertical or up-and-down motion. When moving an object across a baby's field of vision, first move the object horizontally, from left to right, across about six inches of space directly in front of the baby's eyes. Gradually increase the area to twelve inches and then eighteen inches. Next time, move the object vertically, beginning with about a four-inch trail and slowly moving to an eighteen-inch pattern. When your child becomes proficient at this, move the object in a circle, beginning with a small circle and gradually increasing the circle's size.

8

If anyone who visits your baby speaks a foreign language, encourage them to speak that language exclusively to the baby. Because of structures in the brain called LADs (language acquisition devices), it is easier for young children to learn languages than it is for adults. At this early stage, you simply want to accustom the baby to the sounds and cadence of another language. These language "blueprints" will remain in the baby's memory forever and will be recalled every time the baby hears the foreign language spoken.

9
Even little infants love peek-a-boo. Put a cloth in front of your face, remove the cloth, and cry "peek-a-boo!" Peek-a-boo is actually one of the first problem-solving games demonstrated to infants. It allows them to begin to make determinations about the absence or appearance of objects.

10
Remember the one-circle or one-square paper — the three-inch black circle or square on the 9x12 sheet of white paper? Now make a paper with two circles or other shapes and mount it on the wall. When you pass the one-circle paper, say "one." Later, if you pass the two-circle paper, say "two." *Don't* say "one circle" or "two circles," only "one" or "two." The conceptualization of abstract numbers is very difficult for five- or six-year-olds but is child's play for a young infant.

11
When the baby can move her head from side to side, place the rattle on one side of her head, at least twelve inches from her ear, and shake very gently. The baby should begin to turn her head to the sound. Repeat this on the other side of the baby's head. These sound and motion activities may seem simple, but they encourage alertness and inquisitiveness and prompt a baby to explore and reach conclusions about the world.

12
Place three black circles on a sheet of 9x12 white paper and mount the paper. When you pass by with your paper, point to the sheet and say "three." Each week, you'll add a sheet of paper with another circle, square, or other shape until you have ten sheets of paper, each with one to ten shapes. By about the tenth week, you can hold the baby twelve to thirteen inches from the papers. As you walk around the house, point to the papers at random. They may be in different rooms all around the house or apartment. You needn't count in order, nor must

you point out every number every time. For the moment, the baby's mind is merely storing discrete or separate information. One day soon that same mind will begin to put this information together in significant ways.

Let's take a moment to discuss an important point: your reaction to these activities. Many babies whose parents followed my suggestions are now in high school, and their parents still tell me that the early stimulation and focusing activities were a blessing for a somewhat unexpected reason. Not only did these activities begin to build a foundation for early learning, but they encouraged increasing parent-child interaction because the baby was happy and contented so much of the time. When you are happily introducing your baby to his world, your joy shows in your voice, in your expression, and even in your body language. Your baby, sensing your joy, is happy too.

Some parents, however, especially parents who tend to look at things intellectually rather than emotionally, question whether the baby is really "learning" anything from these activities. After all, when you point to the three-circle paper, a one-month-old infant is not going to suddenly yell out, "three!"

Let me be candid. When I first began teaching these activities, I had only two guidelines to follow — these activities had worked for me, and they seemed reasonable. So much less was known about the physiology of the brain two decades ago! Today, I am delighted that reports from the world's most distinguished biologists, neurologists, and other researchers confirm that a child's brain absorbs knowledge in just this way.

Thus, while your baby can't give you the immediate feedback in speech to assure you that these activities really are beneficial, you don't have to take my word alone. If you need "intellectual convincing," go to your public library and check out any book on the physiology of the brain that has been published in the last three years. I'm not recommending specific books, because I don't want you to think that I'm steering you only to scientists who concur with me. Instead, check out any recent books. You'll find several suggestions in the References. When you peruse these works, you'll see that their findings on the structure of the brain and the acquisition of knowledge are displayed in the activities suggested here.

Now, back to basics!

13

At this time, we don't want to ignore a baby's physical development, because a healthy mind certainly depends on a healthy body. An early activity is to place the baby on the floor. This requires a little planning. First, because the baby should not be impeded by tight clothing, be sure that the temperature of the room is warm enough. Hot air rises, which means that a floor is the coolest spot in the room. Try to place the baby on a mat, and, if possible, get down on the floor with her. If you don't, she may begin to cry. If Mom is still a little sore, this is a great activity for Dad. At first, you'll only repeat some of the stimulation and focusing exercises that you did before, but you'll soon see that the baby's reactions are different from those that she had in the crib. She becomes more adventuresome. Perhaps she becomes more distracted. That's good! Don't force her to focus on an object if she's suddenly stimulated by something else. Best of all, her movements will become larger and stronger. She'll thrust her arms and legs into new positions. She may stretch her entire body in ways that you've never seen before. All of these strength and limbering movements are the prelude to crawling and walking, so try to reserve some "floor time" every day.

14

As floor time progresses, increase the number of strength-building exercises. Hold the baby's hands so that he can attempt to pull himself up. Some babies, like some adults, enjoy passive exercise — they want things done to them but are not in the mood to do anything for themselves. Continue to massage the baby. Then, very gently tug at the baby's arms and legs. Finally, try the pull-up again. One day soon, even most "wallflower" babies will want to respond.

15

If you don't have 8x10 photographs of family members on the walls, put them up now. Include a photograph of the family pet. In your walks about the house, introduce the baby to all the members of the family. Soon you'll see that whenever you point to one of these photographs, the baby smiles or laughs.

16

Keep a box of many different articles near the baby's crib. Many young infants will not look at one object for more than a second or two, but they will continue to focus on different objects. Your box may include a spoon, a strainer, a plastic flower, a ribbon or bow, a candle, or nearly any safe and nontoxic object found around the house. Hold up each object and repeat its name. If the baby seems uncommonly interested in a particular object, allow him to touch it or to put it in his hand. Many babies really enjoy this game, which can begin with two or three items and can gradually increase to as many items as your baby will focus on.

17
If yours is the only voice that your baby hears, try to vary it from time to time. Speak in a higher pitch or a lower one. This is an important time for an infant to realize that voices come in a variety of tones.

18
Sing to your baby. Babies exhibit longer attention spans for songs than for any other sounds.

Let's take another time-out. If your son or daughter is now about six weeks old, and you've both passed your six-week checkups with flying colors, perhaps now you both will come into greater contact with other parents and infants. That's why it's important once again to bring up that old subject — comparison. No two babies ever develop in the same way and at the same time. That's one reason why it's impossible to say how much time during the day should be allotted to these activities. The time depends on your interest and availability as well as on your baby's interest and alertness. You should always try to refine your own judgment and common sense regarding your baby.

It's reasonable to want your baby to excel. You've invested emotion and time and pain and money and sleepless nights and everything that you possibly can, and it's only natural to want to reap a little benefit like showing off. The problem is that once you jump on the comparison carousel, it's awfully difficult to jump off again.

Sometimes comparison has less to do with bragging than with calming a parent's fears. Especially if this is your first baby, you may wonder if you're doing everything right. For you, the proof that you are doing everything right can only come by favorable comparisons of your infant with others. The problem is that this approach works only if your baby is at least as proficient as someone else's baby. If not, your fears will become exaggerated.

There are only two proper judges of your baby's progress, and they're not your mother-in-law and your next-door neighbor. You and your child's doctor are the best qualified to make judgments regarding your infant's development.

Most pediatricians will tell you, and they're quite right about this, that development occurs not at a given time, but within a framework of time. If your baby's physician isn't concerned about any apparent lack of progress, then you probably shouldn't be either. However, if you honestly believe that your child's pediatrician is not adequately addressing your concerns, it may be time to shop for another pediatrician, at least for a second opinion. (You may suggest one of the developmental tests listed in the Appendix.)

19

Be sure to place a few objects on both sides of the crib so that the baby can focus on an item, whatever his position. However, don't crowd the infant, because this tends to inhibit stretching and other movements.

20

Add an overhead crib gym to encourage strength and dexterity. When I added a crib gym to Stephen's crib, I found that wherever in the crib I placed him for his nap, when I returned he would be playing with that gym. If you place the gym near the baby's head, place the existing mobile near the baby's feet. Infants vigorously exercise leg and foot muscles by kicking mobiles. You may notice that when your baby sees you watching him, he plays with the mobiles or gym more exuberantly. Infants and children seem to innately enjoy attention, and they recognize (intuitively it seems) the close connection between pleasing you and pleasing themselves.

21

Read your baby's body language. When you begin an activity or pick up an object and the baby begins to smile, that's an A-1 favorite!

22

Some infants are afraid of dogs and cats. If you have a pet, and if placing the child on the floor is a problem, begin even now putting the baby in a playpen. Start by leaving him in the playpen for just a few minutes. You can gradually leave him in the playpen for longer periods of time.

23

Make bath time an exercise time. Gently stretch the baby's arms and legs. Massage the baby's body in the bath and after the bath. Some babies like to be swaddled after a bath, wrapped in a fairly snug cloth, after which they take a long nap. Experiment and see if your baby enjoys this after-bath experience.

24

Massages can also help colicky babies. Very gently massage the stomach and abdomen with a downward motion. This usually helps the baby to expel gas and feel more comfortable.

25

If you take your baby outdoors, you probably keep him in a baby carriage or pram so that he's on his back for the entire expedition. If so, realize that the objects in your baby's sensory field — the wind, the sky, the clouds, leaves on the trees, even a bird — form a kind of mobile for the baby. Point them out and tell the baby their names. The enthusiasm in your voice will encourage him to focus on these objects, and he'll enjoy these outdoor experiences even more.

26

At the end of the first month (or perhaps the second or third), your baby will demonstrate a preference for real people instead of photographs. During this period, she may be making judgments about people. Don't worry, they're only temporary. For example, an infant who always reacted positively to her mother's voice may suddenly grimace or even cry when she hears her mother's voice. Instead, she only smiles when she hears Dad! These occasions may be nervewracking or frightening for a mother. Keep up your spirits and enthusiasm. After a week or two, Mom is invariably back in the baby's good graces.

27

During floor time, use noisy toys like a rattle to invite movement. Because babies tend to move in the direction of a sound, you can encourage a baby to turn on his side by shaking a rattle in the direction in which you want the baby to turn. If the rattle doesn't work, try a squeeze toy. You can also stand up and call the baby's name, and the baby will likely make movements in the direction of your voice.

28

Whether the baby is on the floor or in the crib or carriage, dangle a black-and-white or brightly colored scarf in front of the baby. When he grasps the scarf, gently lift the baby. Most infants love this exercise, which can develop back muscles as well as arm, hand and finger muscles.

29

To encourage grasping, rub the baby's hands together, then place an object like a rattle between them. The baby will exercise his fingers, opening and closing them, attempting to grasp the object. Another way to encourage hand recognition is by cutting two bands of material from a white baby sock and drawing a black band on them with a nontoxic marker. Then place the sock bands on the baby's hands, allowing the fingers to stick out. He'll immediately look at his hands and move his fingers, attempting to investigate the bands.

30

Whenever your baby makes a sound, immediately imitate that sound, trying to establish eye contact when you do. This sends a message to the infant that he has truly communicated with you, and he'll try to increase his sound vocabulary.

31

Consider which of these activities you can distribute to other family members, especially sisters and brothers. Siblings want to help take care of a new baby, and these activities are important in boosting their sagging self-esteem levels. Even very young siblings can gently tickle the baby, sing or hum to the baby, hold up a hand puppet, or perform other simple activities. If you have other children, you can encourage strong sibling bonds by allowing all of the children to care for one another whenever practical.

32
Hold the baby in front of a large mirror and point out his body parts. If he's not interested in looking into the mirror, simply touch him. Do the same thing when the baby is in the crib or on the floor. It's important to perform this and other activities in as many locations as possible. A baby's understanding can expand significantly if his mind isn't locked into a single-location outlook.

33
Increase simple word play. Hold up a single object and say the word for that object. Repeat this about five times during the day for about five days. Then, after a few days' absence, hold up the object again and repeat the word. Many times, your baby will look uncommonly delighted, as though he's located an old friend. Don't overdo this. Build word recognition slowly.

34
Begin or continue exposing the baby to music — classical, jazz, country-western, religious — anything that isn't too loud. The rhythms of most music are at once stimulating and soothing to infants and children.

35
Encourage other family members to hold the baby and to walk with her. A baby who tolerates only one person is an irritation to everyone, baby included.

36
While I never advocate letting a baby "cry it out," recognize that about this time, many babies cry for a little while before falling asleep. Wait a few moments and see. If this is the case, and she then falls asleep peacefully, there's no reason to pick up the baby.

37

If you haven't acquired a playpen by the time the baby is about two months old, consider doing so now. Some individuals have voiced the idea that a playpen invariably restricts a child's movement, but that hardly applies to a young infant. A playpen allows the baby to be safe and contained while being stimulated in the general family environment. Thus, the baby has more opportunity to observe family members and activities. Don't use the playpen as a substitute for floor time; instead, use the playpen as a substitute for a certain amount of crib time. As time goes by, you'll see that the playpen can be like another set of arms. The baby can lie on his back or be propped up, you can safely answer the phone even with pots on the stove and the baby nearby, and you can visit other people's homes without fear of placing the baby on their floors. In short, you'll find many good uses for a playpen, even if your infant is only a few months old.

Above all, stay calm and try not to let minor mishaps dampen your spirits. Every parent makes mistakes; everyone has a bad day. Please know that every parent wishes that he or she had done something differently or not at all. Babies give back their meals, lamps break, the dog chews all your circle posters, phones ring right in the middle of bath time. You find a relative with a cold kissing the baby or your older daughter fingerpainting on her baby brother's belly. Don't worry. Hardly anything happens to a baby that cannot be remedied. Over the years, many pediatricians have admitted that they don't bat 100 percent with their own children. Take heart. The sun will still rise tomorrow, and so will your spirits.

Focusing and Stimulation
at About Three to Six Months

The age between three and six months is a magical time for your baby and for you. You will notice accelerated sensory responses — movements, sounds, smiles, and even laughter — that delight you both. However, a baby's attention span develops with *experiences*, not simply with age. The following activities will bolster and extend your baby's progress.

1

Now, when you take the baby on your travels through the house, allow him to touch some of the objects that you point out. At this age, Stephen had two favorites, the piano and Fredericka, our dog. As you say the name of each object, take the baby's hand and place it on the object. You can also hold the baby's hand in your own and pat or stroke the object.

2

Encourage the baby to lift her head, and help her to do so, if necessary. You can place an object (a rattle, for instance) slightly above her vision level so that she naturally tries to raise her head to focus on the sound. Once she can hold her head up by herself for about thirty seconds, you can roll up a little towel and place it under her chest. This will gently raise her shoulders and head. Gentle head-lifting techniques strengthen neck and shoulder muscles.

3

If you bottle feed your baby, he may enjoy touching your face as he sucks. If so, identity your facial features as he touches them. Then, touch the baby in the same spot and repeat the identification.

4

Even if you have childproofed your home, an infant seat can still be a help when the phone or doorbell rings. If you use an infant seat, to feed your baby, for example, hang small toys from the sides that he can grasp and squeeze as he eats. Not only does this grasping encourage dexterity, but many babies are happier eaters when their hands are occupied.

5

Infants love the sight of bubbles, so buy a jar of bubble mix. Demonstrate the technique by exaggerating your blowing. Even if the baby doesn't immediately join in, following the bubbles as they float in the air is an excellent focusing activity. It's also great fun for older children to share the experience with a baby sister or brother.

6

If you're leaving your baby for all or part of the day, continue to notice the baby's body language when he sees the new care giver. It's always best to ease into the surrogate care situation. At first, leave your baby only for a short time, and show great joy and enthusiasm when you return. Gradually extend the amount of time that you're gone. There may be tears at first, but notice if, after a few days, the baby still seems tense or upset by the time you return. If so, analyze the negative impact that this surrogate care giver may have on your child. It may be necessary to rethink your priorities.

7

Place an 8x10 photo or picture of a familiar object (a rattle or toy, for example) on the side of the crib. Change the picture every three or four days. Seeing familiar objects in picture form acquaints the baby with the fact that there are pictures of objects in addition to objects themselves. This knowledge is important in helping a baby to build concepts of self and of the world. These concepts will later ease the transition to letters, numbers, and words.

8

You may want to alternate pictures with your shape posters. By about five months, you can begin to use red shapes on some posters in place of black circles. Do not mix colors on the same poster. From time to time, say the number corresponding to the number of shapes on the poster.

9

You may notice your baby smiling more and more. Researchers tell us that babies raised in institutions (hospitals or children's homes, for example) often do not smile before they are eight months old. The typical baby in a family setting begins to smile by about two to three months of age. How *frequently* a baby smiles, however, is related to the number of opportunities presented to the infant. Give your baby lots to smile about!

10

For some time you have repeated your baby's sounds back to him. Now, change the tempo. Speak faster or slower, higher or lower, louder or softer. This challenges the baby to develop more sound patterns. Remember, though, that results are usually not immediate.

11
Involve everyone you can in talking to the baby. If you can't rely on other children, then encourage people who you meet in the supermarket or park.

12
To encourage greater awareness and strength of arms and legs, place baby bracelets on the baby's wrists or ankles for several minutes at a time. If these bracelets have charms or bells that make noise, all the better. Congratulate the baby whenever he shakes an arm or leg.

13
Continue to replace black-and-white objects with brightly colored ones.

14
Keep up the conversations at mealtime. Identify each food that you give your baby as well as the spoon. Most babies really enjoy these conversations, and such activity seems to dispel the parents' anxiety about the feeding experience.

> I remember one Sunday morning when Stephen was about three months old and the whole family went out for breakfast. As I fed Stephen his baby food, I told him that this was his favorite rice cereal. The rest of the family chimed in. Clifford pointed to the bacon that he was eating and told Stephen how de-lish-us it was. Another child showed Stephen the butter on his toast. I noticed a lady at the next table eyeing us suspiciously, but on we went. Stephen was enraptured. Finally, this lady turned to her companion and muttered, just within my hearing, "They're all nuts, you know."

15
As part of the floor exercise, gently roll a ball back and forth in front of the baby. Every time she reaches for the ball, congratulate her. Try to have several balls available and alternate their use. A ball collection is one of the best and least expensive investments that you can make.

16

Another floor-time activity is the very beginning of memory development. Show the baby an object (a doll, for example), and say its name: "Doll." Then, put the object on the floor and turn the baby's head slightly away from it. Let go of the baby's head. If he turns his head back to the object, congratulate him. The baby has actually remembered that something was in a location, even if he couldn't see it.

17

As the baby gets a little older, don't turn the baby — move the object. Allow the baby to see you hide the doll in a paper bag and ask the child, "Where is the doll?" At first, of course, he'll simply stare at the paper bag, which is a kind of problem-solving in its own right. Then, take the doll out of the bag and give it to him, praising him all the while. Eventually, when you ask him where the doll is, he will try to grasp the bag and find it. That's a thinking human mind at work! Another fascinating development can to occur with this activity. On some occasions, when you ask where the doll is (or the rattle or the keys), instead of grasping for the bag, the baby will point to the bag and then begin "talking." In his own way, he has decided to tell you where the doll is.

18

Many infants "speak" in response to a question because they begin to understand that when you ask a question, the intonation of your voice suggests a vocal answer. Try asking the baby more and more questions and see if the questions elicit oral responses. If so, they may be your key to encourage speech. If not, be patient and remember PEEEHK (pleasure, excitement, enjoyment, enthusiasm, hugs, and kisses).

19

Begin speaking to your baby in more complete sentences. Use the words "mommy" and "daddy" frequently in addition to the baby's name.

20

The subject of flash cards or picture cards often elicits a strong response. Too often, parents who use these cards *overuse* them, subjecting the child to hours of drilling. The overuse of flash cards is unnecessary and pointless. Used properly, however, they can become a great game for babies and children, encouraging language and memory skills. Start with about five 8x10 cards, each of which has a single picture on it. The picture should be of a familiar object or person. As you show the baby each card, say the name of the object and nothing else. You can do this once, twice, or no more than three times a day. Every three or four days, add another one to five cards to the stack. As the stack becomes large, remove the first cards. It's not necessary to show all the cards all the time, although you'll be fascinated to see that even a baby can sense when certain favorite cards are missing.

21

Begin to make cards with animals. Start with cards that feature family pets — a dog, cat, fish, or bird. Next, include other animals — bears, elephants, lions, tigers, zebras, or anything that you can find. If you can't find color pictures of these animals, buy inexpensive coloring books and color the pictures yourself. Find pictures without distracting backgrounds or other details, and mount them on 8x10 white poster board. Introduce the animal cards into the stack.

I skip ahead now, to a time when Stephen was about five years old, but I want to demonstrate that on many occasions, the activities that you supposedly undertake for your children magically transform themselves into things that you do for yourself. Take the subject of coloring books. I loved them as a child, and, when I began to color pictures for Stephen's flash cards, the old pleasure returned. I found coloring to be very relaxing. I had even enjoyed coloring in my older children's coloring books but occasionally had felt a little foolish. When I was preparing cards for Stephen, however, I had a purpose and was therefore "entitled" to color.

As Stephen grew, and the use of flash cards receded to a memory, I took up my old vice of coloring in his coloring books. One day, for a birthday I think, he received a marvelous jumbo coloring book. That evening, I asked Stephen if I might color a picture, and he replied, with uncommon sternness, "No!" At different times I asked again, but his answer was always the same.

Finally, I decided to have a talk with him about sharing versus selfishness. I went through a long discussion, pointing out how his sisters and brothers had always shared with him and how he should want to share with teachers and classmates when he entered school. Stephen listened in attentive silence. When at last I had finished, he said, to my amazement, "I understand about sharing. I would let anyone color in my book. Anyone except you."

Shocked, I began to run through my mind reasons why my son might want to reject me. Had I been too soft, too hard, too something? Did he feel some underlying, innate resentment toward me? Was it that I worked and had to leave him with a neighbor? Should I take him to a child psychologist? Fearing the answer, but trying to get at the truth, I asked him, "Stephen, why won't you let me color in your book?"

His response was quick. "Mommy, because when you take my coloring books you color almost every picture before you give it back. You never leave anything for me!"

From the mouths of babes and little boys!

22
Once you've introduced the names of the animals — dog, cat, fish, bird, bear, tiger — try to point out real or TV examples. If you have a dog or cat, whenever it goes by, say, "Angela, here is our dog" or, simply, "cat." When you see animals in the park or zoo, or even on TV, point them out by name. Previously, the baby saw the object first (like a rattle) and then the flash card. Now you've shown him that he can see a picture first and then the real object.

23
By about the fifth or sixth month, your baby's favorite colors may be red and blue. Keep this in mind when purchasing new toys, clothes, linens, and other objects that your baby sees every day.

24
Simple challenges provide great opportunities for problem solving. Allow the baby to grasp one object in his hand. Next, place another object in his other hand. So far everything will be okay. Then, offer

him his favorite object. This is where the problem solving comes in — when there are no hands left. It will delight you to see your baby's mind at work. He may simply put down one of the objects or refuse to take the third one. Or he may place one of the objects in his mouth — or even try to grasp it with his foot. One reason why this game is so much fun is that you will probably be laughing hysterically at these antics, and all babies respond with glee when their parents are pleased.

25
During floor time, present simple physical challenges by placing toys slightly out of reach, encouraging the child first to stretch and later to move in order to retrieve the object.

26
When outdoors, encourage the baby to reach for leaves (on nonallergenic plants, of course). Also, encourage spatial concepts. When you hold the baby up to a tree say, "Jonathan, up you go!" Later, say, "Down you come, big boy!" Concepts such as up and down and over and under can best be learned with physical examples.

27
Another good Daddy exercise is a tie-pull. With Daddy wearing a necktie, have him bend down over the baby's crib. At first, the baby may only touch the tie or enjoy its tickling her, but soon she'll be grabbing for it. When she does grasp the tie, Daddy should allow her to pull his head down and should say something encouraging. My husband used to tell Stephen, "You got me!" This not only encourages the actual grasping but begins to teach a baby cause-and-effect relationships.

28
Help the baby to imitate your physical actions. Clap your hands several times, then help the baby to clap his hands. Hug the baby, then help the baby to hug you. Drop something, then help the baby drop something as well. Soon the baby will do these things by himself.

29
Running out of stimulating toys? Remember the terrific toys that you have around the house. Small pots and pans, strainers and spoons,

plastic cups, and containers can all be marvelous fun for a child. If friends or relatives ask what toys they can bring the baby, remember that you can never have enough balls or blocks.

30

If you haven't done so already, start reading to the baby in earnest. Find books that relate to your family and environment. If you have a dog or cat, read a dog or cat book. Read books about brothers and sisters, books about adults and the work that they do, and books about the outdoors and places to go. The animation in your voice will at once soothe and stimulate your child. Not every book has to be a "baby" book. Are you taking a school class, or did you bring reading home from the office? Pressed for time? Read it to the baby. Not only will the baby be pleased by your presence, but the intelligent sounds of speech are never lost on an infant, no matter how young the baby may be or how strange the subject matter.

31

If you and the baby ever feel housebound, go out! Virtually any place is stimulating to an infant. Point out the new objects, the people, the colors, and the smells — cut grass, a red house, white snow, the odor of gasoline. Every time you go out, try to bring one thing home — a ball, an apple, a leaf. Then you can talk about that object and remind the baby of the visit. For example, every time you go to the park, bring home a leaf and talk about that leaf. Soon the baby will associate parks with leaves. Even if you go to a different park, the baby will expect the leaf to be brought home. Making associations is one of the most important activities of the human mind.

The most commonplace locations can be places of magical wonder for a baby. One day, I received a call from the mother of a six-month-old baby who wanted to attend my course. She was nearly hysterical because her husband had left her. Not only didn't she know what to do about her marriage, but, because she had no car, she was heartbroken that she could not attend the course. I regretted that because she lived some distance away, I couldn't offer her transportation.

As a professional counselor, I knew that she had to break the bonds of despondency, and I relied on her love for her baby to accomplish this. "Marian," I said, "it is absolutely imperative that you continue the stimulation activities we discussed. You must!" "How can I?" she cried. "I have no money for a car. I have no money period. Where can I go? I just don't know what to do."

Crossing my fingers, I asked her, "Marian, is there a supermarket nearby?" "Yes," she whimpered in a low voice, " there's one about a block away." I asked her if the baby could sit up by himself, and when she said yes, I told her that she was going to take that baby to the supermarket every single day. She was astounded. I told her to take the baby to the produce aisle and show the baby each kind of fruit and vegetable. She was to say the name of the food and let the baby touch and smell it. Say only one word when you pick up the food. Whatever you buy, I told her, let the baby see it when you get home. Repeat the word. Let the baby see you preparing the food. If you peel a banana, tell the baby that you are peeling the banana. Or mashing the banana. Then, when the baby eats, say, "Jeremy, you are eating mashed banana."

Find the pet department, I told her, and let the baby grasp the dog and cat toys. These toys usually have bells or rattles, so the baby will love them. Go to the book or magazine rack, take down a book, and start reading to the baby. Visit the garden department and point out that different plants have the same parts — the leaf, the stem, the flower.

Let the baby touch frozen food as you say "cold." If you stop for a cup of coffee, tap the baby's finger on the cup for an instant and say "hot." If you take an item from the top shelf, as you reach for it say "up;" as you reach toward the bottom shelf, say "down." Use color names — not apples, but red apples. Take two identical boxes from the shelf and say "the same."

Marian was concerned that the supermarket manager might not appreciate her visits, but I told her to divide her grocery shopping so that she always bought something. She was told to point out the big letters on cereal and soap boxes and to repeat the letters if she brought home the product. If you see another baby, I told her, stop and visit. Most mothers welcome these visits. Begin counting to the baby. Hold up two oranges and say "two;" hold up three plums and say "three;" buy a dozen eggs, *open the carton, and say "twelve" or "one dozen."*

Marian's phone was changed to an unlisted number and I couldn't check on her progress. After a few months, I thought that I might never know how my experiment — devised to combat her anxiety as much as to benefit her child — had turned out. One afternoon, five months later, the phone rang. "This is Marian," she said, and I knew by the tone in her voice, before she said another word, that things had turned out very well indeed. "I just wanted you to know that I've taken Jeremy to the supermarket every day for months. It kept my sanity. And day after day, when I saw him learning all kinds of things, I was so happy and relieved." On she went, hardly taking a second to catch her breath. " I got a job about a month ago and I leave Jeremy with a neighbor. She has been watching children for about twelve years, and she told me that Jeremy is the most intelligent, best-behaved child she has ever seen. She said that he seems to understand everything that she shows him. I'm so grateful."

At that moment, I too was grateful that her efforts had merged with the fates, and I was about to tell her so when Marian interrupted. "And I thought you'd also like to know that Jeremy and I still go to the supermarket together every chance we get."

Stimulation and Focusing after Six Months

This is a truly exciting time because your baby's activity level and learning pace accelerate rapidly. A baby's most remarkable moment occurs when he realizes that he can, to a certain degree, control his own environment. When that moment comes, most infants take off! They want to do more and more and learn more and more. You'll see that they're preparing themselves for two of the biggest events in their young lives — talking and walking.

From about six or seven months to about one year, stimulation and focusing activities adjust to these new priorities. Strength and dexterity exercises assume new importance as the baby's nerves and muscles train for the tasks of communication and locomotion. As babies begin to comprehend that they are members of an ordered universe, problem-solving activities take center stage. No longer are exercises geared toward single-sensory stimulus. Instead, activity combinations that depend on multi-sensory reactions are introduced and refined.

If these months teach us any lesson, it's that the more a baby does, the more that baby wants to do. This is true because a well-balanced program of activities stimulates the brain's communication connections and encourages them to operate. For the parent who needs "proof" that early learning really does benefit a child, these months offer remarkable evidence.

Just don't forget those hugs and kisses!

1

Locating "lost" objects is an excellent problem-solving activity. Cut a small hole in a box and drop in an object; a rattle or the car keys are good for this. Allow the baby to see you drop in the item. Next, shake the box and ask the baby: "The rattle! Where is the rattle?" The baby should point to the box or attempt to grasp it. If so, congratulate her. If not, repeat the exercise once or twice. If necessary, take out the rattle yourself, exclaiming, "Here is the rattle!"

2

When the baby masters this technique, take a larger box and cut two holes in it, one on the top (large enough to drop in an object) and one on the side (large enough to accommodate the baby's arm). Drop in the rattle, shake the box, then remove the object from the side hole. Next, drop in the object again, shake the box, and ask the child, "Where is the rattle? Can you find the rattle?" Using different items, this can be a favorite activity, because most babies love to retrieve objects.

3

Introduce the baby to puzzle concepts. Sets of measuring cups, small plastic measuring bowls, or large measuring spoons are good for this. Work with the baby demonstrating how the objects can nest together. Start by giving the baby only two items from the set, eventually working up to three, four, or five.

4

Play ball rolling. This is especially good if you have an older child or even another adult available. Roll the ball to the baby and have the older individual help the baby to roll it back to you. Keep up the conversation. If the ball goes under a table, say, "Marc, the ball rolled *under* the table." If it rolls under a chair, say, "Marc, now the ball rolled *under* the chair." Because babies like to "chase" rolling balls — even if that means simply leaning out toward the ball — this activity helps to strengthen the muscles that will be used in crawling.

5

Introduce the baby to different foods and cooking techniques. If you have a bowl of different washed fruits, hand each one to the baby. Identify the fruit by name and encourage the baby to feel, smell, and even lick the fruit. Do the same for vegetables.

6

Simple, repetitive, sing-song tunes, such as Pat-A-Cake, This Little Piggy, or ABC songs that you hear on TV or make up yourself are important now. If they are repeated frequently, the baby will repeat them as soon as he is able to speak. Even if the baby can't speak, after a time she may begin to "sing along," sounding out her own version of the song. After a time, sing only the first few lines of the song and see if the baby attempts to complete it on her own.

7

Babies and young children love to play detective; therefore, more advanced hide-and-seek games are a great deal of fun. Hide a biscuit under a napkin, a toy in a basket, a rattle in a pocket, and so on.

8

· When a baby first eats solid food, fingers are the order of the day. First, place the food in the child's mouth. Later, hand the food to the baby or place it on the tray so that she can feed herself. Don't expect a baby to use a spoon without a great deal of practice. First, allow the baby to play with spoons and get to know them. Of course, banging on the table or tray is all that she'll do at first. When you do want to try to teach eating with a spoon, put something on the spoon that the baby likes and that won't fall off easily — a tiny bit of banana pressed into the spoon or a spot of honey.

9

Introduce more body parts to your baby — head, hair, eyes, ears, nose, mouth, neck, arms, elbows, hands, fingers, shoulders, chest, stomach or tummy, legs, knees, feet, toes.

10

Are you still building your flash-card library? If you've abandoned it, retrieve those cards and add as many new categories as you can.

> By the time Stephen was six or seven months old, I had begun to convince myself that he was not retarded. Still, the past year had been such an emotional rollercoaster for me that I remained traumatized. Therefore, I suppose that I was still looking for something that could be called "proof."
>
> By that time, I had been showing Stephen the flash cards for about three and one-half months, and, to tell you the truth, I was running out of ideas for new cards. I had cards for every person, animal, and plant in existence. So I was delighted when I entered a school-supply store and saw that they had a set of insect cards. The name of each insect was on the back of the card, and, as I showed Stephen the card, I read the name of the insect. One day it dawned on me that there were two bees in the stack of cards. One said "honeybee" and the other said "bumblebee." I pulled out the two bee cards and looked at the color drawings of the bees, but I couldn't tell the difference between them.
>
> Then I had an idea, a simple thought really, but one that has been reported throughout the world by journalists who have asked me when I first realized that Stephen was gifted. I held up the bee cards, one in each hand, and I showed the cards to Stephen. Then I said, "honeybee." Stephen immediately reached for the card with the honeybee. Then I said "bumblebee," and Stephen attempted to grasp the card with the bumblebee.
>
> To this day, I don't know if I was more relieved or shocked. I switched the cards behind my back, held them up again, and called out their names. Whatever way I held those cards, Stephen always picked the correct one. How could he tell them apart if I couldn't tell them apart?

*I ran out of the room screaming like a crazy woman, "This
baby is not retarded! This baby is not retarded!"
Now let me ask you, where did you say your flash cards were?*

11

If you see your baby trying to stand up in her crib, however weakly,
help her with standing exercises. You can either place her hands in
front of her to help her prop herself up or approach her from behind
and hold her hands to gently pull her up. Some are reticent to stand
because they're not sure what standing will feel like; therefore, these
activities demonstrate that there's nothing to fear.

12

At about seven or eight months, seat the baby on the floor and give
him a large plastic glass filled with cereal. Allow him to tip it over.
Next, give him a plastic jar filled with cereal and show him how to tip
over the bottle. Soon he'll understand the principle of pouring as you
allow him to pour cereal for himself.

13

When your baby is about seven or eight months old, you may have an
amazing insight. Just as you plan activities for your baby, so your baby
plans activities for you! A favorite activity for parent development has
the baby endlessly dropping objects from the high chair and watching
an obedient parent endlessly picking them up. Babies are happy to
learn that most parents are fairly adept at this. To combat this nearly
endless activity, tie some toys to the rails of the high chair, then place
them on the tray. At first the baby will merely drop them off again,
but he'll soon learn that he can retrieve them too. When he does, your
back will have a rest.

14

Another great activity is emptying things. I first learned about this
in an unexpected way. When Stephen was a baby, I took him with me
to a doctor's appointment. On the way, it dawned on me that I had
forgotten to bring a toy along to occupy him while I was with the
doctor. "Don't worry," offered my daughter Deb, who accompanied us,
"I'll think of something." I was with the doctor for a long time, but
when I returned to the waiting room, I learned that Deb had indeed

found a marvelous toy for Stephen — my purse. Stephen had taken everything out; Deb had put everything back; Stephen had taken it all out again. The best thing to do is to take an old handbag and fill it with safe items. Not only will the baby love to empty the purse again and again, but one day soon he'll even learn to put everything back!

15

Hide small toys under a towel or blanket, but leave one edge exposed. Then ask, "Where did it go?" Seeing an edge sticking out encourages the baby to grasp for — and soon to crawl toward — the object.

16

At about eight months, begin counting in earnest. Count items in the natural environment (the number of eggs on the breakfast table, the number of shirts in the laundry pile). Ask number questions: "What channel is Sesame Street on? Sesame Street is on channel 3." Talk about addresses, times, dates, birthdays, and other "number" items even though it may be a few years before she lets you know that she understands.

17

If you'd like, you can continue your baby's introduction to the sight of printed words. Remember that the baby has already seen printed words in books. You can carefully print the word for an object on an 8x10 piece of white paper or poster board and then tape the card to the object. For example, tape the word "playpen" to the side of the playpen. When you put the baby in the playpen, point to the word and say "playpen" or, "Michelle, this is your playpen" (emphasizing the word "playpen"). You can also place cards on objects that the baby encounters throughout the day. Please remember, you are not now teaching your baby to read. You are simply allowing her to see the sight of printed words and to begin to realize for herself that these printed words correlate with objects in her environment. A growing body of research suggests that children who possess some basic understanding of what a word is later become more proficient readers. Easy does it. *Gradually* increase the number of word cards. If you overdo this activity, you'll tend to drive yourself and your baby a little batty. However, if you begin this activity at a reasonable pace, your baby will likely learn to recognize words earlier and more easily.

18

Now is the time to be scouring the toy store for games, puzzles, books, large beads, large-piece construction toys, and similar items. Stephen had few passive toys, but he had scores of activity toys and learning games, as well as many stuffed animals to encourage his imagination. Did I invest a lot in these items? Yes, I did, but I felt that I earned a good return on my investment when Stephen received scholarships to New York University and the University of Miami Law School. If the choice is to pay a small amount now or a great amount later, I'll pay now every time. You can, however, make quite a few toys yourself. Large macaroni pieces — especially the colored vegetable pastas — make excellent beads. Numerous puzzles and posters can be made from colored cardboard and magazine or coloring-book pictures. Even cereal boxes and other food boxes can teach colors, numbers, letters, and shapes. Cut off the tops of different sizes of milk and dairy containers — pint, quart, half-gallon — and use them for stacking games. Cut off the bottoms and use these containers for nesting games as well.

19

Strengthening the fingers that will one day hold crayons and pencils is an important goal. Happily, the activities which promote finger strength and dexterity are great fun for babies. Place ever smaller pieces of food on her tray for her to grasp. Encourage her to play with dry sand and wet sand, either at the beach or from a sandbox at home. Be sure that the sandbox sand is asbestos-free. Eventually, you can encourage her to imitate simple designs, such as circles or squares, in the sand. If you're adventuresome, prepare chocolate pudding and allow her to play with it in the bowl. Or place a small amount on her tray and let her "draw" with it. Nontoxic children's putties are also great, although clays are still too difficult for babies to handle.

20

Watch TV with your child and repeat some of the letters, numbers, words or sentences used on the show. Stephen and I watched Sesame Street three times a day on Saturday and during school breaks. If you're not available when a program like Sesame Street is on, try to invest in a VCR and tape the show to play back while you feed or dress your child.

21
Encourage sound recognition. "Is the key in the lock? Daddy must be home." "Is the refrigerator opening and closing? Your brother must be hungry again." "Do I hear the mailman? Let's go say hello to him." "I heard the door slam. Is that your sister leaving for school? Let's wave good-bye to her."

22
Read picture books, pointing out the pictures that correspond to the words that you are saying. Babies very quickly adopt favorite books. You'll soon find that as you say certain words, your baby will point to the correct picture!

23
If baby is trying to hoist himself up, place him near low furniture that he can grasp. Also, be sure he's not wearing pants that are tight, especially around the knees.

24
Ask questions that can elicit some type of body-language response that is a physical or verbal (sound) reply. Then take the action that answers the question. "Where is your teddy bear?" (Then, find the teddy bear.) "Do you want to go outside?" (Then, go outside.) "Are you thirsty? Here is some juice."

26
If you don't have much originality in the music department, purchase a song book, because songs, in addition to being great fun, can teach a great deal. What child hasn't learned the names and sounds of all the animals from Old MacDonald?

26
When you go for a walk, call it a nature hike and make it a grand adventure. Try to point out anything that moves — a bird, a squirrel, an insect, the leaves blowing in the wind. Point out the colors — green leaves, red flowers, orange ladybugs. Obtain nature books from the library or bookstore and point out pictures that correspond to the things seen on your walk.

27

At about nine months, a child's sense of humor begins to emerge. Encourage laughter by tickling; by playing peek-a-boo, hide-and-seek, and finger games; and by using squeak toys.

28

Have you added any new balls to baby's ball collection? By now, balls can help a baby learn colors, sizes, weights, textures, and so much more. About this time, too, babies like collections, a trait that will extend throughout childhood. Identify each of the balls by name — red ball, yellow ball, furry ball, soft ball, and so on.

29

Children hear everything and sense the accompanying emotions. Hearing adult conversations can promote a child's efforts to speak. When a baby hears continual arguments, however, the negative sensations may thwart speech for many months. Allow your baby to observe as many conversations as possible (sometimes exaggerating your speech so that the baby can hear each word clearly), but try to save family disagreements for a private spot.

30

Make a duplicate set of shape posters. Then ask the child to match the numbers. For example, show the child the one-circle and two-circle posters and ask, "Which is one?" Or, show the child three posters, two posters with one square and one poster with four squares. Ask, "Which posters are the same?" Of course, you may have to supply the answers for a number of times until the child understands exactly what you are asking and points to the correct posters. Once the child does understand, progress can be remarkable.

31

Make self-motivated activity boxes. To do this, take a shoe box or similar box and fill it with a variety of objects. One box may have small kitchen equipment — a small pan with a lid, plastic bottles, a strainer, and measuring cups and spoons. Another box may have a small ball collection together with a few tiny stuffed animals. A third box may have beads, keys, and other small toys. From time to time, and especially if baby seems bored or cranky, take down the box and pour its contents on the rug. Allow your baby to make his own connections and his own fun. A bath-time box is a good idea too. Fill it with sponges, rubber toys, plastic cups, containers, and so on. If you're creative, bath time will always be a new adventure.

32

Even empty boxes can be great fun. Stephen always received a lot of gifts for birthdays, Christmas, and Chanukah. Yet, as an older baby, his two greatest thrills were tearing off the wrapping and playing with the empty boxes. Cars and trains, planes and castles, all lay idly by while Stephen gathered his imagination and sat in the box, fought with the box, or even wore it as a hat. You can encourage imaginative play by continuing to speak to the baby in an animated voice, alternately praising and questioning and joining in the laughter.

33

Buy or make color-recognition cards. Introduce two colors at a time, starting, for example, with red and yellow or red and blue (understanding the nature of the color white may be too difficult). There are many color games to play. First, point out the red and yellow cards. Then, ask the baby to pick out the red one. Next, turn both cards upside down and ask the baby to pick out the red one.

Certain forms of color recognition seem to be related to the maturation of specific areas of the brain. If the baby isn't interested after several attempts, try again next month. The goal is for the baby to be interested in these games, not necessarily for him to give correct answers. If simple color games are fun, move on to color-object recognition games. For example, hold up a red apple near the red and yellow cards. Ask baby which color is the apple. He'll very likely point to the red card.

34

At about ten months, and especially if you've been practicing finger exercises, you can give your baby a fat crayon or water-based marker pen. The best thing to do, if you'd like to preserve your house, is to buy a roll of brown kraft or wrapping paper at an office-supply store. Roll out a big piece of paper on the floor and place the baby in the middle. Then, demonstrate how to use the marker. Whatever the baby does, remember to shower him with lots of hugs and kisses.

35

Introduce sizes and measures. This is a good activity for the beach or sandbox. Help the baby to fill measuring cups with wet sand. As each is turned over, use words like "less," "more," "bigger," "smaller," "full," "empty," "half-filled," and so on.

36

At bath time, talk to your baby about body parts, water, soap, splashing, and tickling. When you dress your baby, talk about the clothes and their colors. When you're preparing a meal or feeding your baby, discuss the names of the foods, their colors and their shapes.

The activities that follow are suitable for babies about one year old. A baby's interest in certain activities is dependent on many factors: good health, brain maturation, and even personal preference. It is not necessary that you complete in any specific order the activities described in this chapter. Very likely there are favorite activities that you'll repeat again and again and other activities that, for one reason or another, you never try at all. That's fine, but remember that in general, growth relies on an orderly progression of physical and mental challenges. You can't skip to the end of the chapter without passing through at least some of the intermediate steps.

While it is said that babies learn by osmosis — that is, they soak up knowledge like sponges soak up water — certain skills must be *available* for the baby to soak up.

> *When Stephen was a young baby, I never allowed him to hold his bottle himself, nor would I prop up the bottle for him. The bottle was always held. That's because I feared that if he were retarded, he might choke if left alone with the bottle. As a result, even though he could turn the pages of a book or manipulate complex puzzles, he still never learned to hold a bottle. This was made clear to me when Stephen was a year old and was in the hospital with pneumonia. I had fallen asleep on the floor under his crib and awoke to hear Stephen screaming with frustration. The nurse, thinking that a year-old baby could certainly hold a bottle, had given him the bottle, propped it on a diaper, and left the room. Needless to say, the bottle just lay there.*

I realized then what I still know today. A great deal of learning is *not* automatic. There are endless varieties of knowledge that a baby must be taught and encouraged to do, or at least exposed to if learning is to occur. When you engage in more advanced activities with your baby, be especially sensitive to his responses. If he's bored or disinterested, STOP. Try again another day or another month. Remember to avoid SPPPAN: no stress, no pushing, no pressure, no punishment, no anxiety, no negativism!

37
Encourage general body and people recognition. Cut large pictures of people from magazines. Mount the pictures on cardboard, then cut them apart, like a jigsaw puzzle. Help the baby to put the pieces together again.

38
There are numerous color-recognition games that promote both visual discrimination and memory. Take three pairs of the same objects (two blue cars, two red balls, two green crayons, or whatever you have available), and place them in a small box or container. Then remove three objects — two of the same object together with a third, unmatched object. Encourage your baby to find the matching object.

At a paint or hardware store, pick up two copies each of paint-chip cards and have your child match the identical colors. Cut apart old clothes (even doll's clothing) into swatches, and ask your child to select the pieces that match. If the child finds this difficult, you can select two matching swatches and ask your child to select a third swatch that matches. Have the child select from a basket two spools of thread that are identical. Eventually, children can be asked to match color families (all the shades of blue, for example), but this is a more advanced skill.

Make geometric shapes from paper or fabric — red circles, green squares, yellow rectangles, purple triangles — and ask your child to match the pieces. In this activity, conscious color matching is combined with subconscious shape discernment. Take four pieces of paper, three of one color and one of another color, and have your child remove the piece that doesn't match. Have a color of the day. Draw or fingerpaint only with that color; try to spot the color in the natural environment; select and eat foods that are the same color.

39

Once your child is comfortable with these games, you can proceed to more advanced color-recognition games. Give your child several pieces of paper, all of which are the same color; it's best to start with red. Then, ask your child to put one piece of paper on an object in the room that is the same color. Comparing two objects that have the same color but different textures is a sophisticated task. If the child isn't ready for this activity, simply put it away for a later date.

40

Play color lotto. To do this you'll need to make a lotto board. Use a piece of poster board with about a dozen squares that feature different colors (perhaps three red squares, three green, three blue, three yellow; later, you can make new lotto boards with more colors and shades of colors). You will also need about two dozen squares of paper, each of which has one color from the lotto board (in this example, six red pieces, six green, six blue, six yellow). The reverse of each piece should be white. Make two dozen name pieces, twelve with the child's name and twelve with your name. This may sound like a lot of work, but you can easily make this game in thirty minutes, and children love to play color lotto time and again.

To play color lotto, turn the playing pieces upside down. Then, ask the child to turn over one piece. As you say the name of the color, you and the child point to that same color on the lotto board. Whoever touches the correct color first gets to put his name piéce on that square. When the lotto board is filled, the player who has more name pieces on the board is the winner. Needless to say, your child should usually be the winner. If you can convince an older sibling to "allow" a younger child to win most of the time, this is also a great game for children to play together.

41

Mirrors can provide great fun. Practice hand games and funny faces. Especially important are imitation games. Mommy should lift her right arm and encourage baby to do the same, helping her if necessary. Have Daddy make a funny face and ask baby to do the same. Play touch: Mommy touches her eye, baby does the same; Daddy touches his tummy, baby does the same.

42

Play big and little. Daddy's shoe is big, baby's shoe is small; Mommy's shirt is big, baby's shirt is small; eventually, Daddy's shirt is biggest, Mommy's shirt is smaller, baby's shirt is smallest.

43

Chop up a few pieces of vegetables in a bag. As baby pulls out the pieces, identify the vegetable and its color — green pickles, green lettuce, green grapes, green peppers, green asparagus. The first time you play this game, use whole vegetables placed in a box. Continue this game at other times by using smaller pieces of vegetables. Also, use color names when you serve food to your child — brown bread, white bread, and so on.

44

When you go for a walk, if there are any trees or shrubs in the area, take along a paper bag and bring home a collection of leaves to talk about. Point out differences in size, shape, and color or shades of color.

45

Buy animal crackers and pretend to be the animals. Roar, bark, or make similar sounds as each cracker is pulled from the box. When baby pulls out a cracker, can he make an animal sound? Probably yes!

46

Wherever you go, point out sensory things — what you see, what you hear, what you can touch, even what you can smell. When you return home, animatedly review the trip: "What did we hear in the park? We heard the bird! What color was the bird? The bird was blue! What did we smell? The grass smelled very fresh. The garbage smelled terrible!" When you activate your baby's five senses (seeing, hearing, smelling, touching, and tasting), you are actually activating his brain to bring in information from the environment. The more we allow children's senses to work for them, the more intelligent they become. My own book *Looking For a Rainbow* was written expressly to allow children to heighten their sensory abilities.

47

Make jewelry for the family from uncooked macaroni. Multicolored vegetable pastas are especially good for this. Stringing pasta is also a great holiday or birthday activity. Name the colors as you go along. Ask the baby to select a red piece or a green one. Make patterns — two red, two green, two yellow. Gradually make more complex patterns — three red, two green, one yellow.

48

Encourage an understanding of food by making different recipes with the same item, such as an apple. You can make baked apples, candied apples, applesauce, apple pie, and even apple juice.

49

Cut up solid-color fabric pieces into squares and do the same with construction paper. Make two piles, one with the fabric pieces and one with the paper. First, select one piece of fabric, then choose the same color of paper. Place the matched pair clearly in front of the child. Then, make another set. Finally, choose a third piece of fabric and ask the baby to choose the piece of paper that matches.

50

Take an empty plastic or paper egg carton and cut it, retaining only a four-egg section. Take four small toys, balls, marbles, or pieces of food and distribute one in each cup, counting as you go: "One, two, three, four." Don't say "four grapes;" simply say "four." Allow the baby to distribute the pieces also. If he places two items in one cup, simply remove one yourself and place it in the next cup. Gradually add two sections at a time until you have the entire twelve-section carton. Once a child understands numbers from one through twelve, you can introduce words like dozen, half-dozen, and even fractions. (You'll learn how to do this in Chapter 6.)

51

Remember hand and finger dexterity exercises. Jigsaw puzzles, even two-piece jigsaw puzzles, provide opportunities for mental and physical dexterity. Offer construction blocks of various shapes and sizes. Take empty squeeze bottles (ketchup and mustard containers are good), fill them with water, and let your baby squeeze them out during bath time or at the beach. Babies also like to squeeze wet sponges or even rubber-bulbed horns that make funny noises. Also at the beach or sandbox, take a stick (an ice cream stick or wooden stirrer, for example) and begin to draw in the sand — first lines, then shapes, then letters or numbers. Encourage your baby to do the same. Previously, baby used her fingers or hands for this exercise. Now she may be able to use an implement.

52

Start to talk about problems and play problem-solving games. For example, play the "what am I doing wrong?" game. Show your baby two items — a comb and a spoon. Then, brush baby's hair with the spoon. Ask the baby what Mommy is doing wrong, then explain the right answer: "We have to comb our hair with a comb, not a spoon." If your baby does something that you disapprove of, try playing the "what went wrong?" game. Ask: "Why did you write on the wall, Matthew? Didn't you have any paper? Next time, I'll give you paper."

Play "what would happen if" games, especially funny ones. At the breakfast table, as you hold a coffee cup near your head, ask, "What would happen if Mommy poured the coffee on her head? Mommy would get burned and then the coffee would fall off." Many of these games not only teach problem-solving skills but gently introduce a child to the idea that certain behaviors are correct and others incorrect. Incorrect but harmless behaviors should *not* engender punishment; instead, they need explanation and correction.

53

If you have older children, encourage them to join in make-believe games with their younger sibling. Play zoo, for example, with one child climbing on the furniture like a monkey, another roaring like a lion. You can distribute boxes or pillows to heighten the effect. Finally, at bath time, take a ball along so that your baby can play a seal. Don't merely suggest make-believe games to the children — ask them to design the games themselves.

54

Your baby's color discernment is now more sophisticated, even though you won't receive any feedback from her for quite a while.

Therefore, point out many shades of colors: pink on Valentine's Day, bright orange at Halloween, the grey sky on an overcast day, the azure sky on a bright summer day, purple hair ribbons on blond hair.

55
Introduce science experiments. Gather a cupful of snow or an ice cube and continue to check on it as it melts. Mix sugar in water and explain that the sugar didn't disappear, it dissolved, and allow the baby to taste the water. At bath time, push a floating toy under the water and watch it come to the surface. Experiment with things that float and with things that don't. You may want to get an early science book from the library or bookstore so that you can be prepared to offer explanations as to why certain things happen. This is good practice, because as soon as an early learner begins to speak, "why" is going to become a very popular word!

56
Cut out letters from heavy cardboard. At first, make two As and two Bs, cutting out each letter as precisely as you can. Be sure to cut out the "holes" in the As and Bs. Put one A and one B in a paper bag and the other A and B in a second bag. Ask the child to pull out a letter from the first bag. Say, "You picked an A." Then ask the child, "Can you pick out an A from the second bag?" If the child picks a B, say, "You got a B. Can you pick an A?" When the child picks the letter, say, "Great! You matched the A." Then, lay out the two As side by side so that the child can see the pair. Gradually increase the number of letter pairs that you work with. Children who learn to recognize letters by feeling their shapes are also better able to recognize letters visually.

57
You can make your own speaking game with a simple tape recorder. Record all kinds of sounds: doors closing, dogs barking, horns honking, bells chiming, fans whirring, washing machines chugging. Later, play some of the sounds for your baby and identify them. Be aware that some babies do not like to hear sounds separated from events. Therefore, if the baby seems afraid, postpone the activity for another day. Other babies love to hear these sounds, and you'll see that they soon build a mental encyclopedia of favorite sounds.

58

Increase baby's smell encyclopedia too. Allow the baby to smell perfume, baby powder, flowers, sharp smells, and sour smells. Identify each smell. You can increase a baby's mental vocabulary by associating words with sights, sounds, smells, touches, and even tastes. "The cinnamon on the apples has a nice smell. Do you like it, Brian?"

59

If your baby is starting to walk, help him along. Not only can you hold his hands, but you can hold a thick stick in your hands that your baby can grasp much like a walker. Encourage, but don't force. Allow your baby to set the pace.

60

Music is a delight for children. To encourage a child's participation, rather than just listening, make musical instruments from items around the house. If your child plays with pots and pans, suggest that the stainless steel lids, when hit together, sound like cymbals producing a great gong. When struck, an overturned pot or even a wastebasket turned upside down produces the resounding boom of a drum.

61

A musical instrument, such as a xylophone, can be great fun. There are color-keyed xylophones as well as ones with the letters marked on the keys. If you purchase a color-keyed instrument, you can later progress to a letter-keyed one. If you can't find one, you can always tape the letters on each of the keys. An illustrated book of nursery rhymes set to music is a favorite.

62

Simple songbooks featuring songs like these teach your child to play the xylophone and sing along at the same time:

THIS LITTLE PIG

C	C	C	C	C	C	C	C	C	D
THIS	LIT	TLE	PIG	WENT	TO	MAR	KET	AND	THIS

D	D	D	D	D	D	E	E	E	E
LIT	TLE	PIG	STAYED	AT		HOME	THIS	LIT	TLE	PIG

E	E		E	E	F	F	F	F	F
HAD	ROAST		BEEF	AND	THIS	LIT	TLE	PIG	HAD

F	F	G	G		G	G	G	C	B	A	F
NONE	AND	THIS	LIT		TLE	PIG	CRIED	WEE	WEE	WEE	I

E	E	D	D	C
CAN'T	FIND	MY	WAY	HOME

HICKORY DICKORY DOCK

E	F	G	G	A	B	C	E	E
HICK	O	RY	DICK	O	RY	DOCK	THE	MOUSE

F	G	A	B	C	G	C	C	B
RAN	UP	THE	CLOCK	THE	CLOCK	HIT	ONE	THE

B	A	G	G	A	G	F	E	D	C
MOUSE	RAN	DOWN	HICK	O	RY	DICK	O	RY	DOCK

63

Begin to offer your child choices. Making choices challenges problem-solving and memory skills and encourages self-analysis and self-esteem. Ask the child which he would rather have with dinner, carrots or peas. Ask which dress she would rather wear, the red or the blue. Don't simply ask what the child would like for dinner or what dress she would like to wear. Children need to make selections from a limited number of choices, preferably two and eventually three. Choosing for one's own self, instead of having all the choices predetermined, is one of the greatest indications that your baby is now passing from infancy into childhood.

Give yourself a pat on the back, because you certainly deserve one! You have learned that stimulation and focusing activities are designed not merely to teach specific information, but to provide a *foundation* for later learning. These activities blend in easily with a baby's typical daily schedule: eating, bathing, going for a walk. If you believe that childhood is a time for playing and for fun, then these activities have only fortified your belief. Every activity in which you have engaged has been fun for your child and very likely has also been fun for you.

Your commitment to these activities, even if you've pursued them for only minutes a day, ensures that your child will have the *very best foundation that you can possibly offer.* While most activities are not competitive, they still offer your child the single best attribute that he or she will need in order to function in a highly competitive world — self-esteem.

Everything that children can be, everything that heredity and environment and the fates have in store for them, is strengthened and energized through these activities. In the following chapters, you'll learn how to help your child build a strong, intelligent, and happy person on this solid foundation whose building blocks are PEEEHK: pleasure, enthusiasm, excitement, enjoyment, and, of course, hugs and kisses.

CHAPTER   FOUR

Self-Expression Through Speech

Over the years, I have had discussions with psychiatrists and other medical doctors who believe that speech is part of the human biological heritage and that, as a result, it is not necessary to teach children to speak. Children, they say, learn to speak by themselves. If that's true, then why is it that when you gather together a group of six-year-olds — a first-grade class on the first day of school, for example — you find that some of the children are articulate, speaking complete sentences with vivid and descriptive language, while others can barely articulate their ideas at all?

If you were to examine the background of the verbally inhibited group, you would discover, sadly, that these children were rarely, if ever, in the presence of people who genuinely sought to communicate with them. The articulate children, on the other hand, were exposed to a rich and stimulating spoken environment.

As a result of observations such as these, increasing numbers of child-development professionals today believe that while most children can naturally learn to develop some type of speech, in order for children to speak with confidence and precision, they must consistently be presented with challenging speaking opportunities.

Why should a young child have a large vocabulary? The reason has nothing to do with impressing friends and family. The importance of speech lies in the fact that speech is the most powerful means of self-expression possessed by humans. In order to express ourselves — what we think, what we feel, what we like and dislike — we must *talk* about these thoughts and emotions. And the degree to which we are able to say precisely what we think and believe is governed by the breadth of our vocabulary and the facility with which we can use it.

As children grow, the world around them grows in wonder, and the emotions that accompany the wonder — delight, anger, pleasure, fear, confusion, exultation — have only a few outlets: physical movement such as dance, exercise, or banging a fist into a wall; creative activities such as art; and speech. Of these outlets, speech clearly is the one that can be most often relied on, assuming that the child's ability to speak has been developed.

How does "teaching" speech begin? Like all child-directed activities, it begins without formal teaching. When you speak to your child, begin to introduce new words. Try to avoid talking down to a child. When you speak to other family members and friends, include your child in the conversation. If your child spends time with a care giver, consider whether this individual is communicative with children. Certain adults have a great deal of trouble communicating with children. They're fine with other adults, but they're incapable of holding a conversation with a child.

Consider the preposition in that last sentence: speak *with* a child. All too often, adults speak *to* children; rarely do they speak *with* them. Perhaps this unfortunate situation has an innocent start. When we first speak to babies, some of us do just that — speak *to* or *at* them. As the baby grows, some adults find it difficult to shift gears and continue to speak *to* the child, rarely encouraging give-and-take conversation. As a result, some children develop the sorry belief that they are the recipients of conversation ("Roger, eat your vegetables;" "Mary, clean your room") rather than active participants in its creation.

Speech and the Newborn Baby

At what age can a child contribute to a conversation? The answer to this is simple. Children speak from the instant they're born. At first, of course, babies have a limited vocabulary. To express hunger, they cry; to express thirst, they cry; to say, "Hey, I'm cold and I'm wet and I'm miserable," they cry.

Crying is a baby's form of communication and, as with anyone trying to communicate an idea, the baby deserves our serious consideration.

When you sit back and allow your baby to "cry it out," you're sending your baby a strong, negative message — that his or her attempts to communicate thoughts and feelings are meaningless to you. Some child-care authorities suggest that most crying babies, if left alone, will eventually stop crying. They reason that if you let a baby cry things out, he or she will stop crying faster; if you immediately respond to a baby's crying, that baby is only conditioned to cry more frequently.

If we were talking about some kind of detached, scientific experiment, then their observations might be correct. But these so-called experts fail to consider one vital element: When you fail to acknowledge your baby's crying, you are stifling his or her earliest attempts at communication. And babies who learn that their communication attempts are largely failures often have lifelong inhibitions about speech and other forms of communication.

When you respond to your baby's crying, her delight at seeing your smiling face reaps wonderful benefits. She soon begins cooing, gurgling, and screeching, adding these and other sounds to her growing vocabulary.

One way to encourage a baby's vocal communication is by introducing a wide variety of sounds that develop her listening powers. Begin with yourself. Put your face next to your baby's and chuckle, laugh, sigh, and speak. Clap your hands, snap your fingers, or tap a spoon against your hand. As the baby begins to focus on these sounds, explain them: "Jonathan, Mommy's laughing because you made such a funny face." "Listen, Allison, Mommy is clapping her hands."

Become more aware of the sounds around you. While you have learned to filter out many of these sounds, they can be remarkably interesting to your baby. Point out the sounds of clocks ticking, dogs barking, older brother yelling, dad's shaver humming, and the lawnmower grating. As you listen to each sound with your baby, identify the sound — where it's coming from, and who is making it. Babies delight in these sensory opportunities.

Soon an amazing thing begins to happen: your baby tries to duplicate these sounds. At first, of course, the attempts may be so unusual that you don't even realize what your baby is doing. Try to concentrate. When your baby makes a noise, is he listening to a sound that he is trying to imitate? Whenever your baby makes a sound, immediately repeat the sound to him and smile broadly. This assures him that you "understood" what he was trying to say. Then, congratulate him. Nothing encourages speech development like parents' enthusiasm!

Speech is the end product of hearing, recognizing, and differentiating. That is, the baby hears something, recognizes something about the sound, and differentiates that sound from other sounds so that he is able to repeat that sound. That's a wonderful intelligence at work, even if the end product only sounds like "goo-goo-goo."

It's important to supplement your own activities by including other family members. Mom, dad, siblings, grandparents, care givers, and friends should all speak with the baby as frequently as possible. This not only enlarges the baby's sound vocabulary but helps to reinforce the idea that speech is a utility shared by virtually all human beings.

Quickly move from introducing sounds to speaking complete sentences. The best way to do this is to identify the day's activities: "Let's have a nice bath, Michael. I'm going to take the washcloth and wash your beautiful feet. First the right foot and then the left foot. Can you splash your right foot in the water?" Help Michael to splash his right foot in the water. "That's wonderful, Mikey, you splashed your right foot in the water." Continue these activities as you dress the baby, feed him, and change him throughout the day. When the two of you go somewhere, explain where you are going and with whom you will meet.

From the day your child is born, read, read, read. Use every available opportunity to read to your baby. The calm sounds of long sentences and paragraphs are not only soothing to most babies, but babies begin to understand that language is composed of more complex elements than simply "see Spot run." And don't confine yourself only to children's storybooks. You'll be happy to know that you can stretch the moments in a busy day by reading the newspaper to your baby. In a hurry to make supper? Read baby the recipe. Late for class? Read your business-management text aloud. Most babies are wonderfully democratic — they love to listen to anything that you read. From Shakespeare to *Soap Opera News*, from algebra to auto repair, babies love to listen. If you're interested, they're interested.

Early Speech Activities

At birth, a baby's tongue is actually too large for his mouth. As a result, even if a baby intellectually wanted to make certain sounds, his physical anatomy would often make this impossible. In the early months of life, however, these structures begin to develop better symmetry and proportion. At about four months, a baby begins to babble in earnest. If your earlier attempts to coax your baby into soundmaking met with mixed results, these next months should show amazing progress.

It's interesting to consider that babies around the world make the same sounds. However, within the first few months of life, unless these sounds are reinforced, the sounds gradually disappear from the baby's vocabulary. As in all other aspects of a child's life, the parent is the role model. When the parent speaks, the child listens and imitates; when the parent is silent, the child descends into silence as well.

In fact, because babies are so imitative during the early months of life, now is a great time not only to teach one language to your child but, if possible, to teach several languages. That's right. Several languages! Many children have learned to speak three languages by the time they were four years old. More than simply learning the languages, a child will speak the particular language with the person who taught it to him. If Grandma teaches French to Jason, Jason will begin speaking French when he sees her. What's more, because a young child's vocal anatomy is flexible and malleable, the child typically will speak with an accent identical to that of the teacher. Thus, if your housekeeper's native language is Spanish, and if she speaks in Spanish with your daughter, your daughter will likely speak Spanish with a native accent. This is a situation that rarely occurs if your child learns a foreign language in school.

It's important to realize, however, that it may be many months before your child can actually enunciate the words of English or any other language. In these early months, babies listen and babble back their responses. What you're doing now is sharpening baby's listening skills and allowing her to practice sound making at her own pace. Occasionally, your inability to understand exactly what she is trying to say may exasperate both of you. At those times, remember PEEEHK and be assured that the more attuned you are to your baby in general, the more you will understand.

Also important is the realization that not all babbling has meaning. Many babies babble simply because they're happy. Often a babbling baby is simply speaking to himself. Don't try to understand it all, because if you become anxious, you will only discourage this playful gibberish — and that's the last thing you want to do.

As the months progress, and so much of your baby's energy goes into attempting to crawl and walk, speech activities may actually diminish. This does not occur with all babies but happens more frequently than we once imagined. During these times, speak simple words. When you hand the baby her bottle, say, "bottle." If she says "ba ba," repeat the word, "Yes, bottle, bottle." After several days of this, when you give her another bottle, say "warm bottle." If she again says "ba ba," repeat the words "warm bottle." At these sensitive periods, if your baby seems less interested in speech, don't overload her circuits — speak slowly and carefully.

What about baby talk? By baby talk we are not referring to the sounds that a baby makes, but rather the childlike way of talking that some adults adopt. Parents can be very defensive about baby talk, insisting that it makes their child happy. What makes a child happy is the enthusiasm in a voice, not the fact that the person is speaking nonsense. The problem with baby talk is that it encourages incorrect speech. At first, whatever the baby says is greeted with choruses of "isn't that cute." In fact, the more erroneous the pronunciation, the greater the response. Parents and grandparents delight in the malapropisms of their young children. But babies aren't babies forever. And when your young child confronts his peers, he faces laughter and ridicule for the very things that you found so cute.

What's the best way to correct errors in speech? That's easy: simply repeat the word or phrase correctly. Don't chastise. Don't ask "how many times have I told you." Simply repeat the word correctly and let it go at that.

With all of these opportunities for speaking with a child, you might think that all parents would actively engage in these activities. Unfortunately, this is often not the case. As we've alluded to before, some adults are too self-conscious or seemingly too busy to speak directly with their children. And many of these adults assume, erroneously I'm sorry to say, that their child will simply "pick up" speech if the child is surrounded by speaking adults.

Nothing can be further from the truth. Children in institutional settings such as hospitals are surrounded by articulate adults, yet these children learn to speak much later than their nonhospitalized peers. It's not enough for a baby to hear sounds; a baby must be directly spoken to and, better yet, spoken with, if confident speech patterns are to develop.

Speech at Six to Twelve Months

At about six months many babies are able to combine consonants and vowels into recognizable sounds: "mama," "dada," "nana," and "papa" chief among them. Once they feel confident with these words, other one-syllable words can follow, such as "ball" and "dog".

In the months to come, your baby will do best with words that correspond to physical objects in the everyday environment. For example, by ten months, Stephen — like other early conversant children — said words that I could understand: cup, bottle, watch, book, door, chair, car, boat, truck, clock, blanket, doll, block, ball, sock, heat, shoes, cow, mama, dada, bear, horse, cat, dog, drink, banana, cake, apple, toast, cookie, water, milk, juice, and more. These words all correspond to objects in a baby's immediate environment or to pictures of objects found in storybooks. This should reinforce the idea that speech does not come naturally but is the result of being introduced time and again to things or to pictures of things.

There are many ways to make the object-word connection. For example, pat-a-cake is one way to familiarize baby with her hands and with clapping. Bath time is also a fun time for identifying body parts: arms, legs, hands, feet, fingers, toes, head, eyes, ears, nose and mouth. Hide-and-seek is a great way to ask the questions, "Where is the ball?" (the bottle, the stuffed toy, and so on).

When you read illustrated books, be sure to point to the pictures. The first time that you read the book, point and say a single word: dog, cat, man. When you reread the book, gradually add more words. Ask "Where is the cat, Kevin?" Then, as you point to the cat, say, "Kevin, this is the cat."

In addition to words that denote objects, your baby should gradually be introduced to words that describe actions or feelings. "Hi" and "bye-bye," accompanied by waving hands, are good words to start with. Move on to words such as: want, more, have, like, happy, sad, kiss, hug, and so on. Match action words with object words. Once your baby understands the word "ball," talk about hitting the ball, throwing the ball, and pinching the ball and demonstrate these actions. Repeat action words in many contexts — throw the ball, throw a kiss, wave hi, wave bye-bye.

Some babies have difficulty pronouncing certain sounds. "R" and "h" sounds (especially "sh," "th" and "wh") pose problems for certain children. Find opportunities to use these sounds so that your baby can hear them spoken and practice them. Dr. Seuss and similar books can help because they stress many types of unusual sounds that children enjoy mimicking even if the sounds have no meaning.

Because our lives are so busy, many parents tend to set aside time for reading to their children, but then, when other activities occur, all speech stops. For example, you may read to your child for fifteen minutes and then, during the thirty minutes while you prepare dinner, you say virtually nothing at all. Yet these moments offer exceptional language opportunities. Talk about the foods you're preparing. Let the child finger a piece of pasta or a cracker. Talk about veal and beef and fish. Describe actions such as chopping, mincing, slicing, stirring, baking, and frying. Talk about measurements — one teaspoon, two tablespoons, three cups. Children love to participate. When you're preparing dinner, allow the baby to play with his own set of measuring spoons or measuring cups.

Bath time is another superb opportunity. We've already mentioned pointing out body parts, but don't forget action words: splash, drip, sprinkle, spray.

Because you have pointed to things when you mentioned them, your baby understands that language can be used to point things out. At about one year encourage your baby to point things out as well. Tell her to point to her nose or to point to the ball. If she can't, then continue to show her how it's done. She'll soon catch on.

Speech Activities after the First Year

Continue to play "where is" pointing games. Cover your own nose and ask, "Where is my nose?" Stephen used to love pulling my hands apart to point to my nose. Or cover the baby's hair and ask, "Where is your hair? Your hair is all gone!" Baby will delightedly pull your hands apart to locate his hair. When the baby points to the correct object, repeat its name several times. Eventually your baby will try to say these words as part of the game.

Pointing games can continue even after a baby learns to walk. Merely incorporate crawling or walking into the game: "Annie, you point to the ball and I point to the ball, but whoever reaches the ball first wins."

Before the age of two, most words that you introduce are single-referent words. This means that the words relate to only one object. Perhaps you have proceeded from "ball" to "red ball" to "where is the red ball?" or from "box" to "brown box" to "point to the brown box." In every case, however, these words relate to one specific red ball or to the specific brown box.

By the time children are about two years old, they are ready for words that indicate relationships between two or more objects: the red ball is in the box, under the box, behind the box, in front of the box, on the box, next to the box. You also can introduce comparative words: big, bigger, biggest, or fast, faster, fastest, for example.

A box of colored balls is great for this. Begin with two balls. Point out, for example, that the red ball is bigger than the blue ball. Another time, say that the blue ball is smaller than the red ball. Gradually — very gradually — begin to introduce more than two objects at a time so that your child feels comfortable watching and listening to all sorts of relationships.

Next, begin to group the objects by size. For example, if you have five balls, begin to line them up from smallest to largest. Encourage your child to help you. After you've done this several times, leave two empty spaces in the row (the second and fifth positions, for example), and encourage your child to place the correct size ball in each spot. Eventually, you can leave two spaces next to one another and your child should be able to select the correct ball for each spot. If not, try again another day.

In speaking about speech activities, I use the word "eventually" quite a bit. I do this for two reasons. First, it's always difficult to assign a time frame within which certain developments will occur. All children follow their own internal clocks, and what one child does at a year, another child may not do even six months later. Another reason is that most children need to hear a word or see an action a number of times before they catch on to their place in the activity. Be patient. Never tell a child, "Haven't I told you that before?" What if you did? There's no harm in quietly repeating something. If you find that you're becoming exasperated, then immediately stop what you're doing and try something else, even if that something else is a nice warm bath and a nap — for both of you!

By the time children are between two and three years of age, they delight in having conversations with their parents and with anyone else who will speak with them. These natural conversations are the best language-expanding opportunities available. As opposed to planned activities, which are the backbone of speech, conversations offer the benefits of complex and interesting discussions.

There are two components to any conversation — speaking and listening. Try to encourage both. The best way to encourage a child to be a good listener is for you to be a good role model. When your child speaks, listen attentively. It's important to show enthusiasm while she's speaking, but just as important, make comments and ask questions when she finishes. Asking questions is especially important because it *proves* that you were listening and allows the child to offer additional information. From this, your child will deduce that what she says is important to you because you listen to her and because you want to know more.

Read to your child as much as you can, and allow her to handle books and magazines. When you read, ask questions as you go along and encourage her to ask questions.

There are two provisos here. First, don't overdo. Be especially careful about not overtalking or overreading to a child. Too much of anything destroys the joy and spontaneity of the activity. Second, be genuine. Children can spot phony emotions a mile away. If you're really too exhausted to be enthusiastic, then save the activity for another time.

A delightful aspect of conversation is that it is portable and can be carried on anywhere. When you go to the supermarket with your child, talk about the fruits and vegetables, the meats and the milk. If you plan to have lunch out, ask your child where he'd like to go. When you get there, talk about the restaurant: the decorations, the job that each person does, the silverware, the different foods on the menu. You can even point out the other diners: what foods they are eating, the colors of their clothes. In fact, one of the great things about traveling with children is that they pick up new words and experiences without any effort on your part. Once, when Stephen was young, we drove to Disney World but were unaware that a car race at nearby Daytona Beach had caused a dearth of motel rooms. Stephen's dad would stop at each motel and, as he glumly returned to the car, would mutter, "No vacancies." After a few of these occurrences, a frustrated Stephen yelled out, "I want some vacancies!"

Include conversations about emotions. Young children may find it difficult to articulate their emotions, so you may find yourself doing most of the talking. "I know that you felt very sad when we had to take Moppie to the vet, but now she'll feel better," or, "I know that you were angry because we couldn't go for ice cream, but we had to pick up Daddy." Explain words such as sad, happy, angry, scared, and others when the opportunity appears.

On certain occasions, your child may find it difficult to express himself because of physical exhaustion, emotional stress, or some other reason. When this occurs, you can say what you think he means: "Oh, you want to play with your airplane, not with the truck." Don't do this too often, however, or you may stifle your child's desire to work out the words for himself.

I spend a great deal of time counseling parents not to set up time frames for their children, but obviously a point may come when a parent suspects that a problem really does exist. Jamie's parents contacted me because their son, at nineteen months, hardly ever uttered a word despite their unending attempts to teach him to speak. On the phone, Jamie's mother was insistent that she was an excellent mother and that her son lacked for nothing. Was it possible, she asked frantically, that Jamie suffered from some type of learning disability? As always, I told her that I could make no judgment until I visited Jamie.

As I toured Jamie's lovely home, it was difficult to spot anything amiss in his environment. The living room and kitchen had been blocked off to form a huge playroom for the child. Scattered — or rather packed — along the floor were copious numbers of toys: wonderful sets of blocks, musical toys, stuffed animals, and puzzles. A wide, low toy chest held innumerable dolls of every description. Push-and-pull toys made a trail from living room to kitchen and back again. Observing the scene, I began to suspect that I knew the problem.

As I observed Jamie and his mother, my suspicions were confirmed. Whatever toy Jamie wanted, he had only to pick it up. If he wanted to eat, he simply pulled his mother's hand to the refrigerator. When she opened the refrigerator door, he pointed to the food that he wanted. All his favorite foods were gathered at the front of the refrigerator to make pointing easier.

His parents had gone to great trouble and expense to anticipate his every wish, but by doing this they had stifled any need for language on Jamie's part.

To prove the point, I began placing Jamie's favorite items — including his bottle — on tables and shelves where he could no longer reach them. When I moved his bottle, he immediately became frustrated and began to point at it furiously. Asking his mother to leave the room, I then pretended that I did not understand what he was pointing at. He became more frustrated and angry, but I continued to feign confusion: "What do you want Jamie? Tell me what you want." Finally, he yelled out "bottle!" And I yelled out, too, and I hugged him and gave him his bottle. After that, we began a game; he would say the word "block" or "doll" and I would give him the toy and offer boundless enthusiasm. Of course at first he didn't pronounce the words correctly — he didn't have any practice, after all — but I did not let his errors dampen my enthusiasm. I merely pronounced the word correctly and on we went.

Children love this unabashed enthusiasm. At least at a young age they do. One day when I picked up Stephen at law school (he was still too young to drive), he told me that he had won the Book Award given by the American Jurisprudence Association. I promptly opened the car windows and began screaming "Stephen won the book award!" Stephen, I'm sorry to report, no longer appreciated these outbursts and, suitably chastised, I stopped immediately. But at least in private, all children love honest and exuberant enthusiasm.

Many games and activities expand conversational horizons. Hand puppets, for example, stimulate both conversation and imagination. You can make a simple hand puppet from a sock, a few buttons and pieces of ribbon. The puppet can take on all kinds of identities, both human and nonhuman. One day the puppet can be a cook and can ask your child, "Tell me what you want for dinner." Another day the puppet can be a car driver asking, "Where do you want to go today?"

Puppets are excellent for role playing. If a child has had an upsetting experience, the puppet can say that it is sad or angry too and can offer empathy and suggest ways to moderate the bad feelings. The roles of puppets are limited only by your own or your child's imagination.

Rhyme games, with or without the benefit of puppets, are also lots of fun. As a child's vocabulary expands, begin rhyme games. For example, say "spoon—moon;" your child may next pick up with "tune, June," or "name—game—same—came," and so on. If your child likes competition, then whoever comes up with the last rhyme wins.

As your child grows, make word games more complex. For example, what beginning sound doesn't fit: "big, bad, girl, bed." Your child can clap when he hears the sound that doesn't belong or even bang a spoon on the floor. A "find it" game is also fun. You can ask: "can you find something with four legs?" "Can you find something that we wipe our face with?" "Can you find a fruit that is red?"

All kinds of "let's pretend" games encourage speech. For example, you can pretend that you are both on a favorite TV show. Play act what you would say.

Another activity that children adore is a variation of "show & tell" that's played with color photographs of family members taken at various locations: at school, ay the beach, at the park, and so on. Ask your child to describe the people in the picture. At first you can do the describing. Use vivid and colorful words. "Jennifer, remember how blue the sky was at the beach? The waves went boom, boom, boom. Jenny, who is wearing the red bathing suit?" Be as specific as you can. "Who is the lady wearing the blue dress with the bright yellow flowers?" "Yes, that's right, that lady is Nana." Children love to look at photographs of family members, so remember to take lots of photos as often as you can.

Places that hold no special importance to you can be wonderful to a child. Therefore, take photos of the local burger stand, the gas station, the toy store and so on. You can also use photographs to encourage conversation about trips that are not necessarily pleasant. If you take a photo of the pediatrician's office, for example — and even of the doctor and nurse — you can later discuss the visit. Perhaps your son is angry at the doctor who gave him an injection. Discuss why the injection was necessary. "Who is the lady wearing the light blue smock? Yes, she is the nurse. Did she give you something? Yes, a lollipop. What color was the lollipop?"

Encourage conversations about good and not-so-good experiences and your child will learn two invaluable lessons. All of his feelings are important to you, and there are no forbidden subjects — your child can talk to you about anything.

At certain times, and for a variety of reasons, your child may begin to stutter. When Stephen was about four, for no apparent reason, he began to stutter. When this happens, we are inclined either to criticize our children or, more likely, to overcompensate for them. Neither approach is helpful. Unless there is a true speech impediment, these periods tend to be self-limiting if you follow these guidelines:

- Always give the child time to complete the sentence.
- Never suggest going back to the beginning.
- Never tell a child to "say it again and this time say it right."
- Never finish the sentence for the child.
- Don't tell your child to slow down, to be careful, or to avoid saying certain words, all of which serve to make the child more self-conscious than he already is.

In other words, ignore the stuttering as best you can and counsel other family members, especially siblings who can be uncommonly vicious about this, to do the same thing. If the problem persists for what seems to be an unreasonable time, consult a speech therapist.

The Terrible Twos or The Tremendous Twos?

It's been my observation that the terrible two phenomenon occurs with children who want desperately to express themselves but who have never been given the tools with which to accomplish this. Not only do these children enrage themselves and exasperate their parents, but they lose a valuable and highly perishable ability. Language authorities are convinced that the greatest sensitive period for language, the period during which language skills are most easily mastered, occurs between the ages of eighteen months and four years. Once this sensitive period expires, it will never in their lives return. As a result, unlearned language skills will become ever more difficult to master. To encourage the development of skills during this sensitive period, make use of every language opportunity. During this time, two different types of books offer invaluable stepping stones to later language development. These books are rhyme or poetry books and dictionaries. Rhyme and poetry offer young children colorful characters and exciting real or imaginary worlds, all couched in sophisticated and challenging language. Children who are exposed to rhyme and poetry at an early age often show a deeper appreciation for all forms of literature throughout their lives. In my own books (*Rhyme Book*, *Looking For A Rainbow* and *What's Wrong*), I've tried to offer opportunities both for reading and also for play acting. If you're rereading a rhyme, poetry, or storybook to your child, encourage him to act out the story. Also, when children become familiar with rhymes, they enjoy supplying the rhyming word themselves as you read to them. In the years to come, these rhyme and poetry books will probably be the first books that your child learns to read for himself. These early books, introduced during the first years of your child's life, will remain good friends throughout childhood and sometimes beyond. I've often encountered parents who find great joy in reading to their children the very same books that their parents read to them.

Another fine book is a child's dictionary. There are a number of good elementary dictionaries available, but you can also make a dictionary yourself. In fact, it's a good idea to make a dictionary with your child even if you purchase one in the bookstore.

Your own dictionary should be a place for special words, either words related to special occasions or words that seem to engender special delight in your child. The most basic dictionary has no definitions; instead, it simply has a picture of an object together with the name of that object. For example, if your child helps you prepare dinner and, for the first time, sees an eggplant, then you would add the word "eggplant" to the dictionary. On a piece of paper, draw an eggplant (encourage your child to help you draw the picture or have her draw it herself). Then, print the word "eggplant" at the bottom of the page. If you keep these pages in a three-ring binder, you can rearrange the words into alphabetical order. You can also get a set of A-Z tabs at the stationery store. While the effect of alphabetical order may be lost at the beginning, as your child learns the ABCs, she'll come to realize that her very own dictionary is also in ABC order.

If your child spends a portion of the day with a care giver, try to elicit a word for the dictionary when you review the day's activities. Perhaps the care giver read a story about a woodpecker, so the new word can be "woodpecker;" perhaps lunch included celery, so you'll add the word "celery" to the dictionary.

The effect of language activities is cumulative. Every conversation or reading experience builds on those that have preceded it. I realized this when I told a three-year-old Stephen the story of George Washington cutting down the cherry tree. The story seemed to bother Stephen, and he asked me whether George had really chopped down the tree. I thought that he was asking whether the story of Washington was true or if it was a fairy tale like Jack and the Beanstalk. But this was not what Stephen meant, so we talked about the story a little longer. Stephen suggested that perhaps a wind had blown down the tree. I told him no, I didn't think that, because George had confessed to his father that he had cut down the tree. Then, Stephen asked if George had cut down the tree because he was angry at his father for not taking him fishing. So that was it! Stephen's dad had worked late Sunday afternoon, and by the time he had returned home to take Stephen on the promised fishing expedition, it had been raining and the trip had been postponed. The story of George Washington allowed us to talk about feelings of anger, how we can be angry sometimes at people whom we love, and how we don't stop loving them just because we sometimes get angry at them. We also talked about the virtue of forgiveness. It was an enchanting experience for both of us, brought about because Stephen was a good talker and I was a good listener.

CHAPTER FIVE

Teaching Your Child
To Read

I f I were asked to name the single most important gift that you could give your child to ensure personal and academic success, that gift would be the ability to read. I say this not only as a parent myself, but as a lifelong teacher, counselor, drug-education specialist, and educational consultant.

I usually refrain from using scare tactics to pressure parents into adopting a certain course of action, because I recognize that we all prefer to follow the path that logically appeals to us, not one that we have been forced to march along as a result of external fears and pressures. In the case of reading, however, my conscience demands that I unload the biggest guns that experience has afforded me. When I was a drug specialist in an area high school, I learned that 80 percent of young people involved with drugs cannot read on their grade level; 85 percent of children in youth hall reflect this same sorry statistic.

Why should an inability to read almost inevitably lead to problems with drugs? When we first discussed teaching a baby to speak, we considered that the most important means of self-expression is language. To a baby or very young child, language consists primarily of two activities: speaking, the way in which the self is expressed, and listening, the means by which we begin to absorb other selves around us. As a child grows, listening alone isn't good enough. There is simply too much to learn about other people and about the world in general. And the only effective way to learn about that incredible breadth of experience that we call reality is by reading.

In the past, certain "experts" — behaviorists, psychologists, educators — believed that reading was a "natural" function. They believed that as a child matured, reading would simply come naturally. Of course, they reasoned, children would have to be in school or be exposed to books in some way, but if they were, an ability to read was sure to follow. After all, don't most children learn to read?

In recent years, as fewer and fewer children have learned to read with ease and confidence, beliefs such as these have been under increasing scrutiny. If reading were a natural development, challengers asked, then why didn't all children learn to read? No, they thought, children must be *taught* to read.

But, you may be wondering, isn't that what kindergarten and first-grade teachers are all about? One would think so, but when 30 percent of all children who complete first grade *cannot* read on a first-grade level, then it's obvious that letting the schools take care of it is a risky philosophy.

By the end of first grade, children who have been taught to read by their parents or other care givers are usually one to four grade levels ahead of their peers. As a result, *by the end of first grade*, decisions about a child's giftedness, about a child's ability to excel academically, have already been made. That's right! By the end of first grade, a child may already have been labeled a poor performer — the current phrase is "academically disadvantaged." That's quite a sad label for a six-year-old!

Can't poor students "catch up?" My experiences as an educator for nearly three decades show that as a rule, no, they can't. On the contrary, the gap between students usually grows as time goes on. This is true for many reasons, not the least of which is that as the child grows, the classroom becomes a place of increasingly negative experiences, while the necessity to undertake "remedial" work becomes an onerous chore that labels a child a "loser."

Now you don't ever want your child to wear the label of "slow learner," and neither do I, so let's consider how you can help to ensure your child's success simply by teaching him to read. And I use the word "simply" because reading activities are simple, and they're great fun as well.

Stepping Stones to Reading

There are three major components to language, and they are achieved by most children in a predictable order: listening, speaking, and reading. Because reading depends, to some extent, on a degree of listening and speaking comprehension, the activities suggested in Chapter 4 are vitally important.

Even if you're first reading this book long after your child has begun speaking, you should still review the material in Chapter 4. Those activities are designed not merely to allow your child to become an avid talker, but to encourage her to be a considerate and interested listener. In addition, all the activities are designed to strengthen a child's appreciation of language as language. That is, your child will grow to understand that language is a special means of communication. For example, if a child wants a cookie, he has several options. He can point in the direction of the kitchen, he can draw a cookie on a piece of paper and hope that it will be recognized as a vanilla wafer and not a Mr. Sun, and he can even scream and pound his chest. The most effective way to secure a cookie, however, is to say a single word: "cookie."

That's the magic of language. We can say exactly what we think and precisely what we want. Children who can listen and who can speak have been given extraordinary powers with which to mold their environments. When philosophers speak of the power of words to set us free, this is never so true as in childhood. The degree to which the world is comprehensible is largely the result of a child's ability to communicate — to share himself or herself with the world.

Once a child understands what a word is — which for many children occurs even before they learn to speak or at least before they learn to speak fluently — reading activities will prove entertaining and beneficial.

When we began listening and speaking activities with your child, we started with object words, words that indicate real, physical objects with which your child is familiar. Very gradually, we moved on to action words or words that expressed emotional states. That's exactly what we do when we begin reading activities.

Beginning Reading Activities

Many years ago, a woman who had taken my seminar called to tell me that her nine-month-old baby could recognize the word "grandmother." In those early days, I was a bit skeptical, so I went to see for myself and found that the baby did seem to distinguish between the word "grandmother" written on a card and another word written on a card. The baby's mother told me that the child's grandmother visited every day and always said to the baby, "I am your grandmother and I love you." Soon the mother noticed that if she said to her crying infant, "Grandmother is coming to see you today," the baby immediately brightened and cooed. One day, when the baby was about nine months old and the grandmother was in the room for a visit, the mother had an idea. She took a thick, black marker pen and printed the word "grandmother" on a large index card. Then, she asked her mother to hold the card. The baby's eyes darted between the card and her grandmother and she cooed with delight. After a time, if the baby was crying, the mother held up the card with the word "grandmother" and the baby stopped crying. Of course, the case is easily made that the child wasn't reading the word but simply came to associate that card with the pleasant visit of her grandmother. And this is true, of course. But what the mother accomplished, besides delighting both her daughter and her mother, was to introduce the idea of printed words in a pleasurable, nonstressful way.

Your baby should know the meaning of words *before* you attempt to show her the word in printed form. When you begin these activities, never show a child the printed form of an unfamiliar word. After all, you're trying to encourage comprehension, not merely rote or programmed response.

Concentrate on words. Whenever you feed your child, use as many words as possible: lunch, hot (place her hand on the warm bowl), carrots, orange, bottle, milk, white. When you go on any outing, try to present five new words. For example, if you go to the doctor's office, offer: office, doctor, nurse, thermometer, scale.

When should the transition be made between oral and written words? As always, it's difficult to be definite. A child at about ten months can benefit from exposure to written language even before she can speak. The true test is your own and your child's enthusiasm. If speech games are fun, and if you've pursued them for several months, then consider including printed language games. If your child's interest wanes, then delay these activities until she's more familiar with and more excited about language.

> *Paula, who was referred to me by a longtime friend, was dispirited because her daughter, Kelly, had no enthusiasm for language games of any kind. This was especially frustrating because Paula was a writer. Despite the mother's desire to bring Kelly to my office (Paula thought that my advice might be more professional if I gave it in "professional surroundings"), I reiterated my policy that it was necessary to observe a child in that child's natural environment. Often, the physical environment gives clues to the nature of a problem. In this case, however, I could discern nothing amiss. While I sat in a chair and pretended to read one of Paula's short stories, Paula played a typical game with Kelly. A few moments into the game, I knew what the problem was. While Paula never lapsed into SPPPAN, she certainly didn't embrace PEEEHK either. She would have put a saint to sleep. Her matter-of-fact approach might have worked in an adult education class, but it was far too drab to work with a sixteen-month-old. After a few moments' counseling, she brightened her attitude and was on the way to success.*

Begin to label objects in the house, especially objects that the baby encounters every day: diapers, crib, mirror, comb, door, and so on. Labels may be smaller or larger — 4x6 or 8x10 index cards work for most items — but be sure to print clearly using a thick, black marker pen.

As you and baby proceed through the day and encounter the labelled objects, point to the object and say its name. This label game has literally hundreds of possibilities.

1
Clip on cards with the words "Mom" or "Dad." When you refer to yourself, point to the card so that baby can see. Write the baby's name on a card and introduce him to his very own name.

2
If you have been showing words to your child for several months, then at about one year, use colored crayons or markers to write the name of that color on a card. Start with red, blue, green, and black and move on to the other colors.

3
As you go into the mall, tell your child that you will be looking for a certain word: "restaurant" or "store" or whatever. When you see an an example of the word, point to it with enthusiasm.

4
Remember those balls that your child has been collecting? Begin to label the balls. At first, each ball may only have the word "ball" on it. Later, each ball can have a color label. A ball may also have the word "round" or "striped," for example. Finally, when you line up a group of balls, you can label them "small, smaller, smallest," or "big, bigger, biggest."

5
Write the name of a food on a paper plate, then put that food on the plate. After practicing with the same word five or six times, write the word on the plate and ask your child if she knows what food goes on the plate.

6
When you read a story, put a few words from the story on cards. For example, "dinosaur" or "princess" or "castle" are vivid words that your child may remember from the story. The next time you read the story, be sure to take out the cards. When you reach that word in the story, pause for a moment; your child may know what word comes next. Whether he says the word or you supply it for him, be sure to show him the card.

7

Slowly introduce action words, both in the present and past tense: "hug, hugged," "kiss, kissed," and so on. And be sure to demonstrate these words as well!

Language games must be repeated many times to be effective. Go through the games quickly. Keep the pace up so that the games are played with enthusiasm, and don't degenerate into classroom lessons. Avoid negative reactions, whether spoken or nonspoken. If you grimace or frown, your child will soon lose interest.

8

Take everyday objects (balls, a doll) and ask your child what they look like to him. If he says that the ball looks like the sun, then label the ball with the word "sun." Explain that you will label each object with whatever word she says. In this way, your child will understand that her words are very important. Children love to see their own words in print.

9

When your child builds something or draws something, ask what it is and make out a card with that word. If your child offers a nonsense word, write out the nonsense word. Explain what you are doing. If your child says that a drawing is "Batchum Catchum," write out the words "Batchum Catchum" and proudly say "Batchum Catchum" as you place the label on the drawing. If your child starts to laugh, laugh right along with him.

10

A supermarket is like a dictionary of word labels. Before you leave for the supermarket, write out a word on a card — cookie, for example. Then, in the supermarket, find packages that contain the word "cookie." Look for print that is as large and bold as possible. Looking at different ways in which the word "cookie" is printed should prove very interesting. Don't rush. Give your child ample opportunity to study the words. After a time, you may want to take two word cards to the supermarket, but limit yourself to two words if time is short. Think of words that include all sections of the supermarket. For example, the words "cat" and "dog" can be found in the pet-food aisle.

11

Label boxes with the names of certain materials — cotton, wood, metal, rubber, plastic, foam, and so on. Then, play scavenger hunt at home or in the hardware store to find objects made of those materials. Talk about the objects in the box and explain that they are all made of the material named on the box.

12

In addition to storybooks, read everything that you can to your child — recipes, container labels, lists of ingredients, the TV magazine, instructions, or whatever is available during the day. If pictures are available, all the better. Will the cake that you're both making look like the one in the cookbook? Why not? Did you use chocolate icing instead of vanilla icing? Talk about it and write the words "chocolate" and "vanilla" on cards.

13

If there's a safe bush or tree outside, hang cards on different parts of the tree. The largest card may have the name of the tree (ficus tree); other cards may say "leaf," "branch," "berry," "seed," "green," "brown" and so on. Start with three to five cards and add more in the future. On other occasions, label additional trees or plants. Some of the words may be the same (green, branch, leaf), but other words will be different ("flower" instead of "berry," "pink" instead of "white," and so on).

14

When offering food to your child (fruit, for example), offer her a choice. When she decides, give her that fruit and write its name on a card.

15

Begin a word box that contains 4x6 cards (or 8x10 cards for children less than eighteen months) such as the supermarket cards or the food-name cards described above. You can even get a set of index tabs at the stationery store and label the sections: supermarket cards, food cards, tree cards, and so on. Then, when you play a game for the second or twenty-second time, go to the word box and take out the cards. Children love these old friends, and the word box may be a child's first encyclopedia.

16

Children need to see words in every possible format so make a word book too. Label the sections: colors, animals, family, friends, clothing, house, fruits, vegetables, toys, or as many categories as you like. Each page should have pictures of objects in that category (photographs, magazine pictures, or even pictures that your child has drawn). After a picture is pasted in the book, write the word for that picture. Add to the word book as often as you like. If your child draws an especially nice picture, try to find a place for it in the word book.

17

Once your child is familiar with about 100 words, take words from the word box, and, adding cards if necessary, present simple sentences: "Eric eats carrots." "Daddy loves Eric." "Bananas are delicious." "Mommy loves Eric." "Mommy loves Daddy." Give your child sets of three word cards that can make a sentence and have her put them in order.

Moving from Labels to Books

All children should have their very own books, books that are made for them and that contain their favorite words and expressions. That's how the love of reading is encouraged, by our early association with the words that we read. This association comes from reading words about our life, our home, our family, our loves, our dislikes — in short, our world.

The words and sentences in *My Own Storybooks* need not always be short or simple. If your child uses more complex words or expressions, be sure to use them in the storybook.

1

How do you make a storybook? First, think of a theme. If you can't think of one, perhaps your child can: what daddy does at the office, a fishing trip, the trip to the zoo, things we like to do outside. All these and more can furnish the subject matter for storybooks. Then, either you, your child, or both of you together can draw pictures to illustrate the theme. When the drawings are done, write a one-sentence caption under each story. Finally, bind the book together with string, ribbon, or yarn and decorate the cover: *My Own Storybook — Our Trip to the*

Zoo; My Own Storybook — My Trip to Daddy's Office, and so on. Children will delight in these storybooks for years.

2

A *Book About Me* is also fun. Include photos or drawings of the child, mom and dad, grandparents, the family pet, and so on. Label all the drawings, not merely with names, but with other information — hair color, occupations, hometowns and other personal information.

3

Children never tire of themselves. If you've talked about body parts, your child should be able to identify them. Have her lie down on a sheet of kraft paper and trace her outline. Then, ask her to draw in her features and clothes. As you point to different sections and she calls out their names, label as many body parts and clothing items as you can — arm, leg, face, eyes, nose, mouth, belly button, knee, elbow, wrist, hand, foot, finger, toe, shirt, shorts, socks, sneakers, and so forth. Finally, write her name across the top. You can even tape the drawing to her bedroom door.

I know that some parents must wonder if all this labeling really accomplishes what it sets out to do. To answer that, I recall the day that Stephen invited me to meet a law-school friend, Chris Marinello, who was then editor of the law school newspaper (and has since become Stephen's law partner in the firm of Baccus and Marinello). I wondered why they thought it so important that I visit the newspaper office, but when I opened the door and looked around, I burst out laughing. There were labels everywhere! Dozens of them. Labels on the pencil sharpener, on the rug, on the door. A label hung from the ceiling on a piece of string; across the label was printed the word "Air." Wherever I glanced, there was a label. "Mother, Stephen offered coyly, "we just wanted to make you feel at home."

4

Make a poster each week built around a certain theme — animals, foods, flowers, a special holiday. Make drawings or cut out pictures that illustrate the theme and decorate the poster with paints, sparkles, or yarn. Write words that relate to the theme in different color markers. Then, hang the poster in a prominent location such as the kitchen or family room. Save these posters to review and reminisce.

5

Using colored chalk, make a Simon Says playing board on the sidewalk or driveway (indoors, use markers on long sheets of kraft paper). Write about a half dozen familiar words on the paper — cookie, raisin, Mommy, tree — then play Simon Says. "Simon says take one step over the word "cookie"; Simon says take two steps over the word "Mommy". Eventually you can enlarge this to a game of Word Hopscotch, with words replacing the numbers one to ten. Children love this simple game, which combines physical activity with word recognition.

6

From the word box, select about twenty object, action, and emotion cards and turn them over. Each player selects three cards, turns them over, and tries to make a sentence out of them. If the player makes a sentence, she keeps the cards. If not, the cards are returned to the pile. Whoever has the most cards at the end of the game wins. (Obviously, it pays to be fairly liberal in your interpretation of sentences; remember to keep the game fun.)

7

A variation of *My Own Storybook* has your child helping to write a story. After you supply the pictures or your child draws the pictures for the story, begin to write the captions but omit key words and have your child supply the words. Whatever words she says, however inappropriate, is the word that you write down. Don't encourage her to say something else, but simply allow her own imagination to work.

8

Play Find the Word. When your child is familiar with most of the words in the word box, write out a word on a piece of paper and have the child find the word in the word box. If the word box is very large, take out about a dozen words and, as you write the word on a sheet of paper, have your child find the matching card.

9

Make jigsaw puzzles. Paste a color magazine photo on a 5x8 index card and print the name of the object under the picture. Use simple pictures of a dog, cat, house, bird, boy, and so on. Leave a little space between each letter of the word. Cut the picture into pieces so that only one letter is on each piece. Then, ask your child to reassemble the picture. Like magic, if the picture fits together, so does the word!

10

Begin to show the difference between capital (uppercase) and small (lowercase) letters. Print four capital letters across a card. On the next line, print the same four small letters but in a different order. Have your child draw lines connecting the capital letter to its matching small letter.

11

As we discussed, flash cards have come in for some criticism, but I've found that it's the attitude of the parent, not the cards themselves, that may be the problem. Never drill a child. Learning is fun, but tedium is not. I made most of my own flash cards for Stephen, but I've heard from parents who had equal success using only store-bought cards. In any case, the game that worked best with Stephen was a simple competitive game. We used about twenty cards with familiar words. When he turned over a card, if he knew the word, he got to keep the card; if he didn't know the word, I kept the card. After all the cards had been drawn, he got one more chance to identify the cards in my pile. Needless to say, this is another game that I never won.

12

Scrambled Eggs is a word and memory game that uses two sets of cards, each of which has the same words. Begin with six pairs of cards, or twelve cards altogether, and scramble the cards and place them face down. Each player draws two cards. If they match, the player keeps them and tries again. If they don't match, he returns them, face down, to the same spot. Then, the next player goes. Because you help your child remember where the matching words are located, he usually wins. Don't worry — when your child wins, so do you!

13

Make a Bingo card game with words in place of numbers. If several players play, each card should be slightly different. Then, write out each word on a separate piece of paper. Call out each word as it is drawn. When a player recognizes that word on his card, he covers the word with a raisin or penny. The first player to cover his card wins the game. In a variation called Sentence Bingo, the first player to make a sentence with the selected words wins the game.

Reading and Comprehension

Some parents suggest that these early reading activities reveal little more than rote or memorized recognition of certain letters. Comprehension, the true goal of reading, cannot be learned in this way. If these early activities were all that we did, then these individuals might be right. But the immediate goal of word-recognition games is merely to familiarize a young child with the fact that words do exist and that these words denote objects or actions in the child's everyday environment. Once that goal has been reached, we enlarge the scope of activities so that true comprehension occurs naturally, as a matter of course.

I think that almost everyone recognizes that there is something sacred about reading. Perhaps that's why there are so many taboos about it. When Barbara Cox was twenty-two months old, her mother decided that Barbara knew so many words that perhaps she was ready for a simple reader. The problem, Mrs. Cox discovered, was that there were no readers available for twenty-two-month-old babies. I advised Mrs. Cox, just as I have advised you, to create her own storybook. Mrs. Cox demurred. She could not even think of a theme for a storybook, and she hardly had the time. Her own mother was ill, and everyday she bundled Barbara, and Barbara's puppy, into the car and trekked to grandmother's house. As Mrs. Cox attended to her own mother, Barbara sat in her stroller in the rose garden while her puppy ventured into nearby yards to survey a new domain. I asked Mrs. Cox if she had shown Barbara words such as "puppy,"

"garden," "rose," "grandmother," "house," and so on. "Oh yes,"
she replied, "we use those words in our word games all the time."
"Well," I offered, "it looks as though you have the subject for
Barbara's first storybook." Mrs. Cox helped Barbara construct
a seven-page reader and the two of them sat down to read their
creation. Barbara knew most of the words, although her mom
helped out occasionally. "Barbara's thrill when she realized that
she was reading a story was an amazing thing to watch," reported
Mrs. Cox. "When she was finished, she kept jumping up and
down. I don't know who was more excited, me or Barbara, but
that was one terrific day!"

If you've been creating storybooks with your child, now is the time
when your child can truly dictate the story to you. Be a gentle guide
by asking the famous questions, "Who?" "What?" "Where?" Who is the
story about? Where does it take place? What's happening? What do
you think will happen next? If your child simply shrugs, suggest an
event, but try to make it the wrong event. Allow your child to correct
you. Stories don't have to comply with our own sense of reality in
order for them to be valuable to a child.

When you create stories with your child, sometimes probe for an
underlying story. Stories, especially those that children have a hand in
creating, can often serve as springboards for personal reflection and
discussion. Does Ollie Owl look sad? Why do you think Ollie Owl is
sad? Do you think Ollie Owl is sad because his Daddy, Mr. Owl, was
late for work this morning and was very grouchy?

While these storybook activities help to strengthen the kind of mental
agility necessary for true reading comprehension, another element is
crucial. The basis of comprehension is the understanding that language
is an orderly and rational system of communication whose framework,
or "rules," is consistent and understandable.

To understand the rules of language, we move away from random
"look-say" activities and move into the more predictable area of phonics.

The Benefits of Phonics

Reading is, in fact, a three-part exercise that includes the abilities to
read words at sight (which is largely what we have been doing until

this point), to recognize the letters of the alphabet and the sounds that they make, and to combine these talents into true reading comprehension.

Why do we need phonics? A better way to phrase this question might be, why can't we rely on sight reading alone? After all, many school districts rely on sight reading, or "look-say," for 95 percent or more of their reading curriculum. The answer should seem readily apparent. There are simply too many words to memorize.

Sight reading is exciting — at first. The child seems to assimilate words quickly, and even very young children can memorize a prodigious number of words — 100, 200, even more. But language is made up of many thousands of words, and some method is necessary to ensure that a child can deal with all of them. That method is phonics.

Of course, some people still think that phonics is difficult. In fact, this is another example of that old, tired argument: If phonics is difficult for adults, it must be too difficult for children. Nothing could be further from the truth. A child's ability to learn the phonetic rules of language is nearly limitless.

Of course, as in any undertaking, reasonable expectations must apply. For example, when your child first approaches a toy, many times she will not even understand what it is. She may look at it inquisitively, smell it, or pound it on the floor. You don't take away the toy simply because she doesn't understand it. Instead, you allow her to handle the toy, to play with it, and to reach her own conclusions about it. Just because a child thinks that crayons are a new kind of snack doesn't mean that you banish crayons forever. The same is true with intellectual toys — speech, reading, and math. Give your child the opportunity to handle them, play with them, have fun with them, and make mistakes with them. Invariably, these intellectual toys will be among your child's favorites.

Step one is ensuring that your child recognizes the twenty-six letters of the alphabet. If you haven't done this before, then put each letter on a separate 3x5 card and quickly show your child several cards a day while you repeat the letter. You can show different combinations of cards, but be sure that you have repeated all of the letters several times.

Together with your child, make a letter book with twenty-six pages, one page for each letter in the alphabet. Each page is divided into columns like this:

Letter	Sound	Words
A a	ah	apple arrow

If your child is old enough to write, she can write the words; if not, you can help, and perhaps she can draw a small picture to identify the word. If you wish, you can also supply a drawing or picture clipped from a magazine.

You don't have to complete the letter book all at once. In fact, completing the book should be an ongoing experience. Complete all the letters with examples such as these:

Letter	Sound	Words
B b	bh	boy, baseball, butter, but, Bill
C c	kh	candy, cow, come, could, catch
D d	dh	dog, door, dollar, drive, day
E e	eh	egg, elephant, enter, every
F f	eff	fish, feather, food, fly
G g	gh	girl, gift, great, good
H h	hh	house, hen, hard, help, how
I i	ih	Indian, igloo, itch, if, in
J j	jh	jar, jacks, jumprope, just
K k	kh	kitten, kite, key, kiss, Karen
L l	ell	lion, ladder, laugh, little
M m	mm	man, milk, mother, me, many
N n	nn	nut, nickel, night, no, Nancy
O o	ah	octopus, olive, Oscar
P p	phh	puppy, penny, pan, put
Q q	kwh	quarter, queen, quick
R r	rr	river, rocket, red, run, Roger
S s	ss	snake, sugar, sound, say, Sarah
T t	thh	toy, tulip, table, tiger
U u	uh	umbrella, up, until, under
V v	vv	vase, violin, very, Vicky
W w	whh	wagon, water, what, where, when
X x	ks	x-ray, fox, box
Y y	yh	yellow, your, yes, yummy
Z z	zz	zebra, zoo, zipper

In most cases, the earlier words are object words that are more easily understood. Later, more complex words and even names can be added. Review the letter book from time to time and add new examples. In the beginning, you can read the book; then, you and your child can read the book together. Perhaps your child can read some of the words herself. Once your child is familiar with the contents of the letter book, she will happily take over if you begin to read it.

The decision to continue with reading activities is, as always, a personal one. Some parents have asked whether word recognition, as in the "look-say" activities, together with letter recognition, as in the letter book, are sufficient for a preschooler. All I can say, based on three decades of experience, is that *some* learning is better than *none*, but that *more* learning — when done with PEEEHK — is a joy and a blessing to a child. Occasionally, we parents may believe that because certain activities (like phonics) are challenging even to us, they must be uncomfortably difficult for children. On the contrary, children are *more* receptive to learning than we are, and if materials are presented in a gentle, orderly fashion, a child's ability to absorb information is virtually limitless. So do what you can and attempt to overcome your own prejudices so that they don't shortchange your child.

Back to phonics! Next, you and your child will make a phonics book to supplement the letter book. This book will have a number of pages illustrating new facts about letter sounds.

When your child is familiar with the individual letters, point out that letters can make more than one sound. This is especially true of the vowels, a, e, i, o, and u. In fact, vowels make long vowel sounds and short vowel sounds. Long vowel sounds say the name of the vowel, as in the long "a" sound — ate, hate, Jane, made.

Each of the first five pages in the phonics book will illustrate the long vowel sounds of one particular vowel:

    a cake, lake, Jane, ate
    e tree, pea, eat, he, Steve
    i ice, time, pie, iron
    o rope, cold, go, no, open
    u tube, cube, cute, use

You can also add a page for "y," which sometimes acts like a vowel and sometimes behaves like a consonant. "Y" is a very funny letter, because sometimes it makes the long "y" sound (my, by) and sometimes the long "e" sound (carry, Larry).

As pages are entered in the phonics book they can record examples of words that your child encounters during the day. When your child learns a new word, try to find a place for it in the phonics book. The word may be special because of its vowel sound or for some other reason, but putting the word in the phonics book reinforces that all of the activities help your child to understand the world around him. This not only imparts knowledge to your child but also leaves him with a warm and comforting sense of security.

Make a beginning sound, middle sound, and ending sound page. Explain that most words have a beginning, a middle, and an ending sound. For example, the word "bat" begins with the "b" sound, has the short "a" sound in the middle, and ends with the "t" sounds. Each line on the beginning, middle, or ending page should feature two words whose beginning, middle or ending sounds are alike. For example:

beginning sound	bad, ball
middle sound	run, cut
ending sound	hat, hit

When you enter and then review these words, you help to bolster sound and word recognition as well as spelling ability.

Make a magic "E" page. Many times, when you add the letter "e" to the end of a word, it changes to a new word: mad-made, pin-pine, rat-rate, can-cane, fat-fate, bit-bite, Tim-time, spin-spine, hop-hope, pop-Pope, not-note, us-use, cut-cute, cub-cube, tub-tube, and so on. Point out that the short vowel sound becomes a long vowel sound. You can even make a card game with the "before" words. Each player picks a card; if he can say the "after" word (that is, the word with the "e" added), he keeps that card. If not, the card is returned to the deck. The player with the most cards wins.

In time, add the following pages to the phonics book, adding more examples whenever you can:

1. When two vowels come together, the first one says its name and the last one is silent: paid, boat, meat, pie, toe, leaf, pea.
2. When "sh," "ch," "the," or "wh" come together, they make one sound:

shell, sheep, fish, shut; chicken, beach, teach, chin; that, teeth, bath, thank, when, white, wheel, which.

3. C and G love to play tricks, so we call them the tricksters. If they are followed by E, I, or Y, they usually have a soft sound. C sounds like S, and G sounds like J: city, cent, center, pencil, dance, dice, rice; gem, magic, fudge, page, cage, Gene.

4. "Oi" and "Oy" can sound alike: boy, toy, joy; oil, foil, spoil.

5. "You" and "own" can sound alike: cloud, loud, ground, round, out, south, our; clown, gown, brown, flower.

6. "Au" and "aw" can sound alike: haul, Paul, pause, launch; jaw, saw, straw, yawn.

7. Sometimes letters play a joke on you — they're silent and don't say anything at all. Silent B: lamb, thumb, comb, dumb, plumber; Silent H: John, hour, ghost, honest, rhyme; Silent K: knife, knot, knee, knob, know, knuckle; Silent L: half, calf, folk, yolk; Silent T: whistle, often, soften, fasten, listen, wrestle; Silent W: write, whole, wrist, wrong, wrap.

8. Sometimes words make very funny sounds, not at all what you expect, as when "Gh" sounds like "F": laugh, cough, tough, rough; or "eigh" sounds like "A": sleigh, weigh, eight, weight; or "Igh" sounds like "I": high, thigh, fight, light; or "Augh" sounds like "Aw": fought, thought, caught, bought, daughter, ought.

9. "Oo" has two sounds: hood, stood, wood, or boot, school, zoo. You can illustrate these sounds with two sentences: A cookie is a food; the good cow said moo.

English, more than most other languages, has many exceptions to these rules. In fact, about 5 percent of English words do not follow phonetic rules. But this leaves 95 percent of words that do! Very few young children are confused either by the phonetic rules themselves or by the exceptions to these rules.

What's important is to use the phonics book as a record for new words that your child encounters. On occasions when you review the phonics book, write sentences that illustrate some of the rules. Add new facets of the language when you think that they are appropriate. For example, you may want to make a grammar or language book that has pages for interesting parts of the language. One page may feature comparative words: big, bigger, and biggest, together with unusual comparative forms: good, better, best. Another page may feature "ing" words and their root words: go-going, sing-singing, walk-walking. In this last case, you can point out that when we add "ing" to certain words, we have to double the letter that comes before "ing": cutting, winning, hitting.

Games That Encourage Reading Skills

In addition to the letter book, the phonics book, and the language book (which may be combined into one book), games such as these develop reading skills in a sun-filled, pressure-free atmosphere.

1

Select a letter and offer your child a simple riddle whose answer begins with that letter. For example, if the letter is R, the correct answer to a flower riddle might be rose; the correct answer to a color riddle might be red. This game is fun if you elect a different letter each day as that day's special letter. These riddle games encourage comprehensive problem-solving skills.

2

Using 3x5 index cards cut in half, make at least fifty cards, each of which has a letter printed on it. Make at least three cards each for vowels (a,e,i,o,u) and two cards each for the more popular letters (d,l,n,r,s,t). Then, take three of the cards and form a simple three-letter word. Your child will get one point (or one star or one raisin) for every new word that she can make by changing a single letter. (For example, run becomes ran, tan, tar, bar, bat, but, nut, and so on.)

3

If you're going to the doctor, fill your purse with the letter cards. Each time you draw a letter your child keeps the card if he thinks of a word that begins with that letter. If not, you keep the card (but give him a second chance later). If you draw a vowel card, you may ask for a word that contains the vowel. As your child's skills develop, you can ask for words that end in the letter you've selected. Stephen loved this game (probably because I never won!).

4

Draw a baseball diamond and place a letter or combination of letters on each base. If your child can name a word with that letter or letter combination, she advances to the next base and keeps advancing until she cannot think of the correct word or until she hits a "home run." It's then the next player's turn. Whoever scores the most runs wins the game.

5

Play rhyming games and try to build stories out of rhymes: "There was a man whose name was Jack and on his shoulder he carried a _____." Rhyming games are not only great fun for children, but they help to increase awareness of ending sounds.

6

Plan a make-believe party (even if it's a simple two-person affair). How many things can your child bring to the party that begin with a certain letter? For every item that he can name, he gets a raisin or other treat at the party. If you're going to an amusement park, you can play this game and offer nickels or ride tokens for correct answers.

7

Make about fifty word cards, each of which has a simple word on it (include "a," "the," "and," "to"). Then, select about five words to make a sentence. The other cards are placed face down. Each player selects a card and tries to place it over a word in the sentence so that the sentence still makes sense. For example, if the original sentence is, "John had a little brown dog," and the player draws the word "cat," the sentence can read "John had a little brown cat." Each time a player makes a sentence, that player gets a point. The player with the most points wins.

Let's take a moment to consider the concept of winning. I frequently suggest that you allow your child to win these games. Why? The answer is simple. We all like to do things that we're good at and for which we receive enthusiasm and applause. Does your child always have to win? Not always. If you're playing these games with two or more children, it's impossible for one child to win all the time. Even if you're playing these games alone with a child, some children will not even enjoy the unreality of winning all the time. They prefer to savor the true wins that they know they have achieved. Yes, I believe that most children should win nearly all the time, but be sensitive to your child's reactions. If your child does lose a game, offer another opportunity so that these sessions end on a winning note.

8

Games that encourage sentence making are terrific. A variation of "Fish" does just that. Take a deck of several dozen word cards and deal three cards to each player. Turn the rest face down. Each player also has a list of the remaining cards. The object is for each player to make as many sentences as possible. A player looks at his own cards and at the list of available words and then asks for a word that he needs. If the other player has that card, he must forfeit it to that player. If not, the player goes fish. Turns alternate. The player who makes the most sentences wins. (Many young children find it difficult to hold cards in their hands, so you may have to create a little divider between the two of you so that your child can lay his cards on the table without revealing them to you.)

9

Using the deck of letter cards that you previously made, play "Fill-In." Make about twenty word cards, each of which is missing a letter or letter combination. For example: c_te, sil_y, la_gh, cou___. Both the word deck and the letter deck are turned face down. The player chooses a word card and then a letter card. If the letter card supplies the missing letter, the player keeps both cards. If not, both the word card and the letter card are returned to the bottoms of their decks. If a player can fill in the correct letter to make a word, his turn continues. If not, play alternates. The player with the most cards wins.

10

Play "Alphabet," a game that is especially good when travelling in the car. The first player names an object that he sees beginning with A; the next player supplies an object beginning with B and so on.

11

If more than two people are riding in the car, the first player looks for a sign or billboard with the letter A. The next player searches for the letter B, and so on (the driver, of course, is exempt from this game).

12

When your child is familiar with words in print, get a magazine or newspaper with large-print ads. Each player concentrates on one page and circles all the words that begin with a certain letter or that illustrate a certain phonics rule. The player who circles the most correct words wins.

One of the most important things to remember about any of the games in this book is that they are, in fact, games. When adults play games — football, pinochle, spin the bottle — the games rarely have an ulterior purpose. They're played for fun, stimulation, relaxation, or some combination of the three. It's vital that you keep this same frame of mind when playing these games with your child. Children have uncanny sensitivities. When they sense that a game is work for you, then it becomes a chore for them as well. That's why you should play these games with a certain amount of speed and pizazz and only while your mutual enthusiasm continues. If you turn game time into an educational marathon, hoping that the longer your sessions the faster your child will learn, then one day you, like all marathoners, will hit "the wall." Your child — who at first seemed to be doing remarkably well — may become obstinate or disinterested. Both your tempers will grow short, and much of your effort will become undone. Games are designed to be fun. If either of you isn't having fun anymore, then by all means STOP!

Mrs. Armas, along with a group of mothers, had taken my course about three years earlier. I recall that at that time, her son, Luther, was only an infant. I had heard from most of the other mothers in the group and knew that their children, who were a little older than Luther, were reading. When Mrs. Armas called me, she was despondent. Luther, she said, knew his colors. He knew addition and subtraction and spoke in complete sentences. But he refused to read. He would not even look at words.

Knowing that Luther was only three and one-half I encouraged Mrs. Armas to postpone reading activities for a bit, but the mother persisted. She was positive that if Luther did not learn to read now, he might never learn to read. I believed that this was not the case, but I thought that a personal visit might assuage her fears and could just possibly uncover some problem with Luther. Was he dyslexic, I thought, or could he have a health problem that required early diagnosis and intervention? I would see.

I brought with me several gifts for Luther: a ball, a bubble-blowing kit, and a coloring book. Most readers remember these coloring books. You paint the page with water, and colors automatically come up. I also brought along several of my own early readers, such as What's Wrong? and What's Missing?, which had not been available years earlier. Luther was a delight. The moment he greeted me, he stared at my handful of gifts and yelled that he was going to get a cup of water and a paintbrush. "I hope my picture comes up red," he announced. I remarked to Mrs. Armas that Luther had obviously had this coloring book before. No, she indicated, he never had. Then how, I wondered, did he know about the water and the brush? My heart skipped a beat when I realized that there was only one way he could have known — he had read the information on the cover! Luther and I played together — he especially loved blowing bubbles — and we finally turned to the early readers. He laughed through What's Wrong? and What's Missing? but, when we turned to Rhyme Book and its story of Mat the Rat, I told Luther that I was getting awfully tired. Could he, I asked, read the story to me? He read every word! I hugged him and we both laughed and applauded.

So why wouldn't Luther read for his mother? I looked at her word cards. They were so worn that they were dog-eared. As I discussed her methods with Mrs. Armas, I realized that there were no game times with Luther; there were only drill sessions. She had played too few games far too often until Luther wasn't encouraged, but bored. When Luther could not read words or stories, Mrs. Armas read them to him. She read the same stories so many times, hoping that Luther would finally "catch on," that

*the stories bored him as well. Luther found the sessions so unin-
spiring that it never mattered to him to let his mother in on the
fact that he could read. Not only could he read, but, unbeknownst
to his mother, he could write as well. I encouraged Mrs.
Armas to let Luther write whatever he wanted — and not to correct
his spelling unless he specifically asked for help. I also advised
her to move on to more complex phonics games, because Luther
craved challenge, not tedium. Mrs. Armas relaxed and so did
Luther. I asked Mrs. Armas to keep in touch. She called me
three years later to tell me that Luther, who was in first grade,
was reading on a fourth-grade level. I was thrilled to hear that
another case was truly solved!*

Most children who are involved with reading activities decide for
themselves that they want to try their hand at writing. Not only are
intellectual skills needed for writing, but physical skills are needed as
well. Activities that require manual dexterity and eye-hand coordination
— especially those that require assembly or similar mechanical operations — help prepare young fingers to hold crayons and pencils.

A good preface to writing with an instrument is to encourage your
child to write with her fingers. The beach or sandbox is an excellent
place to start. Begin with finger exercises: make lines and circles and
spirals. After practicing these exercises, write words that deal with the
beach: beach, sand, water, shells, pail, shovel, blanket. Encourage your
child to follow your example, one letter at a time. Talk about the way
each letter is made; use words such as circle, half-circle, straight, curved,
right, left, up, and down. Write your child's name — children love to
learn to write their own names.

When you move indoors, clay and fingerpaints are also good finger-
strengthening media. Write your child's name using a heavy marker
or crayon, and encourage him to follow. Make a jigsaw puzzle with the
child's name. When the pieces are cut apart and then put back together,
talk about the way in which the letters are formed. For example, if
your child's name is Joe, "J" is a straight line going down with a curve
to the left; "o" is a circle; "e" is a little line to the right and then a great
big half-circle.

Move on to the letters of the alphabet, encouraging your child to
write words that he can already read. As your child writes, spell out

the letters so that you reinforce the spelling-writing-reading bond. If necessary, draw dots that your child connects to form letters and words. At first, do not use lined paper. Gradually, add heavy lines at least one inch apart with a lighter line in the center (this is sometimes called first-grade paper and is usually available at stationery or school-supply stores).

As your child advances, continue to allow her to select the words or subject to write about. This period of reading and writing activities is perhaps the most critical in terms of child development. Embracing PEEEHK and avoiding SPPPAN is of vital importance.

> *When Stephen learned to write, he would always select one paper to save and show to his father. I never intervened but allowed Stephen to make his own decisions. His judgment of his own work quickly developed. Another mother, Mrs. Jower, was not so lucky. Her daughter Mary returned home from kindergarten carrying papers whose lack of quality was always noted in the negative comments of the teacher. Mary had become despondent, and her mother was fighting angry. Mrs. Jower told the teacher to keep Mary's work on file. According to her mother's wishes, Mary was to decide for herself when — and even if — she would bring papers home. The decision was left entirely with Mary. When Mary returned home, her mother never asked about the papers but only asked more general questions about the day's events. After about two weeks, Mary brought home a paper, the writing on which was very much improved. Mary had jumped off the schoolbus and run to the house yelling, "Mommy! Look at my paper!" Mother and daughter danced for joy. Mary was given time to work through her problem without pressure or negative feedback. She was given the opportunity to succeed, not merely the chance to fail.*

Children who become despondent about the quality of their work may face significant and long-lasting self-esteem problems. On the other hand, children who are congratulated and encouraged build foundations that support them and nourish them throughout their lives.

Teaching Math
To Your Child

A mathematics teacher once remarked that math is the world's greatest spectator sport. He meant that most of us have watched math
teachers whiz their chalk along the blackboard, and we seemed to
understand what they were doing — as long as we were simply watching
them do the work. Once we picked up our pencils, however, and tried
to duplicate the sample problem on our own crisply lined paper, the
world of numbers seemed to fall apart. From these failed attempts,
many of us concluded that numbers were irrational and that mathematics was hard work to be avoided whenever possible.

The larger problem is that while we may try our best to avoid
numbers, numbers do their best *not* to avoid us. Whether we're buying
a house or a hamburger, balancing a checkbook, estimating our arrival
time, or wondering how long it takes to cook a three-and-three-fourths-
pound roast beef medium rare, numbers are an intimate part of our
daily environment. So, if we have to deal with these numbers every
day of our lives, it pays to call a truce and consider them as friends.

If you are not mathematically inclined — if numbers are still gremlins
to you and math a four-letter word — you may wonder how you can
possibly teach math to your child. The answer is simple. At first you
won't be teaching math at all. You'll simply be presenting the natural
environment to your child, and, because numbers are a prominent
feature of our everyday landscape, children absorb numbers and
mathematical concepts as easily as they learn about colors and shapes
and smells and tastes.

Mrs. Kellem, a fellow school teacher, feared that her young daughter, Davida, would grow to hate math as much as her mother had. In fact, Mrs. Kellem herself had a math tutor in high school when it appeared that she would fail to graduate high school because of poor math grades. Knowing that a child who does poorly in arithmetic typically hates school, she asked me how she could avoid this fate for Davida. "Start today," I told her. "Don't waste a moment." Mrs. Kellem demurred that she was too poor a math student to be an effective teacher for Davida. "Don't teach math, talk math," I told her. "You may be surprised to find that you like math too." To make a long story short, Mrs. Kellem began that day to play math games with a delighted Davida who went on to become an excellent student and to be at the top of her class in math. And she is still thanking me.

One stumbling block that you may encounter when sharing math with your child is not that you know too little about math, but that you know *too much*. We've all taken math in school for so many years that it may be difficult to remember the most basic math concepts. Let's review the basic math concepts that you'll use with your child time and again — counting, matching, and seriation (ascending and descending order).

Counting, Matching, and Seriation (Ascending/Descending Order)

Usually we begin teaching math by counting — fingers, toes, toys, what have you. In fact, when you or your child count fingers, you've already completed a mathematical operation. You've matched the fingers; that is, you've decided that all the fingers belong in the same group. When you count fingers, you don't say, "One finger, two eyes, three fingers, four fingers." Nor do you usually count, "One finger plus one finger equals two; two fingers plus one nose equals three." Typically, when you count fingers, you count *only* fingers, and that's because you've matched all the fingers into one single group.

Counting games are practically endless. If you used circle or square charts with your infant (see Chapter 3), you can gradually increase the number of items on the chart, showing your child each chart about twelve times before adding another chart. When your baby is about eight to ten months old, you may have up to fifteen or twenty items on a chart. Once a chart has more than eight or ten items on it, very likely *you* cannot tell how many items are on the chart without counting them. But many babies can. It is still unclear why certain babies have this ability and other babies don't, but this is a remarkable talent shared by very few adults.

At about this time, when your baby is between eight and ten months old, begin to use these charts to teach arithmetic concepts. Show a two-item chart and say, "One and one are two." Show a three-item chart and say, "One and two are three." Show a four-item chart and say, "three and one are four." Show your baby about four or five charts a day for about four or five days. Then, add another chart each day. When you have reached ten charts, begin to eliminate the earlier charts. Once you reach fifteen or twenty items on a single chart, begin again with the early charts, but vary the math facts. Now, when you show a four-item chart, instead of saying, "Three and one are four," say, "Two and two are four." Just as you first said math facts based on ones (one and one, two and one, three and one, etc.), gradually move on to twos, then threes, and so on. Mothers who successfully keep up this pace report that they are amazed at their baby's grasp of addition . . . and even subtraction!

You can share this activity once a day, twice a day, even three times a day, but by all means try it. Remember that you're only spending about two to three minutes each time. Patience is a key, but after several months of this activity, you may begin to see remarkable results. When you lay out two cards and call out a number, your baby may actually point to the correct chart! It now seems that infants under one year of age have an amazing capacity to understand concepts presented in this way. If this stimulation is not offered, the innate ability begins to be lost after about one year of age.

Patience is an important ingredient of success. I have often suggested that whenever you pose a question to or play a game with a child, if the child doesn't *know* the answer, *give* the child the answer. This often prevents a child from becoming frustrated. Some children, however, are natural high achievers. You can see this by their body language as they persist in trying to find the answer for themselves. In these cases, refrain from jumping in with the answer. Give your child enough time to find things out for himself. In all cases, take the course that seems to give your child the greatest satisfaction, because this ensures his continued interest and enthusiasm.

It's important to introduce the concepts of *counting* and *matching* before you begin arithmetic. Even a child less than one year of age who has been exposed to your teaching from birth can learn to identify the shapes of his crackers — circles, squares, rectangles, triangles. Identify the shapes of foods and play simple matching games by matching squares or circles or whatever shapes are available. By the time your child is two, you also can cut out shapes from sheets of colored cardboard — squares, circles, triangles, stars, and so on. Make two of each color, trying to use the colors with which your child is familiar. Mix all the pieces and have the child match the pairs. Gradually increase the numbers of matching items — six red stars, six yellow triangles. When your child is comfortable with this idea, you can greatly expand the number of pieces. For example, cut out circles or triangles of several different colors and ask your child to find all of the circles. Then, ask him to find all of the red pieces, regardless of their shape.

Try to find patterned papers. Wallpaper samples or gift wrap are perfect. Cut out different shapes from each pattern and mix the patterns. Ask your child to find all of the shapes of one pattern. Then, if you're skillful, cut out a dress or shirt from one pattern and then cut out accessories — a tie, a belt, a bow — from the same pattern. Do the same using another patterned paper. Mix all the pieces and have the child locate the pieces that match, placing the bow, the belt, and the other accessories on the matching shirt or dress. Cut out pairs of mittens or other shapes from scraps of wallpaper. Place one mitten on the table and the others in a paper bag. Take turns trying to pick the matching mitten from the bag.

You can also play games that match numbers. Take 3x5 index cards and write large numbers on each of them. Make two cards with the number one, two cards with the number two, and so on. Then, shuffle the cards and place them face down. Each player draws two cards. If they match, the player keeps the cards; if they don't match, the cards are returned to the deck. Alternate turns. When all pairs have been drawn, the player with the most cards wins. Gradually increase the numbers of pairs. As always, remember that children enjoy games that they win.

You can encourage matching of less obvious objects by setting aside a special day to count a particular item — dogs, cats, cars, insects. When you go for a walk, encourage your child to find as many "items of the day" as possible and keep the count going. At the beach or park you can find pebbles or shells to count, and you can even bring these items home for artwork.

Matching items — forming natural sets or groups — is the foundation of mathematics.

Another preface to arithmetic is seriation, recognizing ascending order (which leads to addition and multiplication) and descending order (which leads to subtraction and division). Cut out a variety of shapes and have your child place them in different orders or series: largest to smallest, smallest to largest, narrowest to widest, lightest to darkest, and so on. Measuring cups and other containers are also great for this activity. You can even cut tongue depressors into different sizes and have the child align them.

Next comes pattern recognition — not patterns as in the patterned gift wrap or wallpaper — but recognizable number patterns. The ability to recognize inherent number patterns can increase a child's speed and agility in dealing with numbers. For example, place three blocks in the first row and two blocks in the next row. Then, place three blocks in the third row and two blocks in the fourth row. Finally, place three blocks in the fifth row and ask the child what comes next. Most children will recognize the 3-2-3-2-3-2 number pattern. Gradually increase the complexity of your patterns and use different toys, shells, or other items for variety.

Now your child is ready to enjoy counting! You can once again present black dots on white paper, just as you did when he was an infant, gradually increasing the number of dots on a page to twelve. Fingers and toes have always been used for counting because they're always available for a child to practice the numbers one through ten and eleven through twenty. Count forward and backward: ten, nine, eight, seven, six, five, four, three, two, one, blast off! If your child is talking, encourage her to count after you.

Count many different things besides fingers and toes: windows, chairs, trees, toys, blocks. As your child learns to count after you, begin alternate counting. You say one, she says two, you say three, and so on.

Food is another great place to begin. If you're making cookies and need two cups of flour, count them out: one cup and one cup equal two cups. When the cookies are ready, take two on a plate and offer one to the child. We had two cookies, but you took one; two cookies minus one cookie equals one cookie left or remaining. Count how many pretzels or cookies are in a bag or box.

Make up number stories using a sheet of paper along with a jar of nuts, raisins, or buttons. For example: "Two cows went for a walk in Coral Gables (use the name of your town; whenever you recite a number such as "two cows," have the child count out that number of raisins on the paper). Along came another cow (have the child place one more raisin on the paper). Then, along came a donkey and a fox and a squirrel (have the child place three additional raisins on the paper). Then they all went to John's (use your child's name) house, rang the doorbell, and said, "Let us in!" And John said, "How many are there?" Then, ask your child how many animals are outside. Encourage your child to count the raisins or nuts on the paper and give you the answer.

You can make up similar stories that involve counting animals, people, cars, trees, houses, airplanes, and many other objects. Begin by only adding objects. Later, make up stories that involve both adding and subtracting objects.

Remember to count when you hand things to family members — one towel, two socks, three cookies, and so on. Counting games are easy to devise. For example, make a large set of dice from six-sided containers or large blocks covered wtih contact paper. Number the sides one through six. Each player rolls the dice and begins to build a tower with the number indicated on the dice. After five throws, the player with the highest or largest tower wins. Or draw two large trees on a piece of cardboard or kraft paper. Throw the dice and draw the indicated number of apples or cherries on the tree. After ten throws, the player with the most cherries or apples wins.

These counting games can be adapted for play with several children. There are other counting games that a child can play by himself. Cut out cardboard numbers one through nine. Then, place one to nine nuts or raisins randomly in each cup of an egg carton or muffin tin. The child should count the raisins in each cup and place that number on top of the cup. When all the raisins have been counted, ask the child which cup has the fewest number of raisins and which cup has the most. Can she count the cups in order, from lowest number to highest? If not, count for her.

You can also cut out a quantity of small red and blue discs from pieces of cardboard. Distribute one to nine discs in the cups of the egg carton, but do not mix colors in any one cup. Next, write the numbers one through nine in red crayon on a sheet of paper; next to it make a similar column with the numbers one through nine written with a blue crayon. The child should count the discs in each cup, then draw an X over the correct number and color. Gradually increase the amount of colors that you use so that the child can eventually discriminate among nine numbers and six colors.

A child's understanding of number concepts is not necessarily sequential; in other words, children don't necessarily learn concepts in order. Instead, they tend to skip over certain elementary steps, move on to more sophisticated knowledge, then backtrack to pick up concepts that they may have originally missed. That's why it is *essential* that you do not act as a scorer or judge during these games. All of us, even adults, play games to have fun. If we have fun, we're more inclined to continue the game and improve our skills. On the other hand, if someone is always telling us that we're wrong, we're inclined to abandon the game quickly. Don't sulk or argue when a child makes a mistake. Instead, gently point out the correct answer, suggesting, "I think that the answer may be seven," or, "Don't you think that the answer may be seven?" or, "Let's count the cherries again and be sure that we have the right amount." Children learn best when they feel free to make mistakes and keep on trying; then, when they really learn the correct answer, they remember it.

Some math concepts may be learned in moments; others may take weeks or months to learn. Your only goal is to encourage PEEEHK and avoid SPPPAN. If you consistently present number opportunities, your child will intuitively begin to make connections between numbers. That's why you don't have to teach addition one month, subtraction the next, and multiplication and division a year later. Keep tuned to your child's responses. If she's easily bored, move on to the next step *even if* she doesn't fully understand the earlier concepts.

Many parents ask for a time frame during which elementary math skills can typically be learned. I hesitate to comply because some parents may become too time-frame oriented, pushing a child beyond his immediate inclinations or holding back a child who is eager to continue learning. My own experiences with many different children in a variety of settings suggest that if stimulation activities are started at birth, counting to 100 can often be learned by two years; addition and subtraction can be understood by about age two and one-half; multiplication at about three and one-half; division at about four; fractions at approximately age four and one-half; and simple algebra by age five. Of course, the child who has not had these experiences from birth cannot be expected to follow this timetable. In addition, your own child may learn more quickly or more leisurely. In any case, all children continue to make both progress *and* mistakes as they go along. What I have learned over the years is that virtually all children whose parents practice early learning techniques can learn everything in this book before they begin elementary school.

Numbers typically are symbols for something else. Numbers may symbolize or stand for amounts of money, locations, weights, times, and other important pieces of information. That's why we learn math in the first place, not merely as a form of mental exercise, but because we *need* to know the information contained in the answer to a mathematical problem. Let's look at a few examples that may seem simple to many adults but that have posed major obstacles to children who were never exposed to early math and, as a result, found math principles difficult to understand.

Is there any reason why you might want to know the product of 129×3? Suppose that you want to purchase three loaves of bread, each of which costs \$1.29. If you bring \$3.75 to the store, will you have enough money to purchase the three loaves of bread? Other examples abound. If the time is 3:45 and you anticipate that a chore will take fifty minutes, when will you be finished? If a child has two dozen cookies and expects seven friends to visit, will each person be able to have four cookies? If you decide to make more cookies and place one-half cup of water in a measuring cup, will there be room in the same cup for two-thirds cup of oil? If a child brings cookies to a sick friend and is looking for the address 845 Elm Street, and if the child passes 823 Elm and then 821 Elm, is he going in the right direction? These are the math problems that each of us encounters everyday, and it is with these everyday examples that we begin to introduce mathematical concepts to children.

Almost all of these mathematical concepts begin with an understanding of numbers, so let's review the opportunities to see numbers in the everyday environment.

Numbers are featured on many objects found throughout the house: telephones, clocks, measuring cups and spoons, thermometers, containers, clothing labels, calendars, and even your mail. Point out these numbers to your child and concentrate on the different ways that numbers are presented. (Always be certain that the numbers are large enough for your child to see.) On a telephone dial, the numbers are in order, one through nine. On a thermometer, the numbers are also in order, although a room thermometer, an oven thermometer, and a fever thermometer begin and end with different numbers. At the house-and-garden store, purchase an indoor or outdoor thermometer with large number markings. Explain that a thermometer measures the temperature of the air and that as the needle points to a higher number, we feel warmer; in the evening or early morning, when the needle points to a lower number, we feel colder. Point out the thermometer readings several times each day. The "ranges" of numbers on these items are different, and you can explain why. Measuring cups and spoons also feature numbers in order, from smallest to largest, but these numbers are usually "fractions," or parts of one whole: ¼, ⅓, ½, ⅔, ¾, 1. We'll talk about fractions later in this chapter.

Read magazine ads with your child and point out the ways in which numbers are used: page numbers, prices, sizes, and so on.

A child best understands math concepts when actually using objects that feature numbers. For example, allow your child to help you dial the telephone, or buy a toy phone that features large numbers and ample finger spaces. Don't become impatient if the process takes a bit longer than you might have imagined.

Take numbers outdoors. When you go for a walk, point out the numbers on houses, stores, and street signs. As you walk, point out the consecutive nature of these numbers: 1st Street, 2nd Street, 3rd Street, or the house numbers 821, 823, 825. Play counting games. Count the number of white roofs or red cars or bicycles or trees. Have a contest in which the person who finds the greatest number of an object (the most pencils in the house, the most shells on the beach, the most words that begin with A on signs at the mall) wins.

In the sandbox, wading pool, or garden, allow the child to fill different containers with sand or water and discuss their contents. A one-cup container holds twice as much as a half-cup container. A quart container holds twice as much as a pint container. Try to find containers with different shapes. A taller container may actually hold less if it's very narrow. A wide container may hold more even if it's very low. Help your child pour sand or water from one container to another to illustrate this point.

Many examples should be repeated. Use words that express relationship: bigger, smaller, more, less, fewer, greater, close, far, tall, short, thin, thick, inside, outside, over, under, first, last, empty, full, different, same, and so on. All of these words can relate to number or spatial concepts. Two other relationship words that are important to an understanding of math are "pair" and "set."

Point out natural pairs such as mittens, gloves, and socks. In mathematics, a set is a group of one or more. Point out sets such as sets of dishes, sets of glasses, a set of tableware or silverware, a set of crayons, a set of blocks, and so on. Sets may consist of any number. A set of everyday glasses may include twenty-four; a set of fine crystal glasses may include only eight.

Use numbers as frequently as you can, concentrating first on the numbers between one and ten, and next expanding to at least twenty. When setting the table, remember to say that you need four glasses or five spoons. When making a recipe, give the amount for each ingredient: one-half teaspoon salt, three cups of flour, and so on. Of course, your child should help with these chores whenever possible. Ask your son to distribute the four spoons, one at each place. Ask your daughter to measure the three cups of flour, and let her help you pour them into the mixing bowl.

An easy counting game starts with five or ten marbles and gradually increases to about twenty marbles in a box. Then, roll a die and remove that number of marbles from the box. Narrate as you go: "We started with ten marbles, Amy, and we rolled a six. Let's take out six marbles. Let's look and see how many marbles are left. Four marbles are left." You can vary this game by including many different types of objects in the box — crackers or popcorn, pennies, jacks, or anything available. Food is always a great item to count — popcorn, raisins, carrot sticks.

As numbers become more familiar, purchase or make number games. Make bingo cards that feature nine squares (three rows × three rows) with a random assortment of numbers one through nine; in other words, the numbers may be distributed on two cards as follows:

1	3	4	2	7	9
2	5	6	1	3	5
9	7	8	4	6	8

Next, make cardboard squares with one number, one through nine, on each square. Mix the small squares and begin selecting the numbers one at a time. Each time you call out a number, the player covers that number on the card. Whoever covers an entire row of numbers first wins. At first, use only vertical and horizontal rows. Then, explain what a diagonal row is and include diagonal rows in the game.

Make a number curve game. On a piece of cardboard, draw a double curving line. The lines should be several inches wide and should look like a thick snake. Divide the curve into about twenty squares. Label the first square START and the last square FINISH. On the squares in between, write random directions: GO AHEAD 2 SQUARES, GO BACK 1 SQUARE, and so on. Next, cut out thirty small squares and write a number between one and ten on each square. As you pull one of these small squares, the player moves his game piece (a paper clip, raisin, or colored disk) that number of squares; then, he follows any directions written on the square. Whoever reaches FINISH first wins the game.

These games can be played with two to four players and encourage number skills.

Make a number bag. Begin with the numbers one through four (later you'll include five through nine). Cut out these numbers from stiff cardboard as precisely as you can. You want the child to reach in the bag, pick a number, and identify that number by shape alone. This number bag, which encourages the multisensory identification of numbers, can then be used for many activities.

Draw a tree on a piece of cardboard and cut out about thirty "oranges" from a piece of orange construction paper. Put a tiny piece of double-sided adhesive tape on the back of each orange. Have the child pick a number from the number bag, identify the number before looking at it, then tape that number of oranges to the tree. Both of you can also make a big watermelon. Your child can pick a number from the number bag and tape that number of seeds onto the watermelon.

Select a container together with about thirty of the same object — raisins, dried beans, paper clips, and so on. The child picks a number from the number bag and drops that many items into the container. With practice, a child can use several different containers and objects at the same time. Putting seven raisins in one container and seven paper clips in another container helps a child to see that the same number can relate to more than one set of objects.

Take an egg carton and, with a marker pen, number the segments. Place the numbers 1, 3, 5, 7, 9, and 11 along the top row and the numbers 2, 4, 6, 8, 10 along the bottom row. Continue to play the number-bag games, but ask the child to drop the objects in the proper slot of the egg carton. As the game proceeds, explain that the numbers along the top row are called "odd" and that the numbers along the bottom row are called "even." You can also use a marker to draw two columns on a sheet of paper.

Your child will eagerly grasp the connections that odd and even numbers have to themselves and to each other. Then, when you both walk down the block, point out the house numbers again, indicating that all of the odd numbers are on one side of the street and that all of the even numbers are on the other. In that way, if you know the address where you are going, you'll be able to tell what side of the street it will be on.

One of the most widespread uses of numbers in our everyday experience occurs with money, and it's a good idea to allow a child to handle money whenever practical. Let him place the coins in a fare box, pay for stamps at the post office, or give a donation to a volunteer collecting in the mall. Talk about the sizes, shapes, and colors of money, beginning with coins and moving to bills. Also talk about the relationships between different denominations: "This is a dime. It's worth ten cents. That's equal to ten pennies. You remember the nickel, don't you? The dime is worth twice as much as the nickel."

Make a chart using real or play money or draw the coins on the chart:

5 pennies	= 1 nickel
10 pennies	= 1 dime
25 pennies	= 1 quarter
50 pennies	= 1 half-dollar
100 pennies	= 1 dollar

If your child understands this, add new sections to the chart, offering more equations that illustrate the relationships among coins. For example:

$$5N \qquad = 1Q$$
$$10N \qquad = 1HD$$
$$20N \qquad = 1DOLLAR$$

Do the same for dimes, quarters, and half-dollars. You can even expand the chart up to five or ten dollars by using play money or by drawing the coins and dollars on the cardboard. You can make the charts large enough to display or small enough to bind together into a money book.

Get several small boxes or envelopes and put an amount on each one: eleven cents, for example. Then, give your child a stack of coins and ask her to put eleven cents in the container. She may choose eleven pennies, one dime and one penny, or one nickel and six pennies. If the container says five cents, for example, and if your daughter puts in a nickel, say, "That's great, Susan. What else could you put in if you didn't have a nickel?"

Don't be surprised if your child remembers these facts one day and forgets them the next. One source of number confusion is that American money (like most of the world's currencies) is based on divisions of 100 (100 pennies to the dollar). Other number units, however, are *not* based on 100. While metric measurements are based on ten, most of us are familiar with measurements based on twelve (twelve inches to one foot, thirty-six inches to one yard). Understanding this is good practice for dozens (twelve eggs equal one dozen) but is useless for many other kitchen measurements based on fourths or even thirds. Another way to familiarize your child with number systems based on twelve is to give her a hard ruler and encourage her to measure things around the house.

One way to practice numbers is by playing store. If you've taken your child to a variety of locations where money is exchanged, playing store is a natural. Make a mock grocery, labeling items in certain ways. You may begin simply by labeling items three cents, five cents, and ten cents. At first, you should be the cashier. Later, the child can assume this role. As your child becomes more familiar with money, you can make the prices more sophisticated: two for ten cents, three for one dollar, and so on. If you have a kitchen scale or postal scale, you can even mark some items ten cents/pound or two pounds/one dollar.

Practice counting by using blocks. Ask your child to build a stack of blocks "one more than three" or "two less than five." You can also make a simple counting game with blocks, one die from a pair of dice, and two lengths of string, each about thirty-six inches long (the length of the strings may depend on the size of your blocks and the number that you have available; each player has one piece of string). Each player rolls the dice and places that number of blocks along his or her string. The first player to reach the end of the string wins the game.

Addition and Subtraction

Most of the games and activities that follow rely on the use of "math facts." You can think of a math fact as one-half of an equation. For example, in the equation $1 + 1 = 2$, the math fact is $1 + 1$. In the equation $2 - 1 = 1$, the math fact is $2 - 1$. The same is true of multiplication. The math fact 2×2 gives rise to the equation $2 \times 2 = 4$; in division, the math fact $4 / 2$ or $4 \div 2$ results in the equation $4 \div 2 = 2$. A math fact is like a math problem without the equal sign and without the answer. With this in mind, let's move on to a variety of pleasurable math games!

Marker games are great for demonstrating addition and subtraction. Markers can be any small items — pennies, paper clips, marbles, raisins, jacks, wrapped candy. Raisins, of course, seem to be the safest with very young children, especially if the phone rings in the middle of a game.

Put two markers in one box, one marker in another box, and three markers in the third box. Show your child that $2 + 1 = 3$ by saying: "If we put two and one together, we have the same amount as in box three." Encourage your child to visually follow your actions. Perform other simple combinations using the three boxes: $1 + 1$, $2 + 2$, and so on. Begin to use different items: 2 blocks + 1 block = 3 blocks. If you have one ball and your child has two balls, does he know how many other balls he needs to equal this amount?

These same games work to explain subtraction. Merely take away items instead of adding them. In the beginning, use real items that a child can readily identify.

Give your child blocks and see how many ways she can arrange them (with or without your help.) Begin with three blocks. If she places two blocks together and the third some distance away, write down 2 blocks + 1 block = 3 blocks. If she places all three next to one another, write 1 block + 1 block + 1 block = 3 blocks. Be sure to show her the paper. Gradually increase the number of blocks. After several occasions, you should be able to increase the blocks to about ten. Once she is familiar with the game, eliminate the word "block" when you write. Simply write 5 + 3 = 8.

Begin to accumulate these pages, one equation on each page, into a book: *Debra's Numbers*. From time to time, review a few pages of the book without playing the block game. You can play this game anywhere using shells at the beach, pebbles at the park, or raisins at grandma's house.

Make a chart to use with a pair of dice. The chart should contain about a dozen or so math facts, each of which can be achieved with the roll of the dice (for example, 1 + 1 through 6 + 6). As you each roll the dice, cross off the corresponding equation from the chart (be sure to show your child the equation on the dice and on the chart). If a player rolls the dice and that combination has been used, the player loses his turn. The player to fill in the last combination wins. Of course, you can always make a smaller chart for shorter games or younger children and a longer chart for older children: the number of lines on the chart indicates how long the game will go on.

Another simple game uses a deck of cards, markers, and two small containers such as empty margarine tubs. Each player, in turn, selects two cards from the deck and places the total number of markers in her tub. After all the cards are drawn, the player with the most markers in her tub wins.

Cut a "fish" from a 3x5 index card. Once you've cut about a dozen fish, put a math fact on each one. Make six addition and six subtraction facts. Then, draw two pools with waves for the fish to swim in. Label each wave top in this way.

START   1   2   3   4   5   6   7   8   9   10 (through 50)   FINISH

For older children, the waves can be numbered up to 100. Each player picks a fish and advances or moves back his marker the number of spaces equal to the math fact. Turns alternate, and the first player to reach the finish line wins. You can also play this same game substituting birds on tree branches for fish on the waves.

Play Four-Of-A-Kind. Make cards with a number from four through ten on them and place them face down. Each player selects one of these cards, then tries to collect four cards that contain that math fact. You also need to make about thirty cards, each of which contains a math fact from four through ten. For example: 3 + 1, 2 + 2, 4 + 1 . . . 8 + 2, 9 + 1. Turns alternate. Each player selects one card from the deck. She keeps the card if the math fact equals the number that she needs; if not, she discards the card. Play continues until one person has collected four math facts equal to the original number.

To encourage counting and addition from eleven through twenty or even beyond, play "ladder" or "mountain" games. Draw a ladder with twenty or more rungs. Then, using a deck of math-fact cards, each player selects a card and moves his marker the indicated number of rungs. The first player to reach the top rung wins the game.

Make about a dozen large dominoes from 5x8 index cards. Each card will be divided in half with a number of dots on one half and a number of dots on the other half. Each player gets one card face up, and the remaining cards are shuffled and placed face down. Each player, in turn, picks one card and tries to match the total number of dots on his original card. The first player to do so wins the game. Children who are learning to count and add love to play this game repeatedly.

Try to find occasions for addition in the natural environment. If you're folding the laundry, count the socks with your child. "Three red socks plus four blue socks equal seven socks, Roger." Eventually, when you say "three red socks plus four blue socks," Roger will know that this equals seven socks. You can also ask Roger if he thinks that a sock is missing and what color he thinks that sock is.

Children should actively participate in math games, whether these games are planned or spontaneous. That's why it's important to focus on natural items and to count them, place them in columns, or in piles, match them up, and so on.

There are so many games to play with dice. At the toy store, look for the largest dice that you can find. Some auto-accessory stores have those big dice that people hang from car mirrors, and these may work as well. However, be aware that they are *not* child-proof. Never allow your child to put these in her mouth.

In a simple addition game, each player throws the dice, and his score is written on a sheet of paper. After five turns, the scores are added, and the player with the highest score wins. A variation of this game can be scored with pennies or raisins. Whoever has the most pennies or raisins after five turns wins.

Hide four objects. If the child finds two, how many more must be found in order to win the game?

If it's nice outside, make a hopscotch game, either drawing it with chalk on the sidewalk or tracing it in the sand. Size the blocks so that your child can easily jump from one to the next. A hopscotch game is usually numbered 1 / 2 – 3 / 4 / 5 – 6 / 7 / 8 – 9 / 10. Call out a number and have the child jump to that square (begin with two, for example); then, call out another number (say, three). The child will then be in block five and you can say, "That's very good! Two plus three are five!"

Subtraction games usually follow the pattern of addition games. In the beginning, relate subtraction to counting backward. Count five, four, three, two, one and move on to ten, nine, eight, seven, six, five, four, three, two, one, blast off! When you reach zero or blast off, perform an action that reinforces the counting: Place a piece of fruit in your child's mouth, turn on the bath water, or say good-night and turn off the light. You can begin this counting when your baby is about ten months old. Even if she can't speak, she will still begin to understand what you're saying.

As you increase the numbers used in counting backward, make cards to illustrate these equations; for example, $5 - 1 = 4$, $4 - 1 = 3$ and so on. Graduate to subtraction facts that do not show the answers (for example, $5 - 1$, $4 - 1$).

At the doctor's office, or wherever you play a waiting game, play a subtraction game. Give your child a subtraction fact and ask her to hold up her fingers indicating the right answer. If she's correct, she gets a penny. If she's incorrect, she has to give back a penny. Of course, she gets to keep all of her pennies!

Put four small objects on the table. Then pick them up and hold them behind your back. Next, show your child your right hand, which contains two items. How many items remain behind your back? Repeat with other examples.

Remember the dice games? They can be used for subtraction as well. In the beginning, each player starts with twenty points and only one die is used. Eventually, each player can start with thirty or fifty points and both dice are used. As each player throws the dice, his score is subtracted from the total. Whoever's score reaches zero first wins.

When a child is more adept at addition and subtraction, a combination game can be played. Cards, each of which has a number between two and ten, are placed face down, and each player selects one card. Then the first player throws the dice. If that player can add or subtract the numbers on the dice in any way so that they equal the number on his card, that player wins a round. For example, if a player's card says five, then many rolls of the dice might produce 4 + 1, 2 3, 6 – 1, and so on. The first player to win three rounds wins the game.

Make a board game with your house at one end and a friend's or relative's house at the other. Include about a dozen spaces between them. Make about thirty math cards, each of which has an addition or subtraction fact on it. Players alternate turns selecting one math card from the deck. The player then moves her marker that number of spaces forward or backward, depending on whether the math card is an addition or subtraction problem. The first player to reach the friend's house wins.

You can also play a variation of this game. Using 8½ x 11 sheets of paper, make a "start" line at one end of the room and a "finish" line at the other. Place about a dozen sheets of paper between the start and finish. Each player selects a stuffed animal (or similar toy) as a marker. Play alternates as each player draws a math card from the deck and moves ahead or back the indicated number of spaces. The first player to reach the finish line wins.

Card games, either store-bought ones such as Bingo or War or homemade ones, are great fun. Using a regular deck of cards without the aces or picture cards, place all cards face down. Each player selects three cards. If she can make an arithmetic fact from the cards, she keeps those three cards. If not, they are returned to the deck. For example, if a player selects 2, 3, and 5, she can make either 2 + 3 = 5 or 5 – 3 = 2. The player with the greatest number of cards wins. At the beginning, of course, you can limit this game to addition. Later, you can return the aces or picture cards to the deck as wild cards or to denote any number that you desire.

An addition and subtraction chart (see Figure 6-1) on a piece of poster board can help with addition:

Figure 6-1
Addition and Subtraction Chart

+	0	1	2	3	4	5	6	7	8	9	10
0	0	1	2	3	4	5	6	7	8	9	10
1	1	2	3	4	5	6	7	8	9	10	11
2	2	3	4	5	6	7	8	9	10	11	12
3	3	4	5	6	7	8	9	10	11	12	13
4	4	5	6	7	8	9	10	11	12	13	14
5	5	6	7	8	9	10	11	12	13	14	15
6	6	7	8	9	10	11	12	13	14	15	16
7	7	8	9	10	11	12	13	14	15	16	17
8	8	9	10	11	12	13	14	15	16	17	18
9	9	10	11	12	13	14	15	16	17	18	19
10	10	11	12	13	14	15	16	17	18	19	20

To use the chart for addition, go across the top row and down the left row; the sum is at the intersection. To use the chart for subtraction, always take the smaller number from the larger number. For example, to find the difference between $8 - 2$, go down the left row to 2 and across that row to 8; when you follow that row up to the top, the number on the top row is 6, so $8 - 2 = 6$.

Once your child is familiar with addition facts for the numbers one through ten and has seen equations written vertically, like this

$$\begin{array}{r} 6 \\ + 2 \\ \hline 8 \end{array}$$

then he's ready to add two columns of numbers. When modern young parents who have learned the "new math" think of adding columns of numbers, they invariably think of grouping by tens. Certainly very few people today think of the old-fashioned method of "carrying over." But that's exactly the method that I've used for nineteen years, and I've never seen a young child who had difficulty understanding it. Start with low numbers, like the following:

$$13$$
$$+\ 25$$
$$\overline{}$$

Move on to amounts that produce a carry-over:

$$15$$
$$+\ 37$$
$$\overline{}$$

You can even teach your child to subtract two-digit numbers. This may sound a bit complicated, but I promise you that it can be accomplished quickly and easily. For example, take the problem:

$$73$$
$$-\ 48$$
$$\overline{}$$

Step 1:
Make four cards, each of which will cover one of the numbers.

Step 2:
Then expose the three and the eight so that the problem looks like this:

$$3$$
$$-\ 8$$
$$\overline{}$$

Explain that you cannot subtract eight from three, so you need to move on to Step 3.

Step 3:
In Step 3, the problem looks like this:

$$73$$
$$-\ 8$$
$$\overline{}$$

We need to borrow from the seven, so we take away one, which makes the seven a six; and we add one to the three, which makes it thirteen. At the end of Step 3, the problem looks like this:

$$
\begin{array}{r r}
6 & 13 \\
- & 8 \\
\hline
\end{array}
$$

Step 4:
You can now subtract eight from thirteen, and the answer is five:

$$
\begin{array}{r r}
6 & 13 \\
- & 8 \\
\hline
 & 5 \\
\end{array}
$$

Step 5:
Now you can uncover the four and subtract four from six, and the answer is two:

$$
\begin{array}{r r}
6 & 13 \\
- \ 4 & 8 \\
\hline
2 & 5 \\
\end{array}
$$

So 73 − 48 = 25. Now this may seem like a long and complicated way to do subtraction problems, but parents have reported that their children generally catch on to this method, often within a half hour, and that they ask for more problems to solve. When your child is proficient with subtraction, try a few of these problems. If he seems disinterested, leave them for another day. You may have learned subtraction by "regrouping," but there's no need to mention regrouping to your child. Even if regrouping is eventually taught in school, your child's good foundation in math should place him well ahead of other students.

Before leaving addition and subtraction, two important points should be discussed. The first is the *location* of math activities (and other learning activities, for that matter). When a child is in school, learning takes place within a confined environment, usually at a desk. Your home is not a school, however, and you should not try to duplicate a school setting. It's important to stage these activities in as many different locations as possible — at a table, on the floor or carpet, on a bed, in the kitchen, or even outdoors. In that way, even when you repeat certain activities, they will seem fresh and new. Research has demonstrated that when children learn in a variety of settings, they learn more quickly and the information is retained more easily retained.

Another vital point involves storytelling. Everyone enjoys hearing stories, so try to include math facts as a natural feature of stories. If the farmer in the dell has three cows and two pigs, how many animals does he have? If the wanderer traveled on Monday and Tuesday and Wednesday, how many days did he travel? When sharing an illustrated storybook with your child, be sure to count the various items in the pictures — the numbers of birds on the branches or the number of branches on the tree. If there are six birds and three fly away, how many birds will be left? The ease with which children absorb math is often controlled by the degree to which they see math as a part of their natural environment. Arithmetic games and activities are important and fun, but remember to include other opportunities for numbers as well, whether you're reading a story, walking through the supermarket, preparing dinner, or taking a walk around the block.

Writing Numbers

Children can learn a great deal about addition and subtraction even without their actually writing the numbers. If your child is young, he usually yells out the answers and you write them down. Most children, however, really want to write the numbers themselves, and you can help your child to do just that.

Stephen began to write numbers while we were at the beach. Wet sand is a good medium for writing because it offers support to young fingers. I would tell stories about mommy fish and daddy fish and would write the number one or two in the sand. He would copy my writing. At home, he continued to write numbers in soft clay.

To provide opportunities for writing numbers with large pencils or crayons, make dot numbers. These are outlines of numbers that the child forms by connecting the dots.

You can also take a sheet of paper, mark the sheet into about nine squares, and write a dot number in each square. As your child continues to practice, use two-digit numbers in addition to one-digit numbers.

You can even play a game with these sheets. Prepare "dot sheets" with the numbers between two and twelve. Each player rolls a pair of dice. The player then traces the number on the paper that corresponds with the number shown on the dice. If that number has already been traced, the player throws the dice again. Play alternates, and the first player whose numbers are all traced wins the game (I used to let Stephen trace in my numbers as well).

It's vital to use PEEEHK when your child practices writing. Nothing is more detrimental to a child than a parent's nagging or chastising that some letter or number is not written correctly. Most children honestly try to do their best, but young muscles often lack the strength and coordination to produce talented results. When Stephen spoke at the White House, several TV stations and newspapers reported the story that years before, Stephen's teacher had not wanted him to take advanced math because he could not draw his twos to her satisfaction. While many people chuckled at this seemingly innocuous story, I knew a sorrier truth. Because of this teacher, Stephen did not like to write at all. He often dictated math problems for me to write that he would then solve. This continued until Stephen was nine and entered high school. While I wasn't enthralled by these events, I never attempted to coerce Stephen nor did I make an issue over it. I kept my cool and, in instances like this, so should you.

Multiplication

Multiplication is nothing more than counting groups of equal numbers. You can illustrate this point by using items around the house. Both you and your child can look for groups that have the same number of objects: two groups or sets of glasses, each of which has eight glasses; four rooms, each of which has three windows; five dolls, each of which has two hands; three cars outside near the street, each of which has four tires. Looking for these groups may take days or even weeks.

When your child begins to understand what is meant by groups with the same number of objects, you can begin to work with smaller groups that are convenient for multiplication examples: three rows of blocks, each of which has two crayons on top; three sheets of paper, each of which has four pencils on it; two sheets of paper, each of which has four red dots drawn on it; four containers, each of which has five pennies inside.

Together you can build vertical block towers and horizontal block walls on the floor or table: five towers each with four blocks, three walls each with four blocks, and so on. As the child begins to understand the nature of these groups, give new building directions. Instead of five towers, each with four blocks, *take the same blocks* and build four towers, each with five blocks; instead of three walls, each with four blocks, *take the same blocks* and build two walls, each with six blocks.

Increase the types of objects with which you work. For example, take four stuffed animals and place two raisins near each one. You can even make up a story that the animals are hungry and want to eat lunch; each animal gets two raisins to eat for lunch. Your child can draw five fish on a piece of paper and place three raisins or discs near each one, because each fish gets three pieces of food to eat for lunch. Imaginative stories can feature many other groups: trees with peaches; children with books; houses, each with two cars; and so on.

After you have played these games for a time, at the conclusion of each game, write down the multiplication equation that has been demonstrated. If your daughter drew four fish, each with three pieces of food, write: 4 fish with 3 pieces = 12 pieces of food. If your son made two block towers, each with four blocks, write: 2 towers of 4 = 8 blocks.

Then, begin to expand your child's thinking by drawing three boxes on a sheet of paper and asking, "We need two raisins for each box; how many raisins do we need? Let's draw the raisins and find out." Better yet, hand out three boxes, one to your child, one to Mom, and one to Dad. Have the child distribute two raisins in each box. Then, have the child count the raisins: six raisins. Write: 3 boxes of 2 = 6 raisins. After you've practiced these games for a time, explain that it's faster to write 3 x 2 = 6. Instead of 3 towers of 4 blocks = 12, it's easier to write 3 × 4 = 12.

You'll still have to work with concrete examples for months, but be sure to finish each example by writing the equation that has been demonstrated.

Eventually you can put these equations in a multiplication book, which you can make with your child, creating one page at a time. A multiplication book has thirteen pages (0x — 12x). Label the top of each page 0×, 1×, 2×, 3×, and so on up to 12×. To enter equations on a page, play penny games. For example, on the 2× page, have the child make two rows on the table or floor, each with one penny. How may pennies does that equal? Two rows of 1 = 2. In the book, write 2 × 1 = 2. Next, ask the child to make two rows each with two pennies. Two rows of 2 = 4. Write: 2 × 2 = 4. Of course, even if you have two rows, if each row has 0 pennies, the total will be 0 pennies. The 2× page will begin to read:

$$2 \times 0 = 0$$
$$2 \times 1 = 2$$
$$2 \times 2 = 4$$
$$2 \times 3 = 6$$

Complete the page up to 2 × 12 = 24.

It's good to use different objects for different pages: raisins for the 1× page, pennies for the 2× page, pretzels or candies for the 3× page, and so on. In that way, the child understands that multiplication works for all kinds of objects, not only pennies. Have fun with multiplication. For example, with the book open to the 3× page, you and your child can each draw a man with three arms (if necessary, you can draw the figures). When the drawings are finished, ask him to count the arms. When he counts to six, show him in his multiplication book that 3 × 2 = 6.

You can begin to demonstrate that multiplication equations produce the same answers forward or backward: 2 × 3 = 6 and 3 × 2 = 6. This concept can be illustrated by drawing pictures: 3 houses, each with 2 windows = 6 windows, or 2 houses, each with 3 windows = 6 windows. As you reach the higher numbers, remind your child that she already knows the answer. If 8 × 4 is puzzling, remind her that she already knows 4 × 8; the answers in both cases are the same.

Show your child that in multiplication you can change the order of the numbers being multiplied (factors) and get the same answer (product), but when the equation goes with a story there is a correct way to use the factors in order. 2 × 3 = 6 is of course read, "Two times three equals six." A horizontal multiplication equation is read from left to right just like reading a book. The same equation written vertically looks like this:

$$\begin{array}{r} 3 \\ \times\,2 \\ \hline 6 \end{array}$$

and not like this:

$$\begin{array}{r} 2 \\ \times\,3 \\ \hline 6 \end{array}$$

In other words, the number (factor that is on the line with the times sign is read first, then comes the word "times," followed by the top number (factor). The line means equal (you of course must supply this word) and then the answer is given last.

How many windows do three houses have if each house has two windows? The equation is 3 × 2 = 6 windows, and:

$$\begin{array}{r} 2\ \text{windows} \\ \times\,3 \\ \hline 6\ \text{windows} \end{array}$$

If the question turned around is how many windows do two houses have if each one has three windows, then the equation is 2 × 3 windows = 6 windows, and:

3 windows
× 2
——
6 windows

The first factor read shows the *number of sets*. The second factor read shows the *amount each equal set has in it* and carries the "label," be it windows, money, or any other object.

Starting at the bottom helps when your child does multiplication with several digits and carrying is necessary

4 75
× 682
——

When the book is completed, the child will have a complete multiplication book for equations through 12 × 12 = 144. This book can be used in a variety of ways. When you play multiplication games, and the child gives an answer (such as 5 dolls, each with 2 hands = 10 hands), how can the child be sure that the answer is correct? Simply turn to the 5× page in the multiplication book, and he can see that 5 × 2 = 10. Eventually, the child can play multiplication games by himself. There are a number of good multiplication card games available, including my own "Arith-Matic" game. Multiplication records are also available.

The multiplication book is used to its best advantage if you continue to devise concrete examples that illustrate the equations: 3 scoops of ice cream, each with 2 cherries = 6; 4 palm trees each, with 6 fronds = 24, and so on. To illustrate 12× equations, which involve large numbers, utilize egg cartons, soft-drink cartons, and other natural dozen and half-dozen groups. Tell stories, have the child draw pictures, or play with containers and small objects. Every time you can, concretize these abstract equations by using real objects.

As you proceed with multiplication games, the *point or rationale of multiplication* should always be explained. *Multiplication allows us to count things quickly and easily.* If we had to count all the legs on eight spiders, it would take a long time, but if we know that eight spiders each have eight legs, with practice we immediately know that 8 × 8

= 64. The same is true if we distribute five raisins in each cup of an egg carton. Counting all of those raisins would take a long time, and if we got confused in the middle of counting, we would have to start over. However, because of multiplication, we quickly know that 12 × 5 = 60.

The final page of the multiplication book should be a chart (see Figure 6-2), which gives all equations from 1 × 1 through 12 × 12 in an easy-to-read format:

Figure 6-2
Multiplication Chart

x	0	1	2	3	4	5	6	7	8	9	10	11	12
0	0	0	0	0	0	0	0	0	0	0	0	0	0
1	0	1	2	3	4	5	6	7	8	9	10	11	12
2	0	2	4	6	8	10	12	14	16	18	20	22	24
3	0	3	6	9	12	15	18	21	24	27	30	33	36
4	0	4	8	12	16	20	24	28	32	36	40	44	48
5	0	5	10	15	20	25	30	35	40	45	50	55	60
6	0	6	12	18	24	30	36	42	48	54	60	66	72
7	0	7	14	21	28	35	42	49	56	63	70	77	84
8	0	8	16	24	32	40	48	56	64	72	80	88	96
9	0	9	18	27	36	45	54	63	72	81	90	99	108
10	0	10	20	30	40	50	60	70	80	90	100	110	120
11	0	11	22	33	44	55	66	77	88	99	110	121	132
12	0	12	24	36	48	60	72	84	96	108	120	132	144

As you begin to fill in part of the chart, ask your child for help. For example, when you fill in the 5× line, ask your child if he remembers any of the answers. If not, have him locate the correct answers on the 5× page in the multiplication book. To use the chart to find the product of 6 × 4, for example, find 6 on the top line and follow it down to the point where it intersects or meets the 4 in the left column. The answer, of course, is 24.

Use this chart for review, to find quick answers, and to demonstrate relationships between numbers (4 × 5 and 5 × 4 equal the same number). You'll make better use of the chart if you once again include concrete examples. For instance, have the child make two block towers, each with six blocks. If we want to know how many blocks we have all together, how can we find the answer on the chart? We can either go across to 2 and down to 6 or across to 6 and down to 2; in both cases, the answers are the same.

Much of a child's intuition about numbers, as well as his ability to calculate quickly and without difficulty, are the results of an understanding of multiplication. Play multiplication games frequently, although never so long that they bore or tire your child. A few minutes at a time several days a week is usually best.

Division

Many of us are reasonably adept at multiplication, but we may find division difficult or frustrating. Unfortunately, we often pass our own frustration on to our children. I have frequently encountered tenth-grade children in my classroom or counseling office who had no understanding of division. This is unfortunate and unnecessary, because children naturally use division almost every day of their lives.

Two types of childhood activities call for division — grouping and sharing. Grouping begins in early childhood. I have twelve blocks and want to divide them into two rows. How many blocks will be in each row? There are six children. If we divide into two teams, how many children will be on each team? I have seventeen dishes. How many stacks of four can I make? Will any dishes be left over?

Sharing also begins in early childhood. I have seven candies, and two friends want to share them with me. How many candies will each of us get? Will any candies be left over? That one's for me!

You can recall your own early experiences to provide real-life examples for your child. In addition, divide food at the dinner table. Divide crayons at coloring time. Divide towels among washrooms. You can even divide water among houseplants. If you have a quart of water that equals thirty-two ounces, how many ounces will each plant receive if you have five plants? Will any water be left over? The amount left over is called the remainder.

Just as multiplication was a way of adding things that were already in groups, division is a way of subtracting things into smaller groups. Also, just as there was a special way of writing multiplication equations, so there is a special way of writing division equations. In multiplication, if we had three people, each of whom wanted two cookies, we would need six cookies. We wrote that:

$$3 \times 2 = 6$$

In division, if we have six cookies and three people, each person will receive two cookies. We write that:

$$6 \div 2 = 3$$

If we have seven cookies and threee people, each will receive two cookies, but there will be one cookie left over, or a remainder of one. We write that:

$$7 \div 2 = 3 \text{ R } 1$$

Tell your child that we can also write the same equation this way:

$$2 \overline{)\, 7}^{\,3 \text{ R } 1}$$

When we have a remainder, we divide that remainder equally. In this example, we divide the one remaining cookie between the two people so that each person receives one-half cookie.

Remainders are a good way to begin teaching fractions. For example, if another friend comes along and seven cookies have to be divided among three people, how many cookies will each person receive? The problem is written in this way:

$$3 \overline{)\, 7}^{\,2 \text{ R } 1}$$

Because we have a remainder of one, and we have to divide that remainder among three people, each will receive an extra one-third cookie.

Begin to demonstrate division by offering examples that *do not* contain remainders. As the child gains confidence with division, present examples that do result in remainders. Dividing foods among children and family remains the most realistic way to demonstrate division.

You can also use the multiplication chart as a division chart. Simply go down the left row to the number by which you want to divide (the divisor). Then, go across to the number you wish to divide into (the dividend). The answer is straight up at the top of the row. For example, you have three children and six cookies. How many cookies will each child receive? Locate three at the left row. Go across to the number six. At the top of that row is the number two.

Frequently, a happy bonus will be a child's greater willingness to share with friends and siblings as a means of demonstrating newly learned math skills!

Fractions

Fractions are easy for preschoolers to learn because so many objects in the natural world can be divided into fractions. Cooking and eating, of course, are the premier fraction activities. Begin with simple number concepts while the child is eating. "Let's share the banana — half for you and half for me." The next time, slice the banana into eight slices and say the same thing, "Half for you and half for me." How can you tell what half equals? There are different ways. You can suggest one for me, one for you until the slices are gone. Or you can make two piles, one for me and one for you, and place the same number of slices in each pile. But that takes a lot of time. After a few banana experiments, you'll both agree that it's faster if you know that one-half of eight equals four. What happens, though, when you have a whole banana and you have to share it with Daddy also? Why not slice the banana into nine slices? How many slices does each person receive? Divide the slices into three equal piles, and you see that each person receives three slices. So one-third of nine equals three. The next time this same opportunity presents itself, the child won't have to count out the slices. You'll all immediately know that one-third of nine equals three. Later, reinforce these fraction concepts by dividing raisins, grapes, cookies, or small candies.

To introduce fractions as a purely mathematical concept, begin with strips of posterboard one inch wide and twelve inches long. Leave one strip white. Cut another strip into two six-inch lengths and color them red. Cut a third strip into three four-inch lengths and color them blue. Cut a fourth strip into four three-inch lengths and color them green. Cut a fifth strip into six two-inch lengths and color them yellow. Let your child play with these strips. After she is familiar with them, discuss different fractions by adding and measuring different-colored strips compared to the twelve-inch white strip. For example, how many ways can you combine strips to equal the twelve-inch strip? You can combine one six-inch strip and three two-inch strips. You can also combine two three-inch strips and three two-inch strips. You can think of many more combinations!

When several children are playing, you can reinforce fraction concepts by dividing certain items into equal parts for each of the children to share. For example, if your child is playing with two friends or siblings, divide a granola bar into three equal parts. Explain that you are dividing the bar into thirds so that each person will have an equal amount. Divide nine crayons among the three children and explain that one-third of nine equals three.

You can talk about fractions in several ways: as a part of a single whole (one-fourth of a pie or one-eighth of a pizza); as a certain number out of a group of objects (one-fourth of the cookies or one-half of the crayons); or as the result of division (four children are playing, so we have to divide all the food into fourths so that each person will receive one-fourth).

As your child has more experiences with fractions, write the fractions for him to see. For example, draw a circle that represents a cookie or a pizza and label each section:

$$1/4 \quad\quad 1/4$$
$$1/4 \quad\quad 1/4$$

Make simple puzzles by mounting magazine ads on poster board. Cut the puzzle into fractional parts. Practice with ½, ⅓, ¼, ⅙, and ⅛. Have your child put the puzzle together.

Cut out eight-inch circles from construction paper. Divide one into halves, another into thirds, and so on. Working with one circle at a time, have your child put the pieces of the circle back together. Talk about how many fractional pieces are needed to make one whole circle.

If the circle is cut in quarters, for example, four quarters are needed to make own whole circle.

Graphs

Children love to make graphs. I encourage you to develop this talent because graphs are an important part of math, even though many children never understand them.

Explain that numbers can be presented in many different ways. A graph is a visual presentation or picture that makes related numbers easier to understand. For example, make a graph that shows the numbers and kinds of animals on your block. As you add up the tally of neighborhood pets, you may find the results as depicted in Figure 6-3.

Figure 6-3

DOGS	CATS	FISH	BIRDS
4	5	3	2

You can also put this information on a graph:

Make graphs for other numbers. For example, count the numbers of red, green, orange, and yellow marbles in the marble box. Then, help your child prepare a graph of the results. You can also graph the sexes of people in the family, the types of plants in the garden (flowering plants, trees, shrubs, and herbs), and the kinds of transportation on the block (cars, trucks, RVs, bikes, and motorcycles).

Talk about the graphs. What is the most popular form of transportation on the block? What is the least popular vehicle? There are only three trees in the garden, but there are nine shrubs. Does that mean that there are three times as many shrubs as trees? Why are there so many shrubs? Or why are there so few trees? Your child should know how proud you are of his graphs. Always keep the latest graph in a place of honor.

Telling Time

By the age of two to three, a child is ready to master elementary concepts about telling time; however, a true ability to tell time may not appear until the child is about four and one-half. Make a large cardboard clock with two hands that move. Also, make cards, each of which has a time of day, accurate to one-quarter hour (for example, cards should read 9:00, 9:15, 9:30, 9:45, and so on). Encourage your child to pick out a card at random, and move the hands to that time. At first, you'll have to give examples, but if he's interested, your child will soon understand and a wonderful game will ensue. Next, point out the times of day for major events and set the hands to those times: waking up at eight, taking a bath at eleven, eating lunch at twelve or noon, and so on.

When your child is about four, begin working with a standard or analog clock (the round kind with the numbers one to twelve clearly printed). A digital clock is obviously of little use when explaining number concepts to children. Then, during the day, when you actually engage in the events that you recorded on the play clock, remind the child to look at the real clock: "I think it's time for your bath. Let's look at the clock and make sure. See? It's exactly eleven o'clock." Gradually introduce more sophisticated time concepts, a.m. in the morning and p.m. in the afternoon and evening. Also discuss the fact that each hour has sixty minutes, so that if the clock reads 11 a.m., fifteen minutes later it will be 11:15 a.m.

Problem-Solving and Simple Algebra

I have a copy of an algebra game that I made for Stephen. He was to find the answers to puzzles, each of which had a story. Here are several examples from that game:

$$6 + z = 7$$
$$z =$$

$$4 + x = 8$$
$$x =$$

$$6 - z = 7$$
$$z =$$

$$2 - k = 1$$
$$k =$$

In every case, Stephen filled in the correct answer with his crayon. He was four years old at the time.

Many children who are introduced to early math find algebra to be a natural extension of the math concepts that they already understand. To some adults, this fact may be shocking. Many of us remember algebra from the eitghth or ninth grade, and not all of our memories are pleasant. However, don't prejudice your child with your memories, because children who have been introduced to early-math skills usually find algebra a breeze!

Algebra is nothing more than an extension of everyday problem-solving skills in which we find the value of an unknown. In algebra this is called "solving for the unknown." Perhaps because children love mysteries, and because they love to solve mysteries, they really enjoy algebra.

Before discussing the idea of algebra, offer your child many experiences in problem-solving, like these:

1. Charlie has three crayons. You give him two more. How many crayons does Charlie have now?
2. Charlie starts out with five crayons, but you tell him, "Charlie, please give me three crayons." How many crayons will Charlie have then?
3. Charlie has two crayons. You hand him all the crayons in your hand. Then, Charlie has five crayons. How many crayons did you give to Charlie?
4. Charlie has some crayons in his hand. You give him two more. Now he has five crayons. How many crayons did Charlie have in the beginning?
5. Charlie has some crayons in his hand. You say, "Charlie, please give me three crayons." Now Charlie has only two crayons left. How many crayons did Charlie have in the beginning?

You can and should repeat experiences with these using different items and different number combinations. In the examples above, the math facts all relate to the numbers two, three, and five. In algebra, the equations for these problems would be written like this, where x is the unknown number:

$$1.\ 3 + 2 = x$$
$$2.\ 5 - 3 = x$$
$$3.\ 2 + x = 5$$
$$4.\ x + 2 = 5$$
$$5.\ x - 3 = 2$$

From these simple examples, you can see that x, the unknown amount, can be placed anywhere within an equation. This is one of the beauties of algebra. Just when your child may be getting a little tired of conventional math facts and equations, you open a whole new world of adventure.

When should you introduce algebra? As always, this is an individual decision. Your child should be familiar with the basics of addition and subtraction, and it helps for him to have some understanding of multiplication (and even division). This does not mean that your child needs to know the addition/subtraction or multiplication tables by heart. It simply means that the fun of algebra depends on a basic understanding of math facts. If you've been following the math activities in this chapter for a year or two, and if your child is about four or five years old, now is an appropriate time to begin algebra.

Begin with the simplest example:

$$1 + 1 = A$$

Explain that algebra is like a mystery because you're trying to find out the answer of the unknown. The unknown can be indicated by any letter: A, b, C, X, y, z, or any letter in between. The unknown really means "how many?" So the equation $1 + 1 = A$ can read "1 + 1 equal how many?" Then you can ask, "Michael, I bet you know the answer. One plus one equal how many?" When Michael says two, congratulate him and write his answer this way:

$$1 + 1 = A$$
$$A = 2$$

If Michael thinks that all this is a great deal of fun, offer a few more examples:

$$2 + 1 = L \qquad 3 + 3 = X \quad 3 - 1 = K \qquad 2 \times 2 = B$$

Each time that you write the equation, ask the question in the same way: "Michael, two plus one equal how many?" When Michael offers the answer, write it underneath the equation like this:

$$2 + 1 = L$$
$$L = 3$$

Practice a few equations each day, remembering to use different letters for the unknown. You may want to avoid "O," which looks like "zero," and "S," which looks like "5" and may confuse children and adults alike.

When your child has experienced a wide variety of these expressions (yes, algebraic equations are called expressions), show that the unknown can be in any part of the expression. To make this point, review some of the previous problem-solving examples on page 189 and write their algebraic equivalents.

Then, offer an example, such as 2 + M = 3, and ask your daughter, "Katy, two plus how many equal three?" When Katy says "one," write the answer under the expression:

$$2 + M = 3$$
$$M = 1$$

If Katy doesn't say "one," then try to illustrate this expression with a word problem or, better yet, with a visual prompt. For example, place a small pile of raisins on the table. Then put two raisins near Katy and ask again, "Katy, two plus how many equal three?" If she seems hesitant, slide over one more raisin and exclaim, "Yes, two plus one equal three!" Katy will soon catch on.

In the beginning, or if your child seems to have difficulties, your early examples should all solve for an unknown equal to one. Then, move on to two, three, and so on. Try not to stay on any single number for too long or your child may begin to assume that the unknown must always be that number.

Another way to reinforce these principles is by offering related groups of expressions: 1 + 1 = A, A + 1 = 2, 1 + A = 2. Then, move on to 2 − 1 = A, A − 1 = 1, and so on.

In algebra, pace is important. Never offer more than about a half-dozen expressions each day even if your child wants more. Also, stay with each concept for a least a week before moving on. In other words, when you first introduce addition expressions whose unknown is always one, stay with those examples for about a week. Then move on to unknowns of two, three, four, and so on. After the first two weeks, you can pick up the pace a little. If your child is able to solve addition expressions for unknowns of one, two, three, and four, then move on to subtraction expressions, beginning with subtraction expressions whose unknown is equal to one.

When working with subtraction expressions, use the phrase "how many do we have left?": 2 − 1 = A becomes "when we have two and take away one, how many do we have left?" Again, demonstrate with raisins (or any other marker) if the point is unclear.

In this way, subtraction will pose little or no problem. In fact, after you work with simple subtraction expressions for a week or two (2 − 1 = A, 3 − 2 = B, and so on), you can ask, "Where else can we put the unknown in the subtraction expression?" Your child may very well answer that $2 - A = 1$! If not, use the expression, "How many do we take away?" For example, if we have two, how many do we take away to get one? For $A - 1 = 1$, we vary this to say, "What number, if we take away one will leave us one?"

As your expressions refer to higher numbers you may want to bring out the addition/subtraction chart. The multiplication chart will also help when you introduce multiplication expressions. Early multiplication expressions, such as $2 \times 3 = D$, should pose no problem because your child is familiar with the multiplication equation and understands the meaning of an unknown. When you move on to multiplication expressions whose unknown is in another location (for example, $2 \times A = 6$), then the multiplication chart will surely help. Show your child that you simply go down the 2 column until you reach 6, then go across to the left edge and you see that the answer is 3. Explain that this expression simply asks, "How many times does two equal six?"

If your child is comfortable with multiplication, you can move on to division. If not — perhaps because *you* hesitate to move into the uncharted waters of division — then stay with the addition, subtraction, and multiplication expressions. At some point, however, most children who have learned division facts want the challenge of division expressions. These are taught in much the same way as other expressions, beginning with simple expressions that solve for an unknown equal to 1 or equal to the original number ($3 \div 3 = A$, or $3 \div -1 = A$). Then, slowly move on to more complex examples, using the multiplication/division chart to help you. Remember, however, not to introduce division expressions until well after your child is familiar with division facts.

Many parents have told me that in teaching algebra to their children, they understood it themselves for the very first time! Children love the excitement and mystery of solving for an unknown, and I know that you'll share this special math fun with your child. The rewards are not merely instantaneous, but long-lasting. Your child will very likely excel in math throughout his or her lifetime.

Teaching "Everything Else" To Young Children

Despite the critical importance of subjects such as reading, writing, and arithmetic, life is made up of much more than the three Rs. When I ask parents what they truly want for their children, they offer many specifics. They want their children to develop self-confidence; to develop their talents; to learn about their world through geography, science, and history; to develop their creativity, especially in areas such as art and music; to avoid drugs; to develop "street smarts" for their own safety; and to shun prejudice.

The list is long, but a single question always follows it: Can I teach this to my child? Overwhelmingly, the answer is yes!

> *A first-grade teacher told me that she once thought that very well behaved children might come from repressive environments where children are "sat on." She soon learned that these children were the products of home teaching and that they were well behaved because they were keen with the anticipation of adding to their storehouses of knowledge and experience. "What a pleasure it is to teach these children," she beamed. "They're a teacher's dream."*

Research indicates that the majority of teachers do not teach in the way in which they were taught to teach. Instead, they teach in the same way that they, as children, were taught. This is simply one more example of the idea that actions speak louder than words. Children are influenced more by our actions than by our words. If we say one thing and do another, our children will most likely follow the example of our actions. Admonitions to "do as I say and not as I do" carry no weight.

As a result, our children tend to have the same virtues and vices as we do. Therefore, if we wish our children to act in a certain way and to make certain virtues their own, we must serve as constructive examples.

Encourage your child to befriend a variety of children from many backgrounds. Every person should be seen as valuable and as one who can contribute to society. This or that person may possess a skill that another person does not, but all people possess equal dignity and should be treated in that way. Try to provide opportunities for your child to meet children who are attempting to overcome physical, emotional, or other handicaps.

In our pluralistic society, there is no place for prejudice based on race, color, religion, sex, age, or economic circumstance. Interestingly, this is a view shared by the majority of gifted individuals, many of whom have undertaken a variety of activities to combat racism and other forms of prejudice.

Meeting with, talking with, and playing with a variety of individuals helps to develop a child's self-confidence as well as respect for others. For some parents, however, the question is one of place. Where can my child meet these children? While there are virtually limitless possibilities, several come immediately to mind: activities relating to music, art, drama, and sports, as well as children's events sponsored by your local library, park, zoo, or civic center. The interesting fact about these so-called extracurricular activities is that virtually all children who are thought of as bright or gifted have participated in them. Some people have the illusion that bright children are "eggheads" or "bookworms," spending all of their time in their rooms reading or working with computers. Nothing could be farther from the truth.

In my decades as a guidance counselor, I would estimate that only 10 percent of the high-school students whom I encountered were truly gifted. The students themselves had little in common: they were short or tall; thin or pudgy; poor or middle class; white, black, Spanish, or Asian. Some were the oldest child in the family, but as many were the youngest or a middle child or even an only child. What these gifted students did have in common was that 95 percent of them were early learners and most of them had always participated in extra-curricular activities.

For example, I found that nearly all gifted children could play a musical instrument. Perhaps this is likely because most of these students had been listening to music from birth. Their parents had played records or radios or had sung to them, and music was a natural part of their lives. Many had asked for a toy piano or xylophone which their parents had helped them to play.

Frequently, when a child demonstrates any interest at all in a musical instrument, the question of lessons arises. A young child can begin music lessons as early as age four if — and this is a very big if — the idea of lessons comes from the child. Never, not ever, under any circumstances, pressure a young child to have music lessons or any other lessons. Don't work on the "it's good for him" theory, because nothing good ever comes from ideas like that.

Interview music teachers carefully. Does this individual have experience in teaching young children? Does he embrace PEEEHK and avoid SPPPAN? Will you be encouraged to attend lessons? Never leave a young child alone. If you can't stay for the lesson, send along another adult to supervise.

I have always suggested that if you have to pester a child to practice an instrument, then that child isn't ready for lessons. Sometimes, support for music lessons comes from outside the child's immediate environment (from a neighbor or grandparent, for example). For Stephen, the encouragement was even more remote. We used to go to a fishing camp about four hours from our home. We would all pile into a very old, second-hand camper, and in would go all the fishing equipment and food and books for whatever course I was taking or teaching. Stephen also brought along his accordion. We noticed that as soon as he began to play, groups of raccoons would scamper out from the woods and sit and listen to him. It was a marvelous scene to watch. However, when my older son Cliff began to play, the raccoons would disappear! Needless to say, this raccoon approval gave Stephen all the incentive he needed to become a proficient accordion player.

These provisos for music lessons apply equally well to art, drama, and dance lessons. Whether or not your child takes formal lessons, seek out opportunities for experiences with art, drama, dance, and music. Many museums, libraries, and civic centers sponsor activities and events for young children that not only allow children to practice skills and learn new things, but that allow them to meet a wider cross-section of children in the community. In addition, museums and concerts allow children to see the esteem with which music and art are held; in turn, they will have greater self-esteem for their own musical and artistic efforts.

While lessons and outings are wonderful experiences, the majority of a young child's time is spent at home. Therefore, art, music, and other activities should also be undertaken as part of a child's normal curriculum. Another reason to provide art and music experiences in the home is that some school programs for gifted children do not include the arts. School administrators believe (erroneously, I am sorry to say) that gifted children prefer the challenge of math and science and have no special interest in art or music. How wrong they are!

Most young children love to produce artwork, and you should encourage them to do so. Use fat crayons or markers that are easier to hold and offer large sheets or paper to discourage coloring on a desk or tabletop. If your child expresses dissatisfaction with his drawings, participate in the process. Perhaps you can draw two circles and he can complete a snowman. Or you can draw the same two circles and your daughter can transform them into a cat.

Talk about shapes and colors. When a child is about three, introduce paints. Begin with the primary colors — red, blue, and yellow — and provide containers so that your child can mix her own shades. (Even professional artists find that the bottom half of an egg carton is ideal for this.) The first time that Stephen mixed red and yellow to achieve orange, he squealed with delight!

Whether your child's first shapes are mere scribbles or blotches of color, congratulate the efforts and try to find special places to display these early masterpieces. The refrigerator door is usually a perfect location, although the entrance hall is truly the place of honor.

Always remember that you are a parent, a care giver, not an art critic. Never tell a child "you can do better" or insist that she "remember to color in the lines." Young muscles find it difficult to control pencils and crayons so that end results don't always match either your or your child's imagination. Whatever the result, however, praise it. Even if you provide examples of circles, squares, or wavy lines, a very young child might find these impossible to imitate.

> *Kevin's mother confided her disappointment. She had provided art materials for her son even before the boy was a year old. She would fill empty roll-on deodorant containers with water color, and Kevin would dab or roll them on a sheet of paper. As Kevin grew, she provided other materials — paints, brushes, different kinds of paper — but, in his mother's eyes, Kevin's talents never seemed to improve. What she failed to realize was that Kevin was taking the first steps of an artist. He was familiarizing himself with an artist's tools. One day, when Kevin was nearly five, his astonished mother telephoned me. Kevin had just painted an amazingly detailed street scene with buildings, landscaping, and even a plane in the sky. Where, she asked, had he learned to mix such beautiful colors? Where had he learned perspective? "He was learning all the time," I told her. "You simply needed to give him the time and space to discover these things for himself." If I were to tell you that today Kevin is an award-winning artist, the story would sound too hokey to be true. But true it is.*

One of the best ways to encourage both creative and problem-solving skills is by asking questions. By asking questions, I don't mean that you should endlessly quiz your child. Instead, ask questions that allow your child to formulate his own views of the world. These questions include:

What would you like to do?
What did you think of (that game, that TV show, that person)?
What do you think we should do next?
What do you think we should do about that?
How did you feel about that?
Did you ever wonder about?

Of equal importance, respect your child's answers! Of course, not every response or suggestion makes sense. That's part of what childhood is all about. Allow your child to be creative and inventive, and don't always counter that her suggestions "just won't work." Unless these suggestions are downright dangerous, why not give them a try?

Problem-solving skills can be acquired and refined in many different circumstances: taking things apart and trying to put them back together, observing cause-and-effect relationships, or attempting to accomplish or understand the unknown. Provide as many of these opportunities as you can.

Teaching Personal Safety

Many times, parents ask me about teaching young children "the other things," and by this phrase they mean several different things. Parents comment that the world around us is not all sugar and spice, and they wonder whether they should introduce very young children to realities as sorrowful as crime or drug abuse.

As a former drug specialist and as chairperson of Dade Youth Drug Education, I recognize the need to educate even very young children about the dangers of drug abuse. I'm not saying that you should scare children, but yes, you should educate them. You may find it interesting to know that 80 percent of high-school drug users began using illegal drugs *before* they reached high school, and increasing numbers of children are using illegal drugs as early as *elementary school*.

When you give any medicine to your child, explain why your child is taking that medicine and add that a person only takes medicine if a doctor or parent says its okay. When your child sees you or another family member taking medications, explain this again.

If your child spots a person who is obviously under the influence and asks about him (or her), suggest to your child that this is a person who has abused drugs and alcohol and who now is very unhappy that he or she did. Don't become so heavy-handed that your child is afraid to take any medicine at all. Merely point out the difference between doing something properly and doing it improperly.

Most important, be a good role model for your child. Interviews with teenage drug abusers have found that 85 percent of them believed that their parents abused alcohol. Think about that for a moment!

The area of "street smarts" for young children is controversial. The problem is, if you wait until your child is older, you may miss a vital or lifesaving opportunity. Stephen was mugged when he was only twelve, and I was thankful that we had often discussed the fact that you never put up a struggle to save your belongings. We had always told our children to let things go; they can always be replaced.

Another controversial area is the "talking to strangers" dilemma. Occasionally, parents of children who have been the victims of crime suggest that they should never have encouraged their children to "always obey adults." Other parents, whose children have been lost or hurt and who never asked for help, rued the fact that they had taught their children "never to talk to strangers."

The answer, as in most areas of life, is moderation. Your child should know as much of the following information as possible: his or her first and last name, home telephone number, and a parent's work number. Once a child knows this, the home address can be added to the list. In addition, teach your child about 911 emergency service. Recently, a three-year-old child called 911 to report that his mother was choking. This young tot, trained since the age of two in emergency techniques, summoned the paramedics who saved his mother's life!

What about talking to strangers? The best solution is probably the truth. Most people are good, a few people aren't, but it's hard to tell the difference. That's why it's a good idea to talk to adults whom you know — parents, teachers, neighbors. If a child is lost, she should be able to tell this to a salesperson at a cash register. When you go shopping, point out these salespeople. While there's nothing wrong in telling a child to seek out a police officer if she's lost, there will likely not be a police officer present.

Teaching Your Child About YOU

Did you ever notice that the parents of many of the world's greatest athletes are themselves coaches of that sport? While they may not receive the same publicity, this fact repeats itself throughout the professions. Many of the top people in every field are following in and extending the footprints of their parents.

While there is no necessity that your child follow your career path, and while you should *never* pressure your child to do so, you should certainly recognize that because you are the premier role model in your child's life, everything about you is fascinating.

Be sure that your child understands the work that you do. If at all possible, let your child visit you at work occasionally. Talk candidly about your work, its high points and its low points. The things that you do and the people whom you meet are endlessly interesting to your child. Consider play-acting at home certain events at work. Not only will your child gain better understanding of your workday, but you may release a good bit of tension as well!

When children indicate that they wish to pursue the same career, treat this with moderate enthusiasm, indicating that all of us consider many careers throughout childhood. Never let your child believe that you can be "bought" by such a decision or that your love is conditioned on this choice.

Children tend to change their career ambitions many times throughout childhood, so avoid talking about the relative merit of careers. Don't rank careers on any kind of social scale, and never demean the careers of other adults, especially the parents of your child's friends.

Teaching Thinking Skills

Most behaviorists agree that the key to healthy behavior is healthy thought. Children who can think through their emotions and who can rationally consider ideas and alternatives are the most likely to manifest positive behavior. Children who are continually cranky and who frequently misbehave usually have no other outlet of self-expression.

All of the activities in this book encourage creative and articulate expression, but certain activities transcend subject matter and can best be illustrated under this general category. You can then apply them at any particular instance.

Guessing games, for example, are outstanding (and fun!) ways of concentrating thinking ability. When your child is about two and one-half or three, and if you are waiting in a restaurant for the food to come or waiting in a doctor's office, play guessing games. Give your child three or four clues from which he can deduce the answer:

1. I am on your face, I eat food, words come out of me.
2. I am a woman, I live in the house with you, I give you hugs and kisses.
3. I have four legs, I wag my tail, I bark a lot.

Well, you get the idea! Riddles also develop these same skills.

1. What is it that when it wants you to pick it up, it says "ring, ring, ring?"
2. What is it that when someone knocks, you open it to see who's there?
3. What makes the sound "woof-woof"? "meow-meow"?

Encourage sensory skills. Ask your child to look at you and to study everything that he sees about you. Then, ask him to turn around. Change one thing about yourself — remove a shoe or an earring or add a scarf. When he turns around, does your child know what is different? Or, while your child is turned around, ask him questions about you: "What color blouse are you wearing," "What are two of the colors in your skirt?"

Give your child two or three directions, such as sit up, sit down, then walk around in a circle. Gradually, increase the difficulty of the directions: walk into the kitchen, come back and open the window, play the scales on the piano. This is a good game to play with siblings. You can even play the game yourself, assuming that you "remember to forget" some of the directions so that your child can win the game.

Familiarize your child with the concepts of sameness and difference, left and right, and opposites. When you're out for a walk, point out examples of these concepts. You can even play games with them.

1. My hair is brown. What color is your hair?
2. My eyes are blue. What color are your eyes? What color are Daddy's eyes? Let's go look and see.
3. My coffee is hot. Is your milk hot or cold?
4. A car drives on the ground. What flies in the sky?
5. At the corner, if we turn right we will walk past the school. If we turn left, what will we walk past?

Cut out pictures from magazines that illustrate sameness and difference. Take four pictures, three of which match and one of which is different. Ask your child to find the one that does not match.

In the previous chapters, seriation, what's missing, and what's next were discussed. Draw patterns: three squares, two circles, three squares, two circles, three squares, one circle. What comes next?

Thinking games are not only fun in themselves, but they illustrate to a child the general orderliness of the universe. Once children understand this order, and understand that their environment is not one of random confusion, their self-confidence expands and their behavior and outlook mature. They are not only a delight to others, but, most important, to themselves. These children are bright, articulate, and self-reliant. And isn't that exactly what we've always hoped our children would become?

Teaching Ethical Conduct

Many parents are concerned that their children behave ethically and form good ethical values. This concern is often heightened because we see today that many people, including those from the highest social, financial, and professional categories, display ethical failings.

Of course, the very best way to instill moral or ethical values in a young child is by serving as a good role model. No amount of talk can overcome the actions that your child witnesses everyday. However, even if you do set a positive example, what other things can you do to ensure that your child forms the strongest framework of positive values?

While personal credos may differ from person to person, there are some constants that all of us as human beings share. Chief among these is the Golden Rule: Do unto others as you would have them do unto you. The first step in a child's understanding of the Golden Rule is an appreciation of what "others" truly means.

When you go for a walk with your child, point out the people whom you encounter. Talk about the activities in which they're engaged. Encourage your neighbors to talk to your child and to share their activities, their thoughts, and their occupations. From these meetings, your child can observe that you treat all people with courtesy and respect and that the views of all people should be heard. This tolerance usually extends to your child's relationships with friends and family.

Stephen never exchanged a gift. On one birthday he received three identical games. This was a game that was advertised on TV and was popular at the time. Stephen refused to exchange the gifts because his friends had picked them out. I tried to reason with Stephen that his friends would want him to pick out another gift, but he was adamant that he wanted his friends' choices. I confess that I was proud of him.

Compare and contrast your own environment with the circumstances of people in other parts of the world. Check out a library book on different holidays and discuss why these holidays are important to different people. You can even make or buy a calendar and mark the holidays of different people. Then, when the holiday occurs, take time during the day to remember it. Make a paper dragon or kite for Chinese New Year's. Make a paper ram's horn to blow for the Jewish Rosh Hashanah. Make a country book featuring one page for each country. On the country page, list holidays, famous people, products, and other facts. Cut out pictures from magazines to help illustrate these facts.

Children who study different cultures develop an understanding for other people that is reflected in their attitudes and personal conduct. From these early studies comes an appreciation for history and geography that your library can satisfy easily. Be sure that your child has his or her own library card and that your child checks out books him or herself.

Teaching About the Whole Wide World

Young children especially are marvelous "relaters," that is, they continually relate new experiences to previous ones. You can use this natural tendency to expand their horizons in many areas. You can guide a child's curiosity about other children and adults into an appreciation for foreign cultures, history, and biography.

In much the same way, you can expand children's interest in their own immediate environment into a lifelong interest in the world at large. In Chapter 8, you'll read about many of the places that you can visit with your child. Chief among these is taking a walk around the block. Suffice it to say that when you take a walk with your child, you can talk about many things — events of the day, or what you're planning for dinner, for example. But you can also transform this ten- or twenty-minute walk (or any other outing that you make) into an exciting geography or science investigation.

Talk about the immediate terrain. Does the land slope up or down? Do you live on a hill? Can you see mountains or plains from your home? Whatever the landscape, mention that around the world the land can look very different. When other people go for walks, they may see mountains, forests, lakes, rivers, oceans, or other features of the natural environment. When you return home, select one or two of these words, write them on cards, and look them up in your child's encyclopedia or dictionary.

Begin to talk about the states or countries where these natural features occur. For example, if your child is interested in mountains, talk about Colorado and Nevada, or Switzerland and Nepal, and locate these places on the globe. Perhaps you can even plan a summer vacation to the Rockies.

If you go to the beach, use specific words such as "Atlantic Ocean" or "Lake Michigan." When you find these spots on the map or globe, point out the other oceans of the world or major lakes of the United States.

Make a United States geography or world geography book. Include a page for each country or state in which your child has an interest, indicating its terrain, major bodies of water, the products produced in that area, and something about the lives of the people — what their homes look like, or what they eat or wear or like to do. Cut-out magazine pictures will help to illustrate these foreign places. (An accommodating travel agent can provide wonderful color pictures.) Take your time with projects like this book. You can add new pages for months and even years to come.

Never let anyone suggest that geography is not developmentally appropriate for a young child. Why does a three- or four- or five-year-old child want to know about Colorado or Tunisia? The answers are simple. First, your child lives on the same planet as the people of Colorado and Tunisia, and the more your child knows about the world, the more self-confident she can be about her own place in that world. Second, learning about Colorado and Tunisia is a great deal of fun, and your child's understanding that learning is fun may be the single greatest gift that you as a parent can give.

As with geography, a love for and understanding of science comes from an appreciation of the everyday environment. Because a love of science comes from a sense of wonder, you should be a good role model. Ask your child questions ("What do you think will happen if we . . .") and be sure that your child sees you asking yourself questions as well ("I wonder what will happen if I mix this type of vinegar with the olive oil? I wonder how the salad dressing will taste? I wonder what else I can add to make it spicier?").

There are lots of things to wonder about. If we carve toys out of bars of soap, will they float? Does a sponge float? What about a washcloth? What are balls made of? If Daddy cuts a baseball or golf ball in half, what do you think will be inside? Shall we try it and see? Let's remember to wear safety glasses.

There are many ways to introduce children to science, but one of the best involves animals. Even if you can't have a pet in your home, point out animals that you see in the neighborhood. Talk about breeds of dogs by name (you can get an inexpensive breed book at the pet shop). Ask your child about similarities and differences between breeds: St. Bernards and Huskies both have long coats; Great Danes and Boxers both have very short coats. Why do some breeds have such long coats? Your breed book or encyclopedia will give you the answer that most long-haired breeds originated in cold climates. You can locate these places on your world map or globe and add them to the geography book.

Make as many comparisons as you can. You can talk about baby animals (puppy, kitten, chick, lamb, colt); the feeding habits of different animals; or why some animals have long legs, others have short legs, and some, like snakes, have no legs at all.

Even insects can be a source of wonder for children. If you see a bee, explain that when the bee gathers nectar, which is the food that it eats, pollen from the flower adheres to its body. Then, when the bee goes to drink the nectar from another flower, some of the pollen drops off and falls on the tip of the flower, a spot called the pistil. This fertilizes the flowers, which allows new flowers to bud.

If you need help with this explanation, your encyclopedia, bookstore, or local library can assist you. What's important to recognize is the *pattern* that you are establishing for your child: Observation leads to wonder, wonder leads to research and reading, observation and research lead to understanding. This is a pattern that will be played out literally thousands of times throughout childhood with each experience building on the one preceding it. As a result, each time you take a walk or visit the park, your child will understand more of his environment and will feel more comfortable with it and with himself.

When a child begins to understand concepts of sameness and difference among plants and animals and when she understands that all life is merely the same or different, and not better or worse, then these concepts will inevitably lead to greater understanding of and respect for differences among people.

When you move from analyzing the anatomy of animals to that of people, you can suggest that differences among people are just that — differences — and that people are not better or worse simply because they are different. For example, when you pass a person with a handicap, you can suggest that a medical condition might be the cause. Later, the encyclopedia may help you to explain that the very short man whom you passed in the park has a condition called dwarfism, which may be caused by a disorder of the endocrine glands. The encyclopedia may have an anatomy chart so that you can point out where the endocrine glands are located. Later, you may talk about Pygmies, the shortest people on earth, and Zulus, who are among the tallest, and locate their homes on the map.

Science information contributes to your child's world view and, equally important, to the view of self, but don't forget that most scientific activities, apart from enhancing our knowledge, are just plain fun. Activities such as these provide an afternoon's excitement and loads of happy memories.

1

Blow up a balloon, hold it high, and let it go. As the air rushes out the back, the balloon travels forward. Explain that jet planes fly on the same principle.

2

Make a leaf scrapbook, and, with the help of a plant book, try to identify each specimen. Depending on the part of the country in which you live, why do the same leaves look different at different times of year? Collect four leaf specimens from each tree or shrub, one during each season.

3

If you don't or can't have a cat or dog, try goldfish or tropical fish. Talk about the anatomy of fish, how their gills extract oxygen from water, and the fact that they are cold-blooded, their inside temperature being the same as the temperature of the water. On the other hand, humans are warm-blooded; our temperature is not necessarily the same as the temperature of the air. If you have a fever thermometer and a room thermometer, you can illustrate this point. Perhaps you can overcome any queasiness you might have, because a small snake can also be a good pet.

> *Stephen had a pet snake, a boa named Julius Squeezer. I confess that until Julius came along, I never realized that a child could form such a loving attachment to a snake. At one point, Julius became ill and we took him to the veterinarian, but the vet explained that there was little he could do. He gave Julius medication but concluded that the snake would likely get better on his own. The snake did seem better for a time but then had something of a relapse. Stephen insisted that we return Julius to the vet, which we did, but the vet again explained that there was nothing that he could do to help the snake. Again, Julius recovered. Unfortunately, though, he became ill a third time. When Stephen once again wanted to take Julius to the vet, I reminded him that the vet could not help Julius, and I launched into that sad story, familiar to all parents, where we explain that sometimes pets don't get better and they have to go on to join the other animals in Heaven. A teary Stephen returned to his room, only to emerge moments later with a paper bag that held the entire contents of his now-smashed piggy bank. Tears running down his cheek, Stephen insisted that if I would not pay for Julius to go to the vet, he would. So Stephen and Julius and I and the bag of coins returned to the vet. The vet, who was touched by this scene, offered Julius his very best get-well medicine. It may only have been a vitamin, but Julius did recover. Not only did he recover, but he grew so large that eventually we donated him*

to a traveling zoo so that other children would have the opportunity to know such a fine snake.

4

Fill a glass jar two-thirds full of water, and mark the water level on the outside of the jar. Leave the jar on the kitchen window sill, and mark the new water level each day. Explain that the water didn't simply disappear; it was absorbed into the air by a process called evaporation. Can we see water evaporating, or being absorbed into the air? Certainly! Look at the steam from a teapot (but don't get too close!).

5

Put a few drops of red food coloring into a glass of water, and put in a celery stalk. Watch as the dye is absorbed into the celery. Talk about the human circulatory system and about the fact that blood flows through our bodies with much the same capillary action.

Foods provide many opportunities for science activities:

6

Make a seed box. Whenever you have a fruit with a seed, talk about the seed and put a sample of it in the seed box. From time to time, go through the seed box and see how many seeds your child can identify.

7

Whenever you can, plant a seed to see what kind of plant it produces. Beans are usually good for this if you plant them in a small pot and leave the pot on the window sill. As the bean plant develops, talk about the parts of the plant. Eventually, you may be able to transplant these seedlings in the garden or backyard.

8

When you're preparing food, compare the shapes, colors, and textures of different foods. Talk about the vitamins that foods contain and the different nutrients that we need to remain healthy. When you and your child are in the supermarket, continue these discussions. Point out, for example, that you buy corn-oil margarine because butter has too much cholesterol. You can even extend scientific discussions to nonfood items.

Talk about the chemicals in cleaners, for instance, and the safety precautions that you must take because of these chemicals.

For a child, science provides an explanation of the environment. Instead of always going to the toy store, plan visits to a hobby shop, a pet shop, a garden store, or a scientific-equipment store. Inexpensive items can greatly enhance the fun of science — thermometers, a magnifying glass, a world globe, or a map. Consider the many ways in which you can reinforce scientific knowledge through observation, discussion, reading, and visits to museums. Never think that educational toys somehow deprive children of "pure" fun. Recently, thousands of toys were donated to children across the United States. Each child was allowed to select his or her choice. The top-ten toys selected were all educational toys that enhanced math, reading, or science skills. Children know, perhaps better than we do, that learning truly is the purest form of fun.

Yes, you can teach anything to your child: tangible subjects such as reading, math, science or geography; and intangible virtues such as respect, tolerance, caring, and self-esteem. Best of all, your child's life will become a thank-you for your efforts.

CHAPTER EIGHT

Places To Go and People To Meet

Whenever I introduce the topic of places to visit with a child, parents attending my workshops invariably think that I am referring to places that one visits during extended summer vacations. Certainly, I'm no critic of taking even young children on trips. It would be wonderful if every child could visit oceans and mountains, national parks and forests, wild-animal preserves, painted deserts, the Badlands, great rivers, and tranquil lakes. Doesn't every child want to see Disneyland, the Statue of Liberty, or the Golden Gate Bridge? Of course, children and adults alike delight in vacations such as these. If you can manage it, then by all means do it, and, with proper preparation and a sense of pace, you can certainly take your children along.

But summer vacations are few and far between. And not all of us have the time, the financial resources, or even the stamina for these grand adventures. Most of the opportunities for travel that present themselves to us are simpler and closer to home. The key is to recognize the wide variety of exciting places to visit and people to meet that are in our own backyards and to prepare for these outings so that we maximize their pleasure and learning possibilities. Then, off we go!

One reason why I enjoy discussing places to go is that these excursions offer marvelous opportunities for dads to become more involved with their children. Despite the fact that all the activities described in this book are equally available to both mothers and fathers, the realization is that some dads leave the "inside" activities to their wives, while they shine in the great outdoors. Many dads are by nature goers and doers,

213

and these places to go provide not only adventuresome day trips, but are the stuff of lifelong memories.

Another benefit derived from visiting new places relates to single parents. If you're both mom and dad to your child, then you, perhaps more than others, may need opportunities to get out of the house before you become "unglued." When you just can't look at the four walls any longer, you'll have at your fingertips an exciting array of places to visit that actually reinforce one of the real pleasures of single parenthood: going wherever you want, whenever you want, in the company of your child, without having to answer to anyone else.

Three fundamentals ensure that these outings are pleasurable and memorable experiences while affording the maximum opportunity for learning. First, *preparation is a must.* You can think of the term "preparation" as a kind of insurance policy. Preparation ensures that you have considered the physical and mental requirements for the journey. If your child is very young (perhaps even a baby), more of your preparation will be physical. Ask yourself the following questions.

Is it suitable to bring a child this age to that place? Consider the weather, the temperature, the lighting, the noise, the accessibility to carriage or stroller, and other questions of suitability. Is this the kind of event where a baby or young child may annoy other people? Does the event require an interest or attention span beyond my child's present scope? In the case of very young children, planned events such as lengthy concerts and plays may not fit the bill. What may be less obvious is that even outdoor events may present obstacles if the weather is intemperate or the crowd noise too loud. In most cases with very young children, choose either private destinations or amateur events where more freedom and greater opportunity for spontaneous action are present, as opposed to group tours or professional events, where a child's major occupation is to sit and be quiet.

Once you decide that the destination itself is a good one, make a written list of the things that you'll have to bring along. Remember items such as diapers, changes of clothing, wetnaps, sunscreen, food, water, and toys. However, in your zest to remember everything for your child, don't neglect your own needs. If you're uncomfortable, you'll soon communicate that to your child. As you go on more outings, this list will become second nature. Best of all, as your child grows, these lists will become ever shorter.

However, another type of preparation, mental preparation, blossoms as a child grows. Mental preparation includes the discussions that you have with your child before you actually reach the destination. Such discussions may take place days or even weeks before the event. As your child grows, you'll include his or her desires in the decision-making process, but however you decide on a destination, once you do, you'll want to learn whatever you can about that place.

Will you be going to the beach? Check out a library book on the seashore and talk about shells and seabirds and coastal areas. Going to the ballpark? Discuss a book on the history of baseball or read *Casey at the Bat*. Don't forget to incorporate your own memories of these places. Talk about the time when you went to the beach as a child and first saw a jellyfish or chambered nautilus. Relive the excitement of your own childhood trips to the ballpark when you almost caught a fly ball in the ninth inning. Children love to hear these stories! We adults often hear the saying that "anticipation is the greatest form of enjoyment." That may or may not be true, but anticipation and preparation will ensure the enjoyment that follows.

After preparation, the next key to successful visits is to maintain a flexible attitude throughout the experience. Does it rain at the beach? Don't say that "our trip is ruined." Grab an ice-cream cone at the snack bar and discuss how weather is predicted and how, because of high winds swirling in the upper atmosphere, sometimes weather is not correctly predicted. Stop off at the library or bookstore on the way home and get a book on weather.

Talking is another key to a good visit. Pointing out what there is to see, making connections with other observations, and talking about thoughts and feelings all combine to make any outing a success. The examples below give you many suggestions on how to use sensory stimulation (seeing, hearing, touching, tasting and smelling) to enhance natural feelings of excitement and pleasure and to make every outing a wonderful learning adventure. The more senses that can be used in learning, the more impressions that will be imprinted on the brain.

The final key to successful outings, one that actually maximizes the pleasurable learning aspects of any visit, is to recall the visit time and again. Just as anticipation is a form of pleasure, so is memory. What did the child think of the visit? What did she like or not like? Was anything unexpected? Did you bring home any souvenirs to discuss and exhibit? Is there anything that you and your child wondered about? For example, what kind of bird was it that flew overhead as you were leaving? Why not check out a book on birds from the library and find out?

Reminiscences not only reinforce the pleasure of the place itself, as well as the pleasure of learning about the place, but they invariably progress to a new stage: Where shall we go next? Should we visit the park or beach up the coast and see if there are any different birds there? Should we return to this same park later in the year to see if the trees look any different? Shall we visit the aquarium and see how many kinds of fish live in the ocean just beyond the beach?

So you see that every visit has three components: preparation and the excitement of anticipation; the intellectual and sensory stimulation of the visit itself; and pleasurable recollections of the experience and plans for the next outing. That's a great return on a few hours' investment!

Here are ideas for wonderful places to visit that should be easily accessible wherever you live. I've included my own reminiscences so that you can better gauge whether such an outing is suitable for your child at his or her current stage of development. These examples are designed to introduce you to techniques that maximize the benefits received by children when they visit new places. Once you're familiar with the how-to of these expeditions, you'll likely think of dozens of other adventures to share with your child.

Amateur Athletic Events

Sporting events provide crowds, noise, and excitement. All of this seems great for adults, dads especially, but professional sporting events may be too rigorous for young children. Neighborhood games really are the best place to start. If your child is still in a stroller, for example, and you notice a sandlot baseball or football game, be sure to stop. Explain a little about the mechanics of the game, the rules and regulations of the game, and what the players are trying to do, and stress the words "fun" and "good sportsmanship." Repeat previous information and add new facts each time you return. As your child grows, try to find opportunities to use the phrase "good sportsmanship," and especially try to concentrate on instances where you, your spouse, and any other children practice good sportsmanship.

The importance of physical exercise can be explained the very first time that your child rolls a ball to you. All of us engage in sports so that we can feel PEEEHK (pleasure, excitement, enthusiasm, enjoyment, hugs, and kisses), not SPPPAN (stress, pressure, pushing, punishment, anxiety, and negativism).

If your park has benches or bleachers, round up as many family members as you can, grab a snack, and set out to watch a ball game. If your local park doesn't feature these games, call your city or county Parks Department and ask for the closest park that does. While pre-schoolers should participate in family sports, rather than organized team sports, they still love to watch older children or adults playing baseball, football, tennis, soccer, or any sport that's available.

Read your local sports section to learn if any professional, semiprofessional, college, or high-school teams practice near your home. These practices often are open to the public, and visitors are allowed to come and go as they please. When an athlete, especially an amateur athlete, sees a young child, he or she will often come over for a visit. Such an occasion can be the highlight of a child's year! Your child doesn't know the difference between Joe Namath and a sixteen-year-old high-school quarterback — they're both exciting, memorable, one-of-a kind people.

Speaking of he or she, try to find at least some sports events in which women participate. Whether your child is a boy or a girl, it's important to emphasize that sports are not an exclusively male domain. If you can't find women athletes at the ball park, try the tennis courts, the swimming pool, or the golf course.

Allow your child to continue the sports experience at home, even if this simply means tossing a foam-rubber ball around the house or apartment. In fact, these foam-rubber footballs and basketballs can provide excellent physical development indoors, especially in inclement weather or during the winter. If you're afraid of damage to your possessions, remove these fragile articles. Your child's development is more important than showing off that porcelain lamp.

Visits to sports locales often involve other benefits. We introduced Stephen to carpet golf when he was about three and received a toy golf game as a gift. My husband used to take the three older boys with him to play par 3 golf on a small course near our home, and, when Stephen was about four, his dad took him along as well. Stephen fell in love with golf.

I often went along on these outings (usually with a book in hand so that I could study for my doctoral exam) and I was delighted to see my husband explaining not only the rules of golf, but the makeup of the golf course as well. Stephen's dad explained the kinds of grasses on the course and how they were maintained. One day there were bees on the golf course, and later Stephen and I went to the library for a book on bees.

My husband also liked to pick up the fallen branches near the edge of the course, show Stephen the insects that had burrowed inside, and discuss with him the names of the insects, how they lived, and what they ate. One day, Stephen and his dad found a bird's nest with several tiny eggs. Stephen was so anxious to check on those eggs that my husband, who often worked ten or twelve hours a day at his law practice, would come home early once or twice a week to take Stephen back to the golf course to check on the eggs. We tried to make these outings family excursions, often stopping for dinner or ice cream after we had checked on the eggs.

One early evening, we checked on the nest and, as might have been predicted, the eggs were there no longer. Instead, baby birds had taken their place. Stephen peered at the broken shells and burst into tears. Somehow we had forgotten to mention, or his mind was not prepared to accept, that in order to have baby birds, you need to break a few eggs.

When your child is old enough to join a junior sports league, speak with the coach and learn his or her philosophy and goals. Is the focus on developing mental and motor skills, on cooperating, on having fun . . . or on winning? When I mention that word, "winning," I often hear a chorus of fathers asking what's wrong with winning. Beyond the obvious, that every sport involving a winner must, by definition, involve a loser, my response is that you must consider your child's own wishes and tendencies. Some children, especially those who are well-coordinated and ambitious, love competitive sports. For other children, undue emphasis on winning may be stressful or even boring. These children may prefer playing in their own backyards or in the park and may also prefer individual sports such as bicycling, skating, or the like.

If you're a single parent, be aware that sports events offer substantial opportunities for social involvement with other children and adults.

Sports and storytelling seem to go together. Use storytelling opportunities to stress morals, good judgment, and good sportsmanship. Illustrate the consequences of cheating. You can even make up stories: "Johnny was playing golf and he couldn't get the ball in the hole; nobody was watching him; should he pick up the ball and put it in the hole? Why not?" Your local librarian can also suggest books on the history of sports, on famous sports figures, and on good sportsmanship.

Once you and your child investigate opportunities to watch and participate in sports, visits to the sporting-goods store may become frequent. Let your child handle the equipment and clothing. Ask the clerk to explain equipment that's foreign to you. Find the sporting-books department and show your child that books make every human activity, even sports, more understandable and worthwhile. Finally, easy does it. Try to defeat the temptation to overload your child with equipment. The point of sports is to exercise minds and bodies, not just credit cards!

Pet Shops

The experience of a pet can be wonderful for a child. Dogs, cats, birds, and fish teach valuable lessons — responsibility, dedication, loyalty, and, of course, love and devotion. Pets also teach meaningful, if sometimes sad lessons about life and death. If you've never had a pet yourself, though, go easy. It's often difficult enough to find the time to take care of a home and child. Add a dog or cat to this list of responsibilities and you may become overwhelmed.

Is it possible to have a carefree pet? No, it's not. But tropical fish are among the easiest pets around, and they're ideal for children of all ages. When thinking of a "first pet" for a child, tropical fish can be a fine choice.

Advance planning for a trip to the pet store usually involves a few phone calls. Ask what kinds of pets will be available so that you can discuss them with your child. "Eric, we're going to a store that has lots of birds and fish. They have finches, which are very tiny birds, and parrots, which are large colorful birds. A lot of parrots even talk. Maybe the parrot will talk to you. This store also has lots of canaries that are bright yellow. Many canaries know how to sing." Keep talking as long as your child keeps listening.

Many parents object to the keeping of dogs and cats in cages at pet stores. If you would rather your child not see animals kept behind bars, look exclusively for tropical-fish or bird stores. If you'd like your child to see puppies and kittens in an unrestricted environment, contact dog and cat breeders listed in the Yellow Pages or in the classified section of the newspaper. Explain that you're "only looking" but that you'd like to observe your child's reaction to puppies or kittens.

In most cases, however, the tropical-fish store will be your best bet. Owners of these specialty shops are knowledgeable about their stock and enjoy showing off these beautiful and colorful sea creatures.

Consider allowing your child to bring home a goldfish in a bowl. If you do, be certain that your child listens to the shop owner's instructions regarding the care and feeding of the fish. Explain that taking care of the fish — feeding it and making sure that its home is clean — is a very important responsibility.

Some parents object to fish and other pets because they believe that the death of a pet will have an adverse emotional effect on a child. There's no denying that the sickness or death of a beloved pet can be traumatic for both children and adult. However, there's really no way to shelter a child from death. Sooner or later, every child is exposed to the death of a neighbor, a relative, or even a friend. Through the experience of a pet, children learn that even though we take care of others when they're sick, sometimes we simply can't make someone else well again. If you have particular religious beliefs, you can explain these to the child. Try your best to leave a child hopeful that he will meet his pet again some day, or, if you believe this to be confusing, at least leave the child with the impression that the pet is "safe," that is, free from harm or pain.

Occasionally, I have been asked about hiding the death of a pet from a child. In general, it's not a good idea. Children have a sixth sense about these things, and, in any case, they may hear the bad news from a friend or neighbor. One exception is if the death of the pet follows closely the death of someone else close to the child. Typically, children cannot bear repeated deaths very well, because they inevitably believe that their parents will be next. In such cases, child psychologists suggest that you do not tell the child that the pet has died, but explain that the pet "was wanted by its own family and had to return to the place where it was born."

The experience of living things can produce unexpected results in a child. Stephen loved to fish. Even as a very young child, he had a toy rod and reel and, when he was about four years old, we bought him an actual rod and reel, a little one that would at least hold a small fish. At first, of course, he wasn't much of a fisherman. His brother Michael would catch a fish, and then, as Stephen's dad diverted his attention for a moment, Michael would transfer the little fish to Stephen's line. Stephen would jump for joy: "I caught a fish! I really caught him!"

Sometimes we would hit a school of fish, and, after we transferred them to the bucket, Stephen loved to count them. If we managed to catch a bucket of good-size fish, we brought them home and pan fried them for dinner. Stephen, I remember, loved the taste of fresh fish best of all.

So I was really surprised by Stephen's reaction when, a few years later, we were on a fishing trip and had caught an entire pail of nice-size fish. Stephen peered into the pail and announced that we had better hurry home so that the fish wouldn't die. Stephen's dad asked him what difference that made, since they were going to be eaten anyway. "Oh no, we can't eat them," avowed Stephen. "We have to return them to the water; they're living things." And that's exactly what Stephen did — he released them all into a stream not far from our house.

After that, whenever we went fishing, the ritual was always the same. We had to gingerly remove the hooks from the mouths of the fish so that we wouldn't hurt them. Then, Stephen would put seaweed and some shrimp in the bucket so that the fish could happily survive their trip back to the stream. If we were too far from home, we stopped by the side of the road and returned the the fish to the water.

Of course, we still ate fish after that — store-bought fish, of course — but I confess that our enthusiasm for this dish was never the same again.

The Planetarium

Children's fascination with the heavens begins the first time that they turn their eyes skyward, supported by the sound of a parent's singing "Twinkle, Twinkle Little Star." Many large cities have planetariums and accompanying exhibits that encourage children not merely to learn about the universe but to assess their own place within that universe.

There is much speculation regarding the age when a child develops an understanding of space and of place. Because of this uncertainty, how can you tell if your child is ready for an outing to the planetarium? Look for responses to your suggestions. When you both go outdoors at night, does your child seem interested when you point to the stars and planets, or does she prefer to go back inside? Check out a picture book about the universe from the library. Does your child find the pictures and discussion interesting, or would he rather toss a ball? If you observe or sense any interest, then a trip to the planetarium can be exciting and memorable. Stephen's early visit to the planetarium inspired him at age five to write the song "Orion," the third-place winner in a song-writing contest. Its plaintive refrain ended, "Somewhere, up there, may be a little boy like me."

If you can't locate a planetarium in the telephone book, call a local college or university, or even the meteorologist (or weathercaster) at your local television station for advice.

Like all visits, a trip to the planetarium requires advance planning. Explain that a planetarium is a building that recreates the night sky indoors so that people can study it more closely. If your child has ever been to the movies, you can explain that a planetarium is like a movie of the night sky that is shown on the ceiling of a large room. Also explain that the room will be dark so that visitors can see the pictures of the night sky more clearly. Once prepared, your child is less likely to be frightened when the lights are switched off. Based on information from the astronomy book that you bought or checked out from the library, discuss the idea of stars and planets: some are larger and some smaller; some are closer, but most are very far away. If your child has a ball collection, illustrate these points with various balls. If not, make a simple diagram. As often as possible, refer to the planets by name: Mercury is closest to the Sun; Venus and Mars are closest to the Earth.

When you go to the planetarium, save enough time to see many of the exhibits. When you take a child to see exhibits at a museum or elsewhere, you may have to lift him up and hold him in order for him to see everything.

Whenever you visit a place that has a gift shop, try to make a few simple purchases. Many children enjoy a hat or T-shirt collection that brings back happy memories of exciting visits. In addition, try to purchase an item that will spur on future discussion. At the planetarium gift shop, such an item may be a wall chart of the solar system or a planetary mobile to hang from the ceiling. Books are always great purchases.

In the days after your visit, review your purchases. Hang up the chart or mobile, look through the books, or let your child wear his T-shirt to Grandma's house. A trip to the planetarium is rewarding because its benefits are so long-lasting. Every time your child looks upward into space, his eyes will shine with new understanding and intelligence.

Picnics at the Beach or Park

While visits to specific attractions such as a museum or planetarium are exciting, don't forget that "everyday" visits to the park, beach, or other outdoor playground are equally important.

You may be wondering whether you really need to read a description of *how* to take a child to the park or how to have a picnic. Probably not. However, because these visits are so frequent throughout childhood, you may learn a few ideas that will make these encounters more fun, more exciting, and more conducive to early learning.

The preparation for these visits can teach a child to listen to instructions, follow directions, and proceed in an orderly way. When you arrive at the destination, have your child help with at least a little of the unpacking. Certainly she wants to go feed the ducks or collect seashells, but the necessity of sharing group chores is an important lesson.

Try to learn something about the natural ecology of the places that you visit. By now you know that preparation includes checking out books or referring to the encyclopedia for information on the seashore, the park, the forests, or whatever area you're visiting. If your visits include a county, state, or federal area, check to see if guides or rangers are available to give tours or answer questions.

At the beach, discussions about sea creatures, shells, the ocean, and the tides are all natural. A shell collection is usually a favorite with children, so if you can't find a seashell on the beach, stop at a shell store and buy one. Most shell shops have fascinating exhibits; some even have small aquariums.

At the park, study the plants and animals. Why are there so many trees in the park but so few on the beach? Bring home a few leaf and rock samples. Observe the animals and discuss the importance of animals living in a natural environment. If your child saw birds in the pet shop, discuss why the wild birds are different. For example, if a caged bird gets loose, he may get lost, but a wild bird can fly thousands of miles and never get lost. Why is that? (If you checked out a book on birds from the library, you'll know the answer!) Why is it important that people preserve the animals' environment?

> *Greynolds Park, only fifteen minutes from our home, had a large bird-roosting area and a lake and shoreline well stocked with ducks. Stephen had been feeding bread to the ducks when one of them grabbed his finger. Was he ever mad! He was absolutely furious, shouting at the bird, "Duck not friendly!" He was so angry that he didn't want to feed the ducks anymore.*
>
> *We pointed out to Stephen a duck that was lame, and we explained to him that it would be very difficult for a lame duck to get enough food for itself. This story obviously touched a tender chord in Stephen, because he immediately relented and ran after the lame duck, trying to feed it. The duck, I'm afraid, was in no mood to be chased or fed, and it simply kept running away. Stephen now had a mission, however, and he intended to carry it out. We spent all morning chasing that duck so that Stephen could feed it. At last he succeeded, and I must say that he felt very proud of himself. It was worth the effort to allow Stephen to experience the fact that one gets good feelings by helping out others.*

Parks are also great locations for fantasy play. Simple paddle boats on the lake can provide opportunities for "ocean voyages to China or Japan" or "river rafting on the Colorado." A hill or fort can set the stage for cowboy or soldier games.

A good way to focus on all that's available at the beach or park, especially if several children are present, is with a treasure hunt. Each person gets a slip of paper on which one or more items are written — three leaves, two shells, one acorn, one twig, and so on. Each person gets one or more sheets of paper and returns when he has located those items. Be sure that you accompany any younger children or send along a responsible older child to supervise. When everyone returns, the items can be discussed and compared. For example, if two people found leaves, did they find the same kind of leaves? Why not? What kinds of trees did these leaves come from? Study all, the colors in the environment: not just green, for example, but the many shades of green.

When you're ready to leave the park or beach, place great emphasis on cleaning up. Talk about the beauty of the surroundings and the fact that all of us must preserve that beauty, both for other people as well as for the creatures that call that place home. You may want to save aluminum cans or glass bottles for recycling. Also, if your community recycles newspaper, you can explain that these efforts will protect trees like the ones that grow in the park.

Once you've returned home, you can continue both the physical and intellectual stimulation. Pretend that all of you are the animals that you've seen. Hop like a grasshopper, crawl like an insect, or flutter your arms like a seagull. Relive the beauty of the natural environment by finding stories and poems about the outdoors.

You can take a child to the same place or the same type of place many, many times. With your help, every return visit will be more meaningful. When you visit a new park or beach, compare that location with the first one that you visited. What's different about this new park? Also, if you visit the same park in a different season, discuss the changes. Why are the leaves red and orange? Why have the birds disappeared and where did they go?

You don't have to venture far from home for your child to see extraordinary new worlds.

A Jewelry Store

A mall can be a wonderful place to visit with a child. The sights, the sounds, and even the smells can be tantalizing. As with every other trip, you need to do a few special things to ensure that the visit will have educational value. If your child is in a stroller, or even if he's old enough to walk alongside, little will be gained if you simply whiz by every store.

With a little planning, a visit to a single store can leave your child with a storehouse of information and memories of a fascinating experience. At this point in a workshop, some clever parent immediately interjects, "I know what you're going to recommend — visiting a bookstore."

Clever, but not clever enough. No, the visit that I have in mind is to a jewelry store, showcase to items of incomparable dazzle, all designed to capture the imagination of a child.

Before you go the store, share your own jewelry items with your child. If you have a wedding band, you can discuss who gave you the ring, when you received it, what it is made from, and what the ring symbolizes. If your child is old enough to understand counts and measures, enlighten her to the fact that the purity of gold is measured in karats. Refined gold is twenty-four karats, but nearly all gold is mixed with other metals to make it stronger. Your wedding band may be eighteen-karat gold, meaning that it is three-fourths or 75 percent pure gold.

If you have an engagement ring, explain the kind of stone or stones that it contains. If you were able to locate a book on jewelry making or precious stones and metals, you may be able to locate on a globe or map the countries where these stones and metals are mined. Explain that most precious stones and metals come from inside the earth and are formed from different chemicals that changed over millions of years to form precious gems and metals. For example, if you have an outdoor barbecue and some charcoal briquettes, explain that the charcoal, over millions of years and with the help of intense heat and pressure, becomes a diamond like the one that you have on your finger. Allow your child to handle as many pieces of jewelry as possible.

If you can, schedule your visit for a time other than Saturday afternoon, the busiest time for all mall stores. In that way, you can have lengthy discussions without disturbing other customers, and you may be able to enlist more information from the sales staff.

Point out as many different types of jewelry as possible, and use their specific names: bracelet, necklace, pendant, brooch, anklet, cuff links, tie bar. In addition to the materials from which jewelry is made, you can also talk about its colors and shapes and the reasons why people wear jewelry. In addition to personal adornment ("we wear jewelry because we think that it makes us look prettier"), jewelry has also been used as a substitute for money, as a means of religious identification, to indicate what tribe a person belongs to, and for many other purposes.

If you see silver jewelry or silver tableware, point out that certain precious metals are used for items other than jewelry: for eating utensils, in manufacturing, and even in medicine and dentistry.

Try to see as many kinds of stones and metals as possible, if not on the first trip, then on subsequent trips. You may want to devote one trip to gold and silver; another to diamonds, emeralds, sapphires, and rubies; and a third trip to semiprecious stones such as onyx and lapis lazuli. Be sure to include a look at pearls, one of the few jewelry substances actually produced by an animal (I would like to believe that there is no ivory in your jewelry store).

Seeing costume jewelry can be an interesting experience as well. Most costume jewelry features either wood or plastic beads. It's fun to talk about their colors and shapes and then to locate items around the house, including a child's toys, that are made of the same materials.

Don't be surprised if your child wants to return again and again, because the lure of these items — their beauty as well as the exotic locations where they're mined — fires a child's imagination.

Even very young children can make jewelry at home from beads or uncooked pasta. When Stephen was about five, we bought him a jewelry-making kit, and he loved to make beautiful bracelets for his family and friends. Eventually, his interest in jewelry making blossomed to the point where he taught his fellow SOLVE members how to make ID jewelry that they could sell as a fundraising activity. SOLVE was a high-school club dedicated to good mental health. Its name is an acronym for seek, observe, learn, volunteer, and educate, and they raised money for a number of causes, from funeral expenses for the families of needy students to trips to Disney World. I was delighted when, because of his many activities and contributions, Stephen was presented with the mental health society's annual award by the eminent sociologist and author Ashley Montagu.

Did all of these good things occur because, from the age of about two and one-half, I took Stephen to jewelry stores? Very rarely does a single visit accomplish so much. But the enthusiasm that you bring to these outings combines with your child's own natural curiosity to offer new perspectives and opportunities.

Often during these jewelry-store visits, Stephen's dad would tell tales about miners panning for gold. Once, when we visited North Carolina, Stephen implored us to visit an abandoned mining site. We bought shovels and buckets and, like miners in the old West, gathered two pails of "gold ore" that we kept at home for years as a reminder of an exciting visit.

When you're open to new experiences and excited by the wonderful variety of life, even sad stories can have happy endings. When Stephen was attending NYU, he visited an arcade where he was mugged. The story of the twelve-year-old college student being attacked provided a field day for reporters. "No," Stephen offered, he wasn't frightened because the muggers "looked like professionals and probably didn't plan to kill me. But I am sorry that they took my high-school ring."

A jeweler who read about Stephen's loss offered to replace the ring and, when he learned of Stephen's interest in jewelry making, he took Stephen on a tour of his factory. He showed a delighted Stephen how the bricks of gold were turned into individual baubles and bangles.

So many potentially broadening experiences can begin with trips to the mall. Once you've covered the jewelry store, consider other shops — flower shops, gourmet food and cooking stores, music stores, art galleries or poster shops, high-tech or computer stores, gadget shops, magic stores, and yes, even bookstores.

The Farm

Children love to visit animals, especially large animals. While this may bring a zoo to mind, don't forget about farms, where the possibility exists to visit large animals "up close." Even if you can't locate an animal farm, there may be fruit, vegetable, or grain farms in your area. Any of these locations can introduce a child to the world of food and food production, and, since all children love to eat, they likewise enjoy knowing where food comes from and how it gets to market.

Even if you live in an urban area, a farm may be less than an hour's drive away. If you're unfamiliar with any of these locations, check the Yellow Pages listing under farms or dairies. Many milk producers have public tours of their dairy farm facilities. If none are listed, call your local zoo and ask for their assistance in locating a farm or petting-zoo exhibit. To locate a fruit or vegetable farm, ask your supermarket manager.

If you're thinking that you know the visiting routine by now, and that I'm going to suggest that you check out a book on dairies or farms, well . . . it wouldn't hurt. But you can actually start in a more elementary way. A few days before your visit, begin talking about food. If you're planning a visit to a dairy farm, talk about all the child's favorite foods that are made from milk: milk or chocolate milk, cheese, yogurt, ice cream, and butter. If you're visiting a nonanimal farm, talk about the kinds of foods that you will be seeing: fruits or vegetables, wheat, or corn. Point out as many foods as you can that are made from products that you'll see on the farm.

When you reach the farm, try to take your child through the entire food-making process, from seed planting through cultivation and harvesting, or from milking through pasteurization and even bottling, if that's available.

A short distance from our home was a farm with several large horses and a few cows. We began to visit there when Stephen was young, but still, Stephen's dad would encourage him to touch the horses and see how gentle they were. Jimmy would even hold Stephen and show him how to raise the horse's head by gently trailing his fingers toward the top of the horse's nose.

Stephen noticed the huge veins in the horses' necks, and his dad explained that the blood, which carries oxygen throughout the body, flows back to the heart through those veins.

The explanation must have sunk in, because Stephen next spied a cow and, staring at the cow's pendulous udders, loudly exclaimed, "Boy, does he have a lot of blood!"

Needless to say, an explanation of milking came next.

It's interesting for a child to realize that every food in the supermarket either comes from a farm or is made from ingredients grown on the farm. Thus, whenever your child accompanies you to the grocery store, you can discuss the kinds of ingredients that go into the foods eaten by the family.

If you're not already a label reader, become one. Label readers are good role models for children. When your child asks you what all the chemicals are, you may want to explain that certain chemicals help to keep foods fresh because a lot of time passes between the time that the food is made and the time that it's eaten. You can also point out that you try to buy foods containing very few chemicals — fresh or frozen vegetables, for example. Why not write to a food manufacturer and ask about those chemicals, then discuss the response that you receive. Talk about the relationship between good nutrition and good health. Children are much more inclined to good practices when they understand the reasons for doing so.

The Hardware Store

At the beginning of this chapter, I pointed to the fact that many of these visits are good excursions for children and dads. While the hardware store seems custom-made for that, remember that not only can moms lead excursions to the hardware store, but girls as wells as boys should be the recipients of these visits. Just as men and boys in our society need to know how to cook, women, as well as men, should learn how to change light bulbs, how to assemble a bicycle, and what to do when a fuse blows.

But what can you do if you really don't know anything at all about pliers and wrenches and nuts and bolts and braces and those million-and-one unidentifiable objects in the typical hardware store? What you can do and *should* do is ask questions.

Some parents shy away from early learning because they believe that they are not smart enough for the task. A father may bemoan the fact that he's not a college graduate; a mother with two college degrees regrets that she has no "practical" knowledge to impart to her child.

Many times, how you handle your *lack* of knowledge may be more important than the way in which you share what you *do* know. Nearly every day, each of us is confronted by the fact that we don't know something that we would like to know. We don't know why the company's net profits are down. We don't know why the garden hose leaks. We don't know how caterpillars become butterflies. We don't know when the first snow will fall. While we may not know, *we can find out.*

Finding things out, whether by reading a book or instruction manual, asking questions of a knowledgeable person, or simply taking apart a mechanism and trying to figure out what makes that thing tick, is the key to early learning. *If your child observes you trying to find things out — endeavoring to find out when, where, how, or why — you will be the best role model on earth.*

So tour the hardware store and point out, for example, all the different kinds and sizes of wrenches. If you don't know what they're used for, you can do one of two things: either look for the display of how-to books that explain the uses of various tools or ask a salesperson for assistance.

Those how-to books, incidentally, can provide easy craft or wood-working projects that you and your child will both enjoy. You can build a birdhouse, a dollhouse, or dozens of other items. If this still sounds too complicated, ask if any craft kits are available. These tend to be simple to assemble, even for beginners.

For children of all ages, the hardware store offers a wealth of objects that children can be asked to classify — items made of metal, objects made of wood, things that you use in the kitchen, and products that you use outdoors. You can easily play treasure hunt or other identification games that rely on categorizing or classifying different types of merchandise.

As your child grows, the hardware store becomes a wonderful site for teaching math concepts. Measurement comes first. Rulers and yardsticks, tape measures, and T-squares all teach inches and centimeters, yards and meters. Wrenches and drill bits are great for teaching fractions: one-eighth, one-fourth, three-eighths, one-half. Fuses help to teach addition. If you can't add up the voltages of appliances correctly, the fuse that you purchase may blow and you'll be left without electricity.

When you venture beyond simple mathematics and into geometry, the hardware store features many objects with interesting shapes, all of which must fit together precisely if you don't want your construction to fall down. Nuts must fit bolts and corners must be exactly 90 degrees. If washers don't fit pipes, then yes, the garden hose keeps leaking.

> *One of the great things about early learning is that you never know what the "end of the chapter" will be like. When Stephen was a junior in high school, he took an army recruitment test with the rest of the class. Many of the questions dealt with the uses of tools. Either the army wanted to test a certain kind of practical knowledge, or they needed a lot of tanks repaired that year.*
>
> *In any event, the answers to these tool questions, as well as other practical-knowledge answers, were second nature to Stephen, because there were very few "real-life" situations that he had not encountered or at least discussed.*
>
> *As a result, Stephen scored exceptionally well on the test. So well, in fact, that the army sent a senior officer — not merely the standard recruiter — to interview Stephen and try to persuade him to join the army after graduating from high school.*
>
> *The fateful day came and the officer arrived at Stephen's high school. He stood tall, a fruit salad of ribbons emblazoned on his uniformed chest, and announced in a deep voice, "I'm here from the army to see Mr. Stephen Baccus." All of his classmates watched at the door as a twelve-year-old Stephen approached the officer, extended his hand, and casually remarked, "Hello, Sir, I'm Stephen Baccus. It's a pleasure to meet you."*
>
> *The officer, who had expected a seventeen-year-old, nearly fainted.*

Where Else Can You Go?

You've learned from these examples not merely the kinds of places to visit with children, but also the way to visit them. These techniques of preparation and anticipation, exciting and stimulating experience, and memorable discussion afterward reinforce both the pleasurable as well as the educational aspects of everything from household excursions to summer vacations.

Of course, you can visit and revisit the same places many times. In fact, children feel comfortable revisiting a familiar locale. But some days simply seem to require a new adventure. When it's one of those days, where else can you go?

Many parents ask about museums. There seems to be something about museums that suggests that parents *must* take their children there. Yes, museums can be wonderful places if you consider a few practical matters. First, visiting most museums usually includes a lot of walking. If possible, bring a stroller. Another critical point is that too often parents undertake a grand tour all in one day. Not only is it not necessary to see everything, but it may be better to see only one or two things. You can always return later.

With young children, concentrate on focusing rather than stimulation. If you're at an art museum, for example, concentrate on one canvas. Hold the child in your arms. No child can investigate what he can't see. Talk about the colors and about the kinds of paint that were used. Stand back from the canvas and ask the child to identify how many people or animals or plants are in the painting. What is the main idea or theme of the painting? If the painting is nonrepresentational or abstract, you and your child can mimic the hand motions that he believes created the canvas. Be sure to mention the name of the artist and offer some facts about his or her life.

Whenever possible, visit small museums. Community or college museums may be better places to visit than large, famous museums. The smaller museums require less walking, and you're more likely to find a knowledgeable curator or guide who can answer your questions. If possible, stop at the museum shop and purchase a reproduction of the painting, even on a postcard, to take home. Your child can start an "art collection" in her room from these reproductions.

Other places to visit? Don't forget about zoos, factories, traveling mall exhibits, airports, newspaper offices, colleges and universities, plant and orchid nurseries, amusement parks, produce markets, hotels, circuses and rodeos, science fairs, concerts in the park, churches and synagogues, hospitals, junkyards, TV studios, military bases, cemeteries, inner-city neighborhoods, upscale neighborhoods, breweries, tailors and dressmakers, beauty salons and barber shops, nursing homes, ethnic street fairs, restaurants, police and fire stations, city halls, courthouses, bakeries, fashion shows, dams and power plants, parades, puppet and magic shows, lighthouses, swamps, meadows, oceans, mountains, lakes and rivers, caves, forests, deserts, gardens, famous houses, decaying houses, the place where you first met your spouse, bowling alleys, auctions, car showrooms, boat docks, campgrounds . . .

The possibilities are endless. With just a phone call or two, you can learn how your child can observe a trial, watch a couple being married, or, if hospital policy permits, even look at the newborn babies in the nursery of the hospital where she was born. These visits have practical benefits that were previously unsuspected. If your son needs a tonsillectomy, for example, he'll exhibit less fear about going to the hospital if he's been there before. A visit to a nursing home may help explain why a grandmother or great-granduncle can't come to visit anymore. The world, like a child's life, is filled with an endless parade of events — happy, sad, exciting, and gloomy, the emotions are limitless — and you'll give your child a great head start toward comprehending this natural variety when you enlarge the scope of his encounters.

A Walk Around the Block

Some days it may be impractical to go anywhere. The car may be in the shop or the weather may be threatening. How can you go on an adventure while staying close to home? That's easy. Take a walk around the block. Whether you live in an urban apartment, a suburban townhouse, or a rural cottage, you can still go on an adventure by walking around the block or, in the case of a true rural environment, by going on a nature walk.

If you walk around the block, try to focus on a category of objects. Ask how many different colors the houses are painted. What are the different types of roofs on the houses? Let's count how many kinds of flowers grow on this block. How many kinds of tall trees grow on our block? Are they all alike? Let's find some leaves and compare them.

If your child is a little older, you can expand your categories. For example, people ride in different forms of transportation. See how many the child can spot. Encourage your child to understand that people don't merely ride in cars; they also ride in or on motorcycles, scooters, vans, trucks, buses, skateboards, roller skates, carriages, bicycles, tricycles, and so on.

Whether strolling around the block or going on a rural nature walk, focus on the colors of the environment. A young child can be prompted for objects that are red or green, for example. An older child can be challenged to spot as many shades of green as possible.

You can also help a child to organize sensory knowledge in a more conceptual way. For example, try to classify the colors into "light" or "dark." That's not as easy as merely naming the colors. Later, at home, separate the laundry into "lights" and "darks" to reinforce the experience.

Every walk around the block is a new experience, either because your child is looking for something new or because certain things have actually changed. Noticing changes is a good memory builder. Are any cars new? Are a lot of the leaves a different color? Are there more dogs or cats than last time? Are there people whom we haven't seen before?

What About Those People?

One reason why we visit so many different places with children is to give them opportunities to meet many different people. It's not only that we want them to meet people engaged in a variety of occupations, we also want our children to draw certain conclusions about people in general.

To a great degree, the conclusions reached by your child will result from your own attitude toward people. Hopefully, what your child will learn is that every person does an important job and that all people are worthy of our respect. Many of the moral precepts that we teach children will later be reinforced or disavowed, depending on our child's observation of the ways in which we act toward others.

Working with high-school students for nearly thirty years, I learned that trying to impose a value system on a child, instead of allowing the child to develop a value system based on his own observations, typically backfires by the time that child reaches adolescence. Parents who tell their children to "do as I say, not as I do" are in for a rude awakening. A better motto might be that "actions speak louder than words," because it is by your actions and reactions to the people and situations that you encounter that a child's value system takes shape.

Once, when Stephen was about two and one-half, we had just left a restaurant and were counting our change. I saw that the cashier had given us a few cents more than she should have. I could have let the incident pass ("it's just a few pennies" might have been the obvious thought), but I wanted to teach Stephen a lesson. I emphatically recounted the change, declared that the cashier had given us too much, and concluded that we must return the money because it did not belong to us.

I gave Stephen the money to return. Stephen's brother Michael, then fifteen, picked Stephen up and returned to the cashier, Michael asked Stephen to hand the money to the cashier, which he did, explaining, "Too much change."

Luckily, the cashier made quite a fuss about Stephen's generous act. She praised him to the other customers and even gave him a lollipop.

Many times after that we referred to Stephen's doing the right thing by returning that money. We explained that had he not returned the money, the cashier would have had to put her own money into the register to make up the loss. We even made up hypothetical incidents, asking Stephen how he would react. We always encouraged one thought: Ask yourself how the other person would feel as a result of your actions.

Nearly every place that you go, except perhaps for an isolated nature walk, you will be meeting people as well as visiting locations. Talk about the jobs that people do and, whenever you can, ask that individual to explain his or her job to your child. Most people are enthusiastic to talk about themselves.

Whom should you ask? For starters, try doctors, nurses, salespeople, cooks, waitresses, cashiers, police officers, firefighters, attorneys, engineers, crossing guards, teachers, principals, zoo directors and animal keepers, athletes, vets, carpenters, architects, welders, farmers, musicians, golf pros, bankers, bakers, taxi drivers, truck drivers, pilots, actors, librarians, janitors, security guards, coaches, accountants, photographers, tailors, florists, gardeners, hairstylists, judges, lab technicians, office managers, optometrists, soldiers, secretaries, pharmacists, printers, priests, nuns, ministers, rabbis, computer programmers, reporters, dieticians, painters, lifeguards, forest rangers, social workers, politicians — the list goes on and on.

You can even begin with the parents of your child's friends. Ask them to explain what they do. Also, ask them to bring home materials from their office or factory that help to explain what they do on the job.

Try not to categorize people's jobs into any kind of good-bad or acceptable-unacceptable list. You can discuss the fact that some occupations require more education than others or even that some jobs pay more than others, but encourage respect for all people who contribute to society. Don't make sexist assessments about jobs. A great deal of research tells us that while parents tell their sons that they can become anything that they want, daughters are invariably told only that they will grow up to be "mommies." Women, mommies or not, can be firefighters and pilots, while men can be chefs and ballet dancers and daddies too. In fact, seek out people who transcend sexual, racial or age stereotypes, and point out that with the proper education and training, people can choose whatever occupation they'd like.

As a child grows, she may ask other questions, a typical one being why people work. While it's good to explain economic realities — that people work in order to pay for the things that they and their families need — you should also attempt to explain that what a person "is" is more than what a person "does." Human beings are more than their occupations, and children sense this. Therefore, it's important to confirm their intuitions.

After these visits, try to purchase a memento that will act as a reminder — a child-sized firefighter's helmet, a stethoscope, or artist's paints are good examples.

Many times, when children meet a person whom they really like, they become enraptured with that person's occupation. Never discourage these ambitions. It's not important that you want your son to be a pro quarterback. If he's four years old and wants to wear a fire hat and be a firefighter, then give him your unabashed enthusiasm. The career decisions made by young children tend to change week by week, but their most important function is to test your support for your child's decisions. Give that support without hesitation.

More Suggestions for Post-Visit Activities

In addition to supplying happy memories, visiting places and meeting people provide excellent opportunities for continuing, stimulating activities. You can adapt the following situations to any outing.

If you've managed to bring home pamphlets or brochures from your visit, then cut out the pictures and mount each on a piece of construction paper. If you didn't find any printed material at your destination, cut out magazine or newspaper pictures that illustrate the people or places that you saw. As you mount each picture, discuss what it is. Use this time to reinforce vocabulary words and fix memory impressions about the visit.

The next day, take out one or more of the pictures and play "Where Was I?" Tell something about the place that you visited and ask the child to "guess" where you were. Play "Who Am I?" Take out a "people picture" and mention some of the characteristics of that person. Ask the child to guess who that person is.

Once you've built up a collection of these picture posters from your visits, take out several posters that illustrate more than one place or person and ask the child to match the posters that go together. For example, the planets and stars match the planetarium, while the badge and the uniform match the police officer. You can also place four pictures together (three that match and one that doesn't) and ask your child to eliminate the place or person that doesn't match.

If you find a large, clear picture in a magazine or pamphlet, mount it on poster board and cut it into jigsaw pieces. The number of pieces depends on your child's development. Usually, three to five pieces are good. You may have to demonstrate several times how jigsaw puzzles are put together, but your child should pick up this ability quickly. If not, make a puzzle with fewer pieces.

Start a people and places scrapbook. If your child is very young, use a single page for each visit. You can put pictures of the person or place on that page together with one or two vocabulary words to remember.

As your child grows, divide the scrapbook into more refined categories. At first, simply divide one section for people and another for places. Later, you can divide people into more sophisticated categories, such as people who help make and serve our food (cooks, waitresses, bakers, fishermen, ice-cream vendors, farmers), people who help us when we don't feel well (doctors, nurses, pharmacists, ambulance drivers), people who transport other people or things (truck drivers, taxi drivers, bus drivers, boat captains, chauffeurs, pilots), people who fix things (electricians, plumbers, mechanics, carpenters), and so on.

You can have a scrapbook section for animals that you see in the zoo, in the park, in the pet shop, or on the farm. Each page can have a picture of the animal together with a facing page that lists interesting facts about that animal: where the animal lives, what type of home he has, what kind of food he eats, what the young are called. You can use a book about animals or the encyclopedia for assistance. Don't worry about overloading your child with facts. Some will be consciously remembered, some will be subconsciously stored for future reference, and a very few may be forgotten. Don't gauge your child's ability to absorb facts by your own. In almost every instance, learning is easier for your child than it is for you! Finally, remember that all these visits deserve plenty of PEEEHK and not one drop of SPPPAN!

Our lives are filled with the experiences of visiting places and meeting people. How well an adolescent or adult enjoys or even manages later encounters is largely the result of skills that have been mastered throughout an exciting and pleasurable childhood. So start planning and get going!

Selecting Preschools and Elementary Schools

W hether your child is six weeks old, or even six years old, the decision to entrust a child's care, guidance, and education to another person can be charged with emotional, intellectual, and even physical implications. A child's first day in school or in a child-care facility may produce a profound sense of loss that comes as a surprise to many parents, even those who have looked forward to a return to "freedom." For parents of early learners, there may be a sense that no one can teach your child as well as you do, and often this may be more than a sense. It may be an outright fact.

Yet, that day does come, either earlier because you prefer to return to work or must do so out of economic necessity, or later because your child has remained with you until the time when state law requires school attendance. The decision as to when that day should come for your child is one that no can else can make. You are the person best able to analyze your intellectual, social, and financial needs and to balance those needs with your child's readiness to function for part of the day in a nonparental environment.

As a rule, early learners tend to be socially better adjusted than their peers. Because of their early contacts with a variety of people in a number of locations, these children see new people and places as exciting and pleasurable rather than as threatening or fearsome. Early learners also tend to possess greater self-respect, self-esteem, and confidence; they innately sense that they will be able to cope with even unfamiliar situations.

Some parents question whether the strong bonds between early learners and their parents develop into apron strings that are then difficult
to break, even for a few hours each day. Happily, this is not the case.
Among early learners, the strength of the parent-child bond helps to
underwrite the trust that these children have in their parents. The
knowledge that a parent can always be counted on is vital to a child's
timely integration into a new and expanded learning environment.

Of course, these fortuitous results do not happen by magic, nor do
they occur in an instant. Trust, for example, must be carefully exercised
and tested. You simply cannot leave a child for the first time at a new
school or child-care facility and return eight or nine hours later assuming
that the child has spent the day enraptured in happy activity. No, a
child's successful acclimation to an outside learning environment results
from a course of progressive decisions that have been undertaken with
thought and care.

For example, selecting an early-childhood facility or preschool involves two types of endeavors: selecting the best facility and ensuring
your child's transition to this new environment. The following information suggests the questions that you should ask. The adequacy of the
answers received can best be determined by you.

Selecting an Early-Childhood Facility

How do you select a good preschool or child-care facility for an early
learner? While recommendations from other parents are a good place
to start, any thoughtful decision must be the result of personal observations. When you call a facility to make an appointment for a visit,
try to make a same-day appointment. If the school suggests that this
is not possible, try to find out why. Explain that when you visit you
would like to tour the school and discuss the educational philosophy
as well as the policies and procedures of the school with the director or
other person in charge. It is best to tour the facility during operating
hours so that you may see children participating in the same activities
as will your child.

When you tour the facility for the first time, it's best to go alone or
only with your spouse. Try not to take friends, relatives, or neighbors.
It's *your* judgment that counts, and you can compromise that judgment

if other people keep you on the defensive. If possible, leave your child at home. With a child along, all of your efforts will be geared not toward critical observation but to making your child happy. This tends to make you very nervous. You want the facility to make a good impression on your child, and, at the same time, you want your child to make a good impression on the director. The result is that the visit itself, in terms of observations that lead to decisions, may be a wipeout. Ask questions and note not merely the content of the answers, but the attitude with which they're given. Is the director pleased that you're asking so many questions, and is he or she endeavoring to answer them fully? Or is the director becoming increasingly short-tempered, suggesting that everyone except you knows the answer to such a basic question? When you speak candidly about your child, good points and bad points, does the director answer specifically, or is the response one of "I'm sure he'll fit in" generalities?

Most child-care facilities are broadly divided into two categories: custodial and developmental. A custodial facility merely attempts to keep your child safe, while a true developmental facility seeks to expand the intellectual, physical, social, and emotional growth of your child. How can you tell the difference? Ask specifically about early learning. What is the facility's position on early learning? If you hear a response vaguely suggesting that they believe that "play is a child's work," then early learning will likely take a back seat to random amusement. Of course, developmental facilities rely on play, too, but they use guided play in order to offer potential growth experiences.

Immediately after leaving a facility, make written notes about your tour. Was the facility licensed, and were you given the telephone number of the local HRS office so that you could check on that license? Were you impressed by the director and by the responses to your questions? Was the facility, including bathrooms and kitchen, clean and tidy? Did the children seem healthy and contented? Are there sufficient and appropriate play materials? How are discipline problems handled? What was the ratio of staff to children? Were all children supervised? Is the outdoor play area inviting, well kept, and safe? How are meals and snacks handled, and what foods are served? In what ways is the staff prepared to cope with emergencies?

Finally, how did the staff interact with the children? Is the teacher only an observer, a referee, or a disciplinarian? Does she play with the children? Does she question the children? Does she offer stimulation, focus, guidance, and challenge? Does she accentuate PEEEHK (pleasure, excitement, enjoyment, enthusiasm, and hugs, if not kisses) and eliminate SPPPAN (stress, pushing, pressure, punishment, anxiety, and negativism)? If you're satisfied with the answers to these questions, make a second appointment, explaining that you want to bring your child along specifically to meet the teacher. Your child's introduction to school or child care may have begun long before you began visiting centers or preschools. Perhaps both of you have toured schools or even colleges or universities before. Hopefully, your child understands the reasons why children (and even adults) attend schools of all kinds.

Be sure that your first visit with your child is a short one. It's best not to leave the child alone. Ask to speak to the teacher privately, that is, without the director present. Observe the teacher's reaction to your child. Does she seem genuinely enthusiastic about her position, and is she interested specifically in your child? Does she talk to your child as well as to you? Is she pleased to speak about her own background? Would a child naturally feel secure with her? Do you? When you talk about your own early-learning efforts, does she indicate if she will be able to continue them and how she plans to do so?

At the end of this visit, have a candid discussion with your child. What did he think about the facility and the teacher? Listen to his objections. Answer these objections or questions truthfully. Explain that everyone feels a little uncomfortable about going to a new place, especially if they'll be with people who are, at first, unfamiliar. Suggest that for the first few days you will only be away for a short period of time and that you will return *exactly* at the promised time. Build a wall of trust one brick at a time.

The first few days are critical. Lots of PEEEHK is an absolute necessity. This first school experience isn't merely something that's happening to your son or daughter, it's happening to you as well. Be sure that your child understands that his or her absence requires an important adjustment in your life too. Then, as you continue early-learning activities in the late afternoon or early evening, you will demonstrate to your child that the relationship that you share has been expanded, not replaced.

If you proceed honestly, confidently, and at an appropriate pace, leaving your child for progressively longer periods of time and returning exactly as promised, the strength of the parent-child bond will be matched by a new flexibility as well.

Selecting an Elementary School

Years ago, most kindergartens were independent schools. Today, most elementary or primary schools begin with kindergarten. As a result, for our purpose, when we discuss elementary schools, we'll assume that they begin with kindergarten.

Early-childhood experts agree that by the time your child enters elementary school, the most accelerated period of learning is actually coming to an end. That's why you've devoted your attention to early learning, in order to ensure that your child's most significant intellectual period was met with challenge and excitement rather than with disinterest and tedium. If the most critical period has passed, then does the choice of an elementary school really make any difference? Of course it does, because this school is the place where, year in and year out, children *live the investment* that their parents have made in them.

Many of my workshops and seminars end with a discussion of school selection, and the words that invariably come to mind are "private schools." The problems of many public school systems are so well known that private schools seem an instantly favorable alternative. Are private schools all that good? Some are. Some fortunate private schools have financial resources unheard of in the public school system. They may develop individualized learning programs better geared toward the specialized needs of particular students, especially early learners. Many private schools can afford to hire the best educators, purchase the best equipment, and offer the finest physical surroundings. Whether or not a particular private school *actually does* what it may be financially able to do is something that you must decide.

Again, personal visits are a must, and many of the questions are the same. What are the teachers' qualifications? What is the educational philosophy? Are there written policy guidelines that you can see? What specialized learning programs are available? Are bright students encouraged to skip grades, or are they given additional learning challenges while remaining in their own grade? Are computers available, and do these computers enhance teacher contact or replace it? What are the values of the school? What values does it wish to impart to students? Is the school socially or ethnically restrictive, and what effect will this have on your child's development? Are all of these questions met with enthusiasm or with indignation?

For many parents, good private schools are either not available locally or are not financially practicable. If that's the case, how can you maximize the effectiveness of your community's public schools?

First, whether you're searching out a private or a public school, allow yourself sufficient time to make an informed decision. A several-month search and evaluation period is best. In the case of public schools, call your county school board and ask for the name and phone number of the assistant superintendent in your school region. Make an appointment to meet with this individual, and, when you do, be candid about your early-learning efforts and about your expectations for the future.

Ask about the reputation of the elementary or primary school closest to your home. Ask to see test results from that school indicating where its students rank in relation to other elementary students in the county. What special programs are available at this school? Is gifted learning at least as important as remedial instruction?

If it's not, ask what other schools are available. Can your child go to a nearby school in another district? Many county school systems have magnet or pilot schools that feature innovative programs: accelerated or gifted learning; specialized educational philosophy; or special area emphasis, such as computers, science, art, or music. Other magnet schools may feature outstanding, even award-winning teachers and support personnel. So why don't all parents send their children to these schools? Usually, a tradeoff is involved. Today, most magnet or pilot schools are in underdeveloped or inner-city areas, a result of the school boards' attempts to reduce the failure and dropout rate of high-risk students.

Providing educational opportunities for gifted students, most of whom have been early learners, has become a national concern. Teaching techniques designed specifically for gifted children are now practiced in many schools throughout the United States and around the world.

In 1978, when I completed the research for my doctoral dissertation on the history of giftedness in children, I concluded that the best way to educate gifted children was to keep them *with their peers* five days a week. At that time, I shared my research with the coordinator of the gifted program in my home county, and he replied, "Interesting, but it will never happen here." Well, ten years later it has happened. Every school area in that county has the same five-day program for gifted children that I suggested.

If your school district doesn't have this type of program, then there are alternatives. Ask if your district has a program in which children spend part of the week in a gifted program and the remainder of the week at their home school. Another alternative is the traveling resource teacher who visits all area schools, offering expanded and challenging learning opportunities for gifted students.

Acceleration, or skipping a grade, is a controversial topic. All the research seems to point in one direction, while the public's fancy points in another. There seems to be great public concern that younger children cannot successfully interface with older students. This belief is so pervasive that I refused to allow Stephen to accelerate until my research demonstrated to me that he would suffer no emotional or social consequences as a result of skipping grades. Stephen's experiences fully support the bulk of research suggesting that *if a child wants to be accelerated and is socially and emotionally well adjusted*, the results are typically quite favorable. The challenge of and interest in school is maintained.

If you still decide against acceleration, or if your school district does not offer this option, consider enrichment programs. An enrichment program is any educational opportunity beyond the usual for a child's grade or age. Enrichment teachers, who may specialize in areas such as language arts, science, math, foreign languages, music, or art, typically make use of varied materials to encourage creative thinking and problem-solving strategies. Most enrichment programs are conducted in a group setting. Another option is independent study, in which a child is allowed to undertake special reading (usually in the library) or to work on a special project after completing the regular classwork.

A final option, and one that an increasing number of schools are happy to offer, is single-subject advancement. In this case, children remain with their regular class except during one period each day. For example, a first-grade student who is very proficient in math may go to a second-grade math class for the hour; another student who is especially interested in science may study with a second-, third-, or even fourth-grade science class.

Today, your desire to explore gifted programs for your child should be met with enthusiasm by the administrators of your school district. Gifted children are always a boon to any school, and in many school districts there is a genuine, ongoing effort to provide diversified programs for these talented students.

One of the best ways to learn about any school, public or private, is to ask the superintendent, director, or principal to which school it sends most of its graduates. In the case of an elementary school, to which junior high school or middle school do most of the children go? Once you've learned this information, contact the director or principal of the junior high school. Ask how students from that particular elementary school are faring in the junior high. Are they brighter than their peers, average, or below average? Does the elementary school seem to produce students who are interested in learning, or are there a disproportionate number of students with untreated learning disabilities or discipline problems? One of the best critics of any elementary school may be the junior-high principal who copes with the earlier school's graduates.

Analyze all available alternatives and recognize that you may have to compromise. If, for example, private schools are not an available option, consider a neighborhood public school teamed with a private after-school program or even a personal tutor for a subject in which your child is especially interested.

Since you've become a devoted, if only part-time, teacher yourself, you may even want to consider home-based learning. Today, more and more parents, especially those who have been involved in early learning, decide to educate their children themselves, either alone or in concert with a group of neighborhood parents. Most children in a home-based school are of elementary school age, and these children are evaluated by the school board each year to ascertain that their educational progress is on track. If you're interested in learning more about home-based teaching, your local school board will have information relating to the licensing of a home-based school.

Whatever decision you reach, remember that a child's success in school is largely the result of parental interest and involvement. As professional educators begin to replace your teaching efforts, step back but don't step away. Encourage your child to share the experiences of the school day, pleasures as well as problems, and don't merely ask if homework is complete. Ask about it, ask to see it, read it with interest, offer a few suggestions, and give a lot of praise. If there seems to be unnecessary drill work, speak to the teacher and ask if these assignments can be replaced with more appropriate and challenging work.

Remember when you first began to set the stones of the early-learning foundation? You wondered if your child could really absorb, retain, and use the information that you tried to impart. Now you know. As you see your child's structure grow ever taller, ever closer to the sun and sky, you see that early learning was, in fact, a birthright, a glimpse through the doorway at the beauty, the power, and the wonder of the world. It was you who opened the door, and now, as your child walks through that door with pride and confidence, I know that you will agree with me that no other investment will deliver so great a reward.

Questions That People Always Ask

Stephen Baccus

Throughout this book, you have been introduced to much of Stephen's life, although in admittedly disjointed fashion. The reason why I'd like to fill in a few gaps is not so much the result of motherly admiration, but because I want to leave you with the best possible picture of the ways in which early learning can contribute to the development of a multifaceted, completely integrated, whole and happy child.

The aspect of Stephen's soul of which I am most proud is not his academic achievement, even though this has garnered the most press coverage. No, I reserve my sturdiest pride for Stephen's voluntary willingness and enthusiasm to help others. While parents can encourage such conduct, each child must ultimately decide for himself what value he places on service to others. In Stephen, I'm happy to report, a sense of community involvement has always been forthcoming.

As with most children, many of these activities were school-sponsored, and Stephen not only washed the usual cars, but sold enough bagels and brownies and candy canes to keep the area dentists financially healthy. The most memorable events, however, have been those times when Stephen employed his love for performance — acting, singing, dancing, and playing an instrument — for the benefit of a worthy cause.

Stephen performed for the Hallandale Cultural Art Series and for the Promenade in the Park, a benefit for Fort Lauderdale artists. He visited nursing homes on tour with the British Ballet Company and also with the Generation Gap group. He planned, directed, and performed in shows for the Achiever's Club, a group of physically and emotionally handicapped citizens, and for the retarded clients of the Suniland Training Center. Ronald MacDonald House, the Special Olympics, the Children's Cardiac Association, and many other organizations that assist physically, emotionally, intellectually, and financially disabled persons were the recipients of Stephen's efforts.

Often, Stephen was willing to carry on with a one-man show when others cancelled at the last moment. He was the sole performer for the Salvation Army's Edison Center Christmas Show for needy families, for the Easter Seal show for handicapped persons, for the City of Hope, and for the combined United Cerebral Palsy Organization fundraising benefits.

Never one to let ethnic or religious differences stand in his way, Stephen performed for Black Awareness Week and for the Afro-American Kwaanza Festival as easily as he entertained at the St. Louis Catholic Church, the South Miami Methodist Church, and the Boca Raton Synagogue.

Charity and community performances, however, have not consumed all of Stephen's "free" time. On the contrary, Stephen, a dues-paying member of four performing unions, has appeared in five motion pictures; three TV specials; a TV series, numerous TV, radio, and print ads; countless university films; and more than a dozen major stage performances — everything from *Winnie the Pooh* and *Pinocchio* to *The King and I, Auntie Mame,* and *The Rothschilds.*

On occasion, even a rave review may have a startling impact on me. Put yourself in my place and imagine the confusion of emotions that you might feel if you read these words about your own child. The play in question is *Tomorrow the World.*

> *Stephen Baccus portrays Emil with sinister coldness and quiet boldness. As a Nazi of unflinching evil, his back is arched with ramrod precision, his movements calculated, . . . a believable product of his teachings and a frightening one.*

In addition to performing, Stephen, who has so often been the subject of press attention, has also tried his hand at the fourth estate. He has served as staff writer on publications as diverse as *Children's Express*, a syndicated column appearing in newspapers and magazines throughout the United States, and *RES IPSA LOQUITUR*, the newspaper of the University of Miami School of Law.

Stephen's global concerns were evidenced in his serving as announcer for the "Children of the World" event; as high-school organizer of International Youth Year, a group of projects sponsored by the United Nations; and as a major speaker at the PAVAC rally for nuclear disarmament.

Even today, he voluntarily serves as presiding judge at the Nova University Law School mock trials for second-year law students and undertakes other volunteer services for an early alma mater, Miami Carol City Senior High.

At this juncture, you may rightly ask if I pushed Stephen to accomplish all of these things. The answer is simple. Never, at any time, did I push Stephen to do *any* of these things. In every instance, his activities were the extension of his own interests. His desires and accomplishments are truly his own and should in no way be considered the product of a "pushy" or "stage mother." As Stephen's mind expanded, I merely opened doors and allowed him to peer beyond the threshold. Any decision to take the first step into a new world was always his own. In many instances, he opened the doors himself, venturing into areas that even I could hardly have imagined.

As with any young person, most of his time has been spent not so much in having "fun" (his own description of performance), but in academic pursuits. The awards have been many. Few children or adolescents have days named for them, as the mayors of Miami and Dade County, Florida, and the borough president of Manhattan did for Stephen, nor are they spoken of in the *Congressional Record* or invited to speak at an educational symposium held in the White House. Yet, like everyone else, Stephen has had to work with determination to achieve his goals and has confronted obstacles. Character, I believe, is more frequently revealed during these cloudy intervals.

Stephen entered New York University at age twelve and decided, by the time of his graduation at age fourteen, to pursue a legal education.

It has always been his ambition to combine into a single career his appreciation for the law, his love for entertainment, and his sophisticated background in computers. Law school was the first step. However, because the New York State Board of [Bar] Examiners would not allow a candidate under the age of twenty-one to take the Bar exam, and would not allow anyone of any age to take the Bar exam who began law school before the age of eighteen, Stephen decided to look outside the state of New York for a law-school education.

Stephen entered the University of Miami School of Law at the age of fourteen, the youngest law student in the country, and graduated at the age of sixteen. Even though he then took the Florida Bar exam and passed, the Florida Board of [Bar] Examiners had a minimum age requirement of eighteen for admission to the Bar.

While Stephen petitioned the board for an exception, he reasoned that he could not allow two years to pass if his request were refused, so he returned to NYU at age seventeen to pursue a master's degree in computer science. Midway through the master's program, the Florida Bar acceded to his petition. Stephen returned to Florida, was sworn in as an attorney, and returned to New York to complete the master's program.

Stephen then returned to Florida and, at age eighteen, opened a law firm in the Miami area. The refusal of the New York Bar to allow his admission was a sticking point, however, and Stephen felt compelled to challenge their preemptory decision. His suit in the New York state courts was not upheld. Therefore, Stephen filed a class-action suit in the federal courts alleging age discrimination on the part of the New York Board of Examiners and of the New York Court of Appeals, which had upheld the authority of the Board of [Bar] Examiners.

In a landmark decision, United States District Court Judge Gerald L. Goettel, reversed, in part, the decision of the lower court, stating that "the prospective Mozarts of the legal profession deserve better." Agreeing that the Bar examiners could still prohibit anyone under the age of twenty-one from taking the Bar exam in New York state, Judge Goettel ruled as unconstitutional that part of the law which prohibited Stephen, and any other law students who might one day be in his circumstance, from ever taking the Bar exam because they had entered law school before their eighteenth birthday. Stephen turned twenty-one on February 25, 1990, and took the New York and Massachusetts Bar examinations in April 1991. He passed both.

One hot August day, when Stephen was eleven or twelve, he wanted to swim in the pool and attempted to recruit a few neighborhood children to join him. None was available. A few had already gone to the beach, one had a cold, and another had gone to the library. Stephen returned home so downhearted that I volunteered to go swimming with him. Stephen hugged me tightly and called me "the best." I told my husband that I would always remember that day, because so very soon he would no longer want to spend his time with me.

As I complete these brief biographical notes, I consider the man that my son has become. An admired attorney, entertainer, computer whiz — that's good. A respected and caring member of the community — that's better. A happy and healthy human being continuing on life's journey with intelligence, dedication, and good cheer — that's the best!

Stephen has been the subject of hundreds of TV, radio, and print interviews reported throughout the world. Everyone from the son of the President of the United States to an entire news-production team from Australian television has been in our living room. Following are some of the most typical questions that Stephen has been asked:

From the *Good Morning New York* TV show:
    Comm[entator]: Stephen, how do you see yourself?
    Stephen: Basically I'm just an average boy who likes to do whatever other kids like to do, but I learn a little faster.
    Comm: How come you're in college at age twelve?
    Stephen: I exhausted all the high-school courses except calculus, which I'm taking now, so there was no reason to stay another year.
    Comm: Were you ever pressured to achieve?
    Stephen: No, I just wanted to learn things. But I don't care to sit in classes where I know the material.
    Comm: Do you feel that you are happy?
    Stephen: Yes, I'm definitely happy with the life I have now.

From *That's Incredible*:
    Comm: In the last few days we saw you fly a plane, perform in a show, attend college, and catch and throw a football with great accuracy. How do people react to you?
    Stephen: OK, at first they may be in awe of me, but that quickly

disappears as they get to know me.

Comm: How do you account for that?

Stephen: Well, I act just like everyone else does who is my age. I may be a little more mature, but my friends don't act as if I am.

From *Channel 1 News (Italy):*

Comm: When did you notice that you were ahead of other children your age?

Stephen: No particular time. I guess little by little I found out I could do things academically a little better than the other students in my classes, starting from nursery school, which I started at two and one-half.

Comm: How did that make you feel? Superior?

Stephen: Not at all. I just learn faster and maybe remember more.

From the TV show *Kids Beat:*

Comm: How come you're graduating high school this year and you're only eleven?

Stephen: I will be twelve when I graduate, but I was to enter kindergarten when I was five. I skipped that and was put in first grade; then I skipped fifth, sixth, seventh and eighth grades and I am going to college on early admission.

President Reagan's son, Ron Reagan, flew to Miami to interview Stephen for *Parade Magazine:*

Ron: What about acceleration in school?

Stephen: School has never been terribly challenging. Learning faster helps a lot. To fend off boredom, I got involved in a lot of extracurricular activities, joining clubs and getting involved in projects.

Ron: Do you feel any special responsibility to society?

Stephen: Not a special burden beyond the notion that everyone has the responsibility to do what he can for society.

Ron: Would you like to run for the Presidency one day?

Stephen: OK, that might be fun.

Ron: Do you like to be compared to the great geniuses?

Stephen: No, that's an embarrassment.

On another day, the questioner was (now former) Mayor Koch of New York:

Mayor Koch: Do you think you might be interested in going into politics?

Stephen: It might be interesting. Yes, I think I would like that.

Mayor Koch: If you do, I know that you will participate vigorously, and that's what it takes to succeed.

From NBC's *The Today Show:*

Jane Pauley: Stephen, have you ever not passed a test?

Stephen: Yes, I didn't know there was to be a math test because I was absent. [I] did not study for it and I failed.

Jane: How does a boy of seventeen get a fourteen-page resume?

Stephen: Oh, that's because I am also in show business, and it contains both my performance and academic careers.

Jane: What do you want to be, an actor, lawyer, or computer scientist?

Stephen: I would like to be all three.

Jane: I see in the papers that you don't have a stunted social life. Tell me about your actress girlfriend, Danielle Brisebois.

Stephen: We met when I did a show with her and have been friends ever since.

Jane: Stephen, when do you sleep?

Stephen: During law school. It was hard, but I managed.

Appearing on *The David Letterman Show,* the host offered Stephen the chance to do a comedy routine:

DL: Besides college courses, [I know that] you're interested in acting. How about a sample? You don't want to miss this chance to try out your act on national TV. Stephen decided to have a go at comedy: You know, I'm from Miami, but I do like New York, except for one thing. It's our apartment. It has five rooms. It has two closets, a bathroom, a living room, and a mailbox. We live in the mailbox. It's the one with the window.

New York has many bargains, and my mother buys anything that's marked down. Yesterday she brought home an escalator.

From *Time and Place,* an English TV show:

Comm: Did you have any time to play when you were growing up, or did you study all the time?

Stephen: I remember playing all the time. I believe that my parents taught me as I was playing.

Comm: What memories do you have of your childhood?
Stephen: I remember it as one of having fun, going places, playing with my parents, my brothers and sister, and my friends.
Comm: What methods did your parents use in teaching you?
Stephen: Because everyone asks, I believe that my mother is writing a book about that. I think that they pointed things out to me and explained things to me and took me to a lot of different places that I enjoyed going to and actively pointed out things to me.

Some interviewers don't even listen to their guests. The following is an example of a dull show with a disinterested host. Stephen tried, to no avail, to liven things up a bit:
Comm: How did you get so far in school at such a young age?
Stephen: I cheated.
Comm: Oh yes, some children do that. You have done so much; when do you sleep?
Stephen: In the winter.
Comm: Yes, that's a good time.

No one takes a back seat to Johnny Carson, and Stephen enjoyed his visit to *The Tonight Show:*
Johnny Carson: I hear you are taking the bar this weekend. Are they very difficult?
Stephen: I believe they can be.
Johnny Carson: Let's get back to the beginning. I heard you took algebra in the second grade.
Stephen: Between the second and third grades. I went to a nearby high school and took algebra in the summer. But when I went back to third grade, I had to do third-grade math because the teacher said that I didn't make my twos correctly.
Johnny Carson: When you were in high school — kids can be cruel — did you get any kidding?
Stephen: Yes, but only in fun. Occasionally I would hear, "He's really twenty-five but smoking stunted his growth." Once, a big, tall football player picked me up and ran down the hall with me under his arm, yelling, "I want your brain! I want your brain!"
Johnny Carson: That's funny.
Stephen: I wasn't scared until he started to punt!

Johnny Carson: Did you go to the senior prom?

Stephen: Yes. Someone once told my mother that she would not let her son skip grades because he would miss out on his prom, so my mother suggested that I go to my prom. I took a friend. She was eleven, I was twelve, and she was a head taller than me. It was fun.

Johnny Carson: I hear you're IQ is 190.

Stephen: Oh, that's been said, but above 155 it's not really accurate.

Johnny Carson: I know someone who has an IQ of 190: the band.

Johnny Carson: What kind of law are you interested in?

Stephen: Computer law. It's a new field and I would be interested in handling cases in that field and in entertainment law.

On Johnny's show, Johnny, of course, has the last word.

Johnny Carson: Ever think of divorce law? I can put you on a retainer.

From a news telecast at a peace rally in Central Park. A thirteen-year-old Stephen was interviewed by Joseph Papp, best known as the producer of Shakespeare in the Park:

Joseph Papp: We are here today to listen to the kids.

Stephen: I'm here as one of the representatives of today's youth. I would like to suggest a worldwide nonpolitical organization whereby other nations would travel to our country and vice versa . . . mobilize senior citizens to help . . . against war and violence in any form . . . . start in elementary school.

As in many interviews, Stephen was asked on *The Larry King Show* if he had ever failed a test. Stephen mentioned that old math test he had failed after an absence from school and then continued:

Stephen: I tried a chemistry CLEP test. That's where you take a test to see if you can get credit for a university course without taking the course, and I didn't make it.

Larry King: Were you depressed?

Stephen: No, I'm not afraid of failure. If I can't do something, I try a little harder.

On *The Dick Cavett Show*, Dick asked Stephen about criminal law:

Dick Cavett: After hearing the three most famous criminal lawyers today, do you think that you would like to go into criminal law?

Stephen: Not really. I think, and my father said also, that the people you deal with tend not to be the best people.

As a postscript, let me add that Stephen's first case, when he opened his law firm, was a criminal case.

The interview on *CBS News* asked two familiar questions:

Comm: Do any of the students resent you because you learn so quickly?

Stephen: No, I don't think so. I do have to study like the rest of the students, but I believe that I catch on more quickly and remember more.

Comm: Do you have a photographic memory?

Stephen: No, I wish I did. It would make things easier.

By the time Stephen appeared on *The Gary Collins Show*, he was awaiting the results of the Bar exam and Gary asked:

Gary Collins: When did you decide you wanted to be a lawyer?

Stephen: I really don't remember, but I think it was in the last year of college. A law degree is always good to have no matter what field you go into.

A ten-year old Stephen was interviewed on the local *PM Magazine*:

Comm: I heard that your mother thought you were playing with sand the other day. Do you want to tell us about that?

Stephen: Oh yes, it was really gunpowder. I was mixing this to launch a rocket.

And, as always, that most-asked question:

Comm: Do you feel that you're missing out on anything?

Stephen: No, I love what I'm doing. I love acting, performing, dancing, my classes in high school. I'm very happy.

These same thoughts were expressed in an interview two years later on the national edition of *PM Magazine*:

Comm: What is life like for you at the university? How are you treated?

Stephen: I believe that I'm treated just like any other university student, only shorter.

Comm: Do you feel that pressured to work very hard?

Stephen: No, I just go at my own pace.
Comm: Do you feel that you missed out on your childhood?
Stephen: If I did, I don't know what I missed.

Many interviewers ask about Stephen's love for performance:
Comm: Which do you like better, performing on stage or in movies?
Stephen: They are both fun, but I think that I prefer the stage because you see the reactions from people. You can see the smiles on their faces, or when I entertain for the elderly, you can see them moving to the music.
Comm: Do you join in any physical activities or hobbies?
Stephen: I play football, baseball, basketball and, with my brothers and Dad, I play golf. I guess you could say that my hobbies were magic and computer games.

On *Mother's Day*, Joan Lunden asked if Stephen would recommend his life of achievement for other students:
Stephen: It would depend on the student. For me, it was the best thing to do.

One *ABC News* commentator asked how Stephen's "fan club" first started:
Stephen: The kids in my neighborhood started it. The president is the girl next door. Then my high school joined in. Then, when I went to NYU, an article was published that mentioned the club and its address. I received mail from everywhere.
Comm: How did that make you feel?
Stephen: I feel very flattered.
Comm: Are they all from school children?
Stephen: I would say about 80 percent are from young females, but about 15 percent are from young males and some are from parents.
Comm: What do they write about?
Stephen: Parents ask for suggestions about their children. Students ask how to get along with their parents. Some write about individual problems. And some are just what I guess you would call love letters.
Comm: Any proposals of marriage?
Stephen: Oh, yes!

As a mother, I have always been heartened by the love and respect for one another that Stephen and his siblings share. Witness this response from the Boston TV show *People Are Talking*:

Comm: How did you get to law school every day? You live in Miami; the school is in Coral Gables.

Stephen: My older brother, Clifford, drove me. He worked two blocks away from home, but he would get up an hour and a half earlier, drive me to school about forty to forty-five minutes away, drive back, and then go to work. My parents would pick me up. Or sometimes Clifford would, if I stayed late at night studying at the library which is open until three a.m.

A great moment was Stephen's appearance on NBC's *Main Street*. The other guest was Warren Burger, retired Chief Justice of the United States Supreme Court. Host Bryant Gumbel asked Stephen about his difficulties attempting to take the New York State Bar exam:

Bryant Gumbel: I hear that you're having some problems with being permitted to take the [New York] bar exam. Do you believe that's against your constitutional rights?

Stephen: Yes. The law states that I can never practice law in New York because I had to be eighteeen when I started law school.

Bryant Gumbel: What are you going to do about that?

Stephen: I'm suing the New York State Board of Examiners.

Finally, Stephen was interviewed by *FUJI Japanese TV Network* in New York City, which sent a crew to Miami for Stephen's law-school graduation. The footage was televised throughout Japan as an inspiration to Japanese youth.

Comm: What is your dream?

Stephen: To do the things I like to do.

Dr. Florence Baccus

Many of the questions that I'm asked focus on the popular misconception that bright children are somehow unhappy or are shunned by their peers. And I'm sorry to admit that many professionals are to blame for these erroneous beliefs. Some of these individuals, however, are willing to admit that they've been wrong.

For example, Stephen appeared on a TV interview show with a well-known psychiatrist. The interviewer stated that he had heard that very bright children typically had problems with school, with their parents, and with their friends. The psychiatrist agreed that this was "absolutely true."

Later, a twelve-year-old Stephen appeared with me on the show, and we candidly answered the interviewer's questions and offered our opinions on the subject of early learning. Toward the end of the show, the host asked the psychiatrist to return. The gentleman walked back on stage, threw out his hands to the audience, and admitted, "Well, I was wrong. This boy is a delight. I guess I've been seeing the wrong kids! Psychiatrists do have clients who have problems. I have to rethink my beliefs."

Turning people into believers about early learning takes up most of my professional life, and these questions about social adjustment, or others that focus on discipline or parental pushiness, are among the most popular, as you'll see below. Many times a parent asks the most thoughtful questions:

Parent: Why did you allow Stephen to win almost all the games that you played with him?

Dr. Baccus: Because the games that I played were mostly learning games, and I wanted him to have a good feeling about playing the games. Self-esteem is most important. Children have to have a good feeling about what they are doing or they don't want to do it. That doesn't mean there were no struggles to win. Many times it was hard work, just as it is hard work for a baby to learn to walk or to pick up a raisin from a dish or to build a tower with blocks. But soon I couldn't beat him no matter how hard I tried!

Parent: But when he played with other children, what happened then?

Dr. Baccus: At first there were no competitive games. Then he usually did win, but remember that he said he did fail at some things and he would just try harder. Also remember that he had a good role model on how to be a good loser — me! Of course, acting is a profession where you learn to lose gracefully or you quickly get out of it. Many times Stephen was promised a role, but something would happen — a contributor to the production had a nephew who wanted the part, or the movie was never made. Jerry Lewis hired Stephen for another movie that he was going to make after *Hardly Working*, but it was never produced. So life is full of failing situations.

Another parent asked that familiar question about pushiness. You will note that sometimes it's the child, not the parent, who does the pushing:

Parent: How do you know when your child is doing too much? My eight-year-old seems to want to do too much. She wants to join every club and take every after-school activity. I'm exhausted just taking her places.

Dr. Baccus: I know that those are hard decisions to make, but you have to look at your daughter and see both her mental and physical condition. Does she seem to be fine physically? Is she eating and sleeping as usual? Is she tired during the day? Is her school work the same as always, and are her grades and conduct in school and at home the same? If everything seems to be OK, except you, then perhaps you can car pool or make arrangements with a neighbor to take her. Also, if just plain common sense — your mother's instinct, the best instinct in the world — tells you that it's too much, then listen to your instincts and tell your daughter to save an activity for a later date.

Parent: What can I do to punish my child? She really needs it, and I'm tired of spanking her because it happens every day.

Dr. Baccus: I really don't believe in spanking, except when everything else does not work. But that usually does not happen. If your child is misbehaving as often as you say, I would try to *anticipate* what she is going to do in certain situations and avoid or change what is about to happen before it does. Ask yourself some questions. Why is she misbehaving? Does she have a strong will that can be channeled? Can you establish some rules with your child that cover the really big things: (1) You do not hurt other people; (2) You do not hurt property; (3) You are not rude or fresh. Then the child must know that for breaking these rules there will be punishment. The punishment need not be spanking. It can be removing the child from the scene, by putting her into another room or place where she will be alone for a while. Or it could be withdrawing privileges. A misbehaving child does not feel good about herself. If you start your child in a planned early-learning program, where she consistently meets success, she will feel good about herself.

Parent: Didn't Stephen ever misbehave?

Dr. Baccus: It depends on who the observer is. If you observed him at night, when he didn't want to go to sleep, you might say that he was misbehaving. My experience with my other children taught me that this, too, will pass, so I didn't make a big issue of it. I placed an extra cup of water on a high table that he could reach, put toys in his bed, did not turn out the light, and let him fall asleep when he wanted to. He was out of excuses or reasons to call me. When it was time for him to dress himself, he could, but at times he took so long, dawdling over something. I would go into his room and take a minute to dress him without a word. I never said things like "you are the slowest thing on earth" or "I don't have all day for you" — things that I had said to the other children. I knew that this, too, would pass, so why make an issue of it.

Parent: What is your opinion of Saturday morning TV? My child watches hours of cartoons, but at least I'm able to get the housework done.

Dr. Baccus: My own preferences are for *Sesame Street* and nature shows. Certain science shows or biographies of interesting people are also good. Avoid programs that don't challenge a child or encourage his imagination but that merely glorify inane action or violence.

Watch TV shows with your child as often as you can. As for the housework, try to enlist the services of a housekeeper, a home-cleaning service, or even a neighbor's child who's looking for a little extra spending money. If these suggestions aren't practical, then let the housework take second place.

Parent: I work full-time and I'm tired when I get home. Plus, I can't afford any housekeeper. How did you fit early learning into your schedule?

Dr. Baccus: Before Stephen was born, when I came home to three children under the age of six, I was tired and worn out, too. We had a full-time housekeeper, but despite that, and especially on the weekends when she wasn't there, the exhaustion and the yelling were nonstop. By the time I had Stephen, I was more than ten years older. I continued to work full-time, and by then we had no housekeeper at all. I still came home exhausted, but I always had time for Stephen. Where did I find the time? I made the time. There are two secrets about time. You have to optimize, and you have to prioritize. If I was really tired when I came home, I took Stephen into bed with me and read to him or we watched TV together. Later, when I was rested, we engaged in more physically demanding activities. *Most important of all, I turned typical daily activities — preparing dinner, doing the laundry, shopping at the supermarket — into learning experiences.*

Parent: I have heard of children who went to college early and who had problems there. What did you do to ensure that Stephen did not have any of those problems?

Dr. Baccus: The students who have had problems were students whose parents sent them away to college. I am against that! Stephen did go away to college, but I went with him. I took an extended leave, and Stephen and I lived in an apartment. He then joined activities with children his own age — a children's singing group, an acting group, and so on.

The question of Stephen's acting and performing career has always given rise to questions like this one, posed to me by *CBS News*:

Comm: Why do you allow Stephen to entertain so much? Isn't that a waste of time? He is so brilliant. Certainly you don't want him to be an actor.

Dr. Baccus: If he was my first child, or only child, I might agree with you. But I have brought up four grown children, and I have learned by experience that it is best for your children if you allow them to be what they want to be. I urged one of my children to take a good government job over his protest that he did not like that type of work. He became ill and nearly developed ulcers. I urged another child to go into a profession that was financially secure, and she finally left home with much trauma.

Again, the question of enforcing my goals on Stephen was asked by a commentator on *Italian TV News*:

Comm: What are your goals for Stephen?

Dr. Baccus: The same that they were the day he was born: to be healthy, happy, and to use to the fullest the intelligence that he was born with.

Even though I mention intelligence last, doubts persist. In a TV interview, Pat Boone asked Stephen to comment on an *Encyclopaedia Britannica Newsletter* article that dubbed Stephen the world's smartest boy. Stephen answered that he didn't believe that such a label was correct. Then, Pat asked me if it was my intention to make Stephen the most intelligent child in the world.

Dr. Baccus: No, it was to have my son become a very nice person, and in that respect I believe I have succeeded.

Pat Boone: Mama of the world's smartest boy, I think you are right.

Tests That Measure Child Development

Throughout this book, I have indicated the obvious fact that children develop at different rates. While it is usually incorrect to compare children's development with that of their peers, or to compare your child's development with that suggested in books, at some point you may suspect a problem. When that happens, be sure to contact your child's physician. You should know that the following tests are available to measure various facets of child development. These tests should be administered and interpreted by trained professionals.

Neonatal Behavioral Assessment Scale: 3 days – 1 month
Inventory of Home Stimulation: birth – 3 years
Marshall Behavioral Development: birth – 6 years
Gesell Development Schedules: 4 weeks – 5 years
Piagetian Scales: from infancy
Albert Einstein Scales of Sensorimotor Development: 2 – 8 months (prehension); 5 – 25 months (spatial relationship)
Bayley Scales of Infant Development: 2 months – 2½ years
Object and Person Performance Scale: 6 months – 2 years
Minnesota Child Development Profile: 1 – 6 years
Parent as Reader Scale: 1½ – 5 years
Carolina Developmental Profile: 2 – 5 years
Revised Gesell Preschool Examination: 2½ – 6 years
McCarthy Scales of Children's Abilities: 2½ – 8½ years
Parent-Child Interaction Rating Procedure: 3 – 4 years

Personality Inventory of Children: 3 – 5 years
Hannah/Gardner Preschool Language Screening Test: 3 – 5½ years
Woodcock-Johnson Psychoeducational Battery: from 3 years

Annotated Early-Learning Bibliography

U nless you have access to a university library, many of the sources listed below may not be readily available. I offer them to show you that for many decades, serious research into all facets of early learning has been and continues to be undertaken throughout the world.

Ausubel, D. P. 1967. Cognitive structure: learning to read. *Education* 87, 544-548. Declared that the failure to stimulate a child in early life was irreversible.

Bloom, B. 1982. The role of gifts and markers in the development of talent. *Exceptional Children* 48(6), 510-522. Found that special abilities only show themselves as a result of opportunities and encouragement supplied by parents.

Bloom, B. 1964. *Stability and Change in Human Characteristics*. New York: John Wiley & Sons. Found that 50 percent of the deviation in childhood IQ occurs between birth and the age of four.

Callaway, R. *Report of the Ontario Institute for Studies in Education*. Toronto, Ontario, Canada. Found that an economic cross-section of 600 three- and four-year-olds easily learned to read.

Clark, B. 1988. *Growing Up Gifted*. Columbus, OH: Merrill. Found that late learners are generally at an incredible disadvantage in school; as a rule, they never catch up to early learners.

Colvin, S. 1915. What infant prodigies teach educators. *Illustrated World* 24, 47-52. A study of prodigies revealed that all were educated from the first months of their lives.

Fowler, W. 1962. Cognitive learning in infancy and early childhood. *Psychology Bulletin* 59, 116-152.

Fowler, W. 1962. Teaching a two-year old to read: an experiment in early childhood learning. *Genetic Psychology Monograph* 66, 181-283.

Goertzel, V., and M. Goertzel. 1962. *Cradles of Eminence*. Boston: Little Brown. A study of eminent people which revealed that all were the products of stimulating early environments.

Hayward, A. 1985. *Early Learners*. Los Angeles: The Education Institute. Suggests ways to promote an early learning environment.

Hollingsworth, L. 1926. *Gifted Children*. New York: Macmillan. Found that virtually all gifted children were educated from the first month of life.

Karnes, M., and A. Schwedel. 1987. Differences in attitudes and practices between fathers of young gifted and fathers of young non-gifted children. *Gifted Children Quarterly* 31, 79-82. Fathers of gifted children read to their children three times as long as fathers of non-gifted children; also, fathers of gifted children took their children on more frequent trips and encouraged more unusual questions from their children.

Maclean, P. 1978. Educating the triune brain. *In* J. Chall and A. Mirsky, eds. *Education and the Brain*: The 77 Yearbook of the National Society for the Study of Education, Part I. Chicago: University of Chicago Press. Substantiates that empathy and concern for others is a function of the prefrontal cortex of the brain, which, if not stimulated and developed in early childhood, may never function properly.

Mustaine, L., and B. Zeigler. 1976. Effects of experience on the behavior of the young infant. *Neuropadiatrie* 8, 107-133. Found that the first four years of life are the most critical for the development of learning ability.

Pines, M. 1979. A head start in the nursery. *Psychology Today* 13(4), 56-58. Found that the period between eighteen and twenty-four months is the most critical time for teaching a child not to hurt others.

Podgoretckaya, N. 1979. A study of spontaneous logical thinking in adults. *Soviet Psychology* 17(3), 70-84. Dismisses the observations of Piaget, stating that Piaget merely observed children in an environment that failed to encourage early development. Cites biological differences (the growth of dendritic branching and quantity of glial cells) in the brains of advanced or accelerated children that were not present at birth but that were encouraged to develop.

Pressey, S. 1955. Concerning the nature and nurture of genius. *Science* 31, 123-129. Found that parents can create genius by providing children with encouragement and challenge.

Restak, R. 1986. *The Infant Mind.* Garden City, NY: Doubleday. Determined that complex brain development in children was the result of abundant childhood experiences and environment.

Satir, V. 1972. *Peoplemaking.* Palo Alto, CA: Science & Behavior Books. Found that problem children tend to come from problem families and that largely problem-free children come from nurturing, highly functional families.

Scarr-Salapatek, S. 1974. Comment on individual and group differences in I.Q. scores. *In* P. Rosenthal, ed. *Annual Editions: Readings in Human Development.* Cuildford, CT: Dushkin. A child with low IQ scores is often the result of a family that restricts or fails to encourage the growth of intelligence.

Terman, L. 1947. Mental and physical traits of a thousand gifted children. *Genetic Studies of Genius*, vol. I. Stanford, CA: Stanford University Press. Famous study tracing 1,000 gifted children over thirty-five years which found that all subjects who were gifted were stimulated early in life.

Teyler, T. 1971. An introduction to the neurosciences. *In* M. W. Wittrock, ed. *The Human Brain.* Englewood Cliffs, NJ: Prentice-Hall. Determined that certain brain processes that are present at birth will deteriorate if they are not stimulated in early childhood.

Trotter, R. 1987. The play's the thing. *Psychology Today* 21, 26-34. Found that infants have tremendous ability to imitate and to learn from the moment of birth.

Wittrock, M. 1980. *The Brain and Psychology.* New York: Academic Press. Traced the physiologic differences in the brains of gifted children.

Index